POLITICAL ACTION AND SOCIAL IDENTITY

Class, Locality and Ideology

Edited by Gareth Rees, Janet Bujra, Paul Littlewood,
Howard Newby and Teresa L. Rees

First published 1985

Published by
THE MACMILLAN PRESS LTD
Houndmills, Basingstoke, Hampshire RG21 2XS
and London
Companies and representatives
throughout the world

Printed in Hong Kong

British Library Cataloguing in Publication Data
Political action and social identity
1. Political sociology
I. Rees, Gareth, *1949*–306'2   JA76
ISBN 0–333–37336–7
ISBN 0–333–37337–5 Pbk

Contents

Preface and Acknowledgements

The papers collected together in this book (and its companion, *Restructuring Capital: Recession and Reorganisation in Industrial Society*) were all presented at the 1983 British Sociological Association Conference, held at University College, Cardiff, on the theme 'The Periphery of Industrial Society'. The papers have been revised by their authors, in the light of discussion at the Conference and comments from ourselves.

In selecting rather a small number of papers, we have found it impossible to be *representative* of the enormous diversity that was presented at the conference. Rather, we hope that this collection is illustrative of some of the contemporary developments in the analysis of the determinants of political consciousness and action. More specifically, as the subtitle indicates, the volume is focused upon the interrelationships between class, locality and ideology in the determination of such action: interrelationships which manifest in a particularly acute form at the 'periphery of industrial society'. Accordingly, what follows is not simply of interest to academic social scientists, but also is relevant to many practical political debates which are current. However, it may be, of course, that this is not the 'relevance' which has itself now become such a pressing political concern.

In preparing this volume we have been helped by a number of people; it is a pleasure to record our thanks publicly. Anne Dix at the BSA office was the lynchpin in organising the conference which has made this volume possible; Mike Milotte, also at the BSA office, has been a most effective liaison with the publishers; and Anne-Lucie Norton has been a tolerant and supportive editor at Macmillan.

GARETH REES
JANET BUJRA
PAUL LITTLEWOOD
HOWARD NEWBY
TERESA L. REES

Notes on the Contributors

Janet Bujra is a Lecturer in the Department of Economic and Social History and Sociology at the University College of Wales, Aberystwyth.

Philip Cooke is a Lecturer in the Department of Town Planning at the University of Wales Institute of Science and Technology, Cardiff.

Steve Cornish is a Senior Lecturer in the Department of Administrative and Social Studies at Teesside Polytechnic.

Graham Day is a Lecturer in the Department of Economic and Social History and Sociology at the University College of Wales, Aberystwyth.

Chris Gerry is a Lecturer in the Centre for Development Studies at the University College of Swansea.

Paul Littlewood is a Lecturer in the Department of Sociology at the University of Glasgow.

Howard Newby is a Professor in the Department of Sociology and Director of the ESRC Survey Archive at the University of Essex.

Liam O'Dowd is a Lecturer in the Department of Social Studies at the Queen's University of Belfast.

C.G. Pickvance is a Senior Lecturer and Director in the Urban and Regional Studies Unit at the University of Kent at Canterbury.

M.R. Redclift is a Lecturer in the Department of Environmental Studies and Countryside Planning at Wye College and the Institute of Latin American Studies, University of London.

Gareth Rees is a Lecturer in the Department of Sociology at University College, Cardiff and in the Department of Town Planning at the University of Wales Institute of Science and Technology, Cardiff.

Teresa L. Rees is a Research Fellow in the Sociological Research Unit at University College, Cardiff.

R. James Sacouman is an Associate Professor in the Department of Sociology at Acadia University, Wolfville, Nova Scotia.

Graham Suggett is a Research Fellow in the Department of Economic and Social History and Sociology at the University College of Wales, Aberystwyth.

1 Introduction: Class, Locality and Ideology

GARETH REES

Britain's modern economic crisis has been paralleled by a political one. The massive restructuring of economic activity which has been characteristic of the last twenty years or so[1] has been matched by equivalent upheavals in the sphere of politics. The gathering economic storm of the later 1960s engendered what now appears to have been a brief refulgence of nationalisms in Scotland and Wales (Nairn, 1981). The more severe economic rigours of the 1970s have likewise given rise to new political forms and forces: the 'New Right' has emerged with a vengeance in the shape of Mrs Thatcher's two post-1979 Conservative administrations; whilst what is purported to be the 'centre-ground' of British politics has been occupied by the new Social Democratic Party (SDP), more latterly in alliance with the resuscitated Liberals (Gamble, 1981; 1983). Moreover, of course, such developments have by no means been confined to Britain, but are echoed in the characteristic developments of other Western European states and, indeed, those of North America.

The other side of this coin – and here perhaps the trends are especially marked in Britain – has been a decline in those traditional institutions which were created by working people to represent (in some sense) their interests: in British terms, the Labour Party and the trades unions. In straightforward electoral terms, voting for the Labour Party has fallen very dramatically from the 'plateau' it had achieved between 1945 and 1970, when its support never fell below 43 per cent of the total vote, to the low point of 1983, when it achieved a mere 28

1

per cent. It goes without saying, of course, that these figures gloss over much more complex processes. Political scientists are thus currently locked in debate over the 'dealignment thesis' (for example, Sarlvik and Crewe, 1983) and, more generally, the relationships between 'class' position (however defined) and electoral patterns have been the subject of controversy (for example, Dunleavy, 1979, 1980; Harrop, 1980).

On the Left, too, these upheavals have called forth a rather more urgent (though not more acerbic) questioning and debate. Amongst the more important indigenous contributions here have been those of Hobsbawm (1981; 1983) and Hall (1983), who have sought – in rather different ways – to relate the decline in Labour Party support to an historically informed analysis of changes in the character of the British class structure and the social formation more widely. Most particularly, both commentators have agreed that Labour's decline cannot be accounted for by some mechanistic 'reading off' of politics from the class structure, or, even more grossly, the economic structure on which the former rests. Rather, such secular, structural changes are *mediated* by particular forms of ideology and political consciousness. Hence, for example, the emergence of new political forces – nationalisms, the New Right, the SDP – should be situated in a context set by the *limitations* and *failures* of the cultural and ideological forms of earlier years: crucially, the labourism and narrow wage militancy which have characterised much of the mainstream Left's activities in post-War Britain (and elsewhere).

The significance of this debate, moreover, has been highlighted by the emergence of wholly new political concerns, whose articulation is quite simply inimical to these earlier ideological forms and the institutions which gave expression to them. The efflorescence of a politics of ecological crisis, of nuclear war and, above all, of gender relations has necessitated a thoroughgoing re-examination of accepted views of the relationships between production, civil society and the state. Left intellectuals have at least begun the task of thinking through the implications of capitalist restructuring and the emergence of new forces in civil society for appropriate forms of socialism: forms which cannot but be radically distinct from the bureaucratic, remote and – at worst – dominating institutions of labourist 'social democracy' or, even more starkly, of the 'already existing socialism' of the Soviet bloc (Bahro, 1982; Gorz, 1982; Williams, 1983).

Sociological analysis, of course, is deeply implicated in all of the issues that have been touched upon here. At the most general level, they pose afresh the problem which in traditional terms has been known as the relationship between 'social structure' and 'individual action': the still unresolved relationship which has shaped the character of sociological practice since its inception. More specifically – and certainly more usefully – recent contributions have secured quite fundamental redefinitions and re-evaluations of many of the central concepts and categories. Nowhere, for example, is this more clearly seen than in the impact of the work of feminist sociologists in the reconstruction of the politics of gender relations, especially in respect of the more conventional politics of class relations (for example, Gamarnikow, Morgan, Purvis and Taylorson, 1983a and 1983b; Siltanen and Stanworth, 1984). What has been involved here is not simply the introduction of a 'new variable' into the analysis of politics, but rather the reconstitution of what the latter comprises.

Equally, important – though certainly less spectacular – advances have also been made in the redefinition of the interconnections between the *social structure* and *spatial relations*. More precisely, it is increasingly recognised that the class structure itself varies significantly in character from place to place. Giddens (1979) makes the basic point quite succinctly:

> In class society, spatial division is a major feature of class differentiation. In a fairly crude, but nevertheless sociologically significant, sense, classes tend to be regionally concentrated. One can easily instance the contrasts between the north and south of England, or west and east Scotland, to make the point. Such spatial differentiations always have to be regarded as time-space formations in terms of social theory. Thus one of the important features of the spatial differentiation of class is the sedimentation of divergent regional 'class cultures' *over time*: class cultures which today, of course, are partly dissolved by new modes of transcending time-space distances (p. 206).

These latter comments are especially significant for my present purposes, in that they begin to indicate some of the ways in which the political activity which is an articulation of class structure does not derive from some pure type of 'consciousness of class position', but actually gains expression in forms which are mediated by the social relations which characterise particular localities.

Raymond Williams (1983) has addressed essentially the same issue, but in the more specific context of the expression of the class position of working people through trade unionism and, less frequently, socialism. Hence, whilst wage-labourers in modern industry have demonstrated a remarkable degree of homogeneity in their attachments to unionisation and some degree of association with socialism, it is not possible to reduce that attachment to some sort of immutable, universal principle. Workers' class position is cross-cut by other forms of social relationship, which makes infinitely more complex the determination of political responses. The essential notion adduced here is that of 'bonding': 'the institution and exercise of those relationships which are capable of maintaining the effective practice of social life as a whole' (p. 166). The 'bonding' generated out of the labour movement itself was inserted into pre-existing structures of social relations which themselves provided bases for such 'bonding': kinship and family networks; national and regional loyalties; religious affiliations; and so forth. Moreover, there continues to be a significant interaction between different forms of 'bonding'.

> In one kind of community – the South Wales mining settlements, or the Clydeside shipyard communities – there is a predominantly common working situation and workplace but also a relative simultaneity of other major social bonds. Through their still significant individual differences, the people of such communities are simultaneously fellow-workers, husbands and wives of fellow-workers, neighbours, interlinked extended families. Other kinds of bond, as of being consciously Welsh or Scots against a dominant 'English' system, or (though here in more complex and at times in divisive as well as uniting ways) of religion, provide

positive and in some cases supporting resources. Though always incomplete and internally contentious, such communities have taken the active practices of the labour movement and of popular socialism to the highest points that, within Britain, they have yet reached (Williams, 1983, pp. 168–9).[2]

In this way, then, the spatial unevenness of productive relations coalesces with the local particularities of other dimensions of the social structure to generate characteristic forms of political expression in such communities.

Williams' (1983) analysis is richly suggestive: especially in so far as it marks out a terrain on which real, concrete political expressions are shaped by an *interaction* of class position, rooted in productive relations, and other forms of social relationship; and, moreover, both these sets of attachments develop in ways that are *spatially* uneven. However, this is clearly not to suggest that the analysis is wholly unproblematical. Most significantly, the central conceptualisation – of 'bonding' – remains relatively uninterrogated. Hence, we are presented with a set of 'bonding' institutions (family, kinship, locality, nation, etc.) which precede historically the conditions which gave rise to the emergence of the labour movement (with its own basis of 'bonding'), but which are not wholly eclipsed by the appearance of the latter. What the argument does not make clear are the precise nature and origins of these apparently enduring relationships of 'bonding'. Likewise, the sphere of production – and the 'bonding' to which it gives rise – remains relatively unexplored.

These are omissions which become especially significant later when important distinctions are drawn between different bases of 'bonding' in terms of their political implications. Hence:

> Wage-bargaining groups compete with their employers, but their employers also, by necessity, compete with each other. The sources of a different ethos are then primarily in those other social bonds, those ultimately deeper attachments and purposes, which capitalism tries to push into a lower

importance, or where necessary to cancel. It is then in what happens or can happen in these other practices and relationships that the resources of a wider socialism have to be developed. It is a matter of what happens in the primary care of people, in families and neighbourhoods and communities. It is a matter of what happens in the organised services of health and education; in the quality of our public information and entertainment (Williams, 1983, p. 171).

It is impossible not to recognise the perversion of the potential of labour movement 'bonding' by the pursuit of a narrowly competitive ethic. However, what is more contentious is the delineation of an area of social relations which can be insulated in the way suggested. In analytical terms, the problem arises from a failure to explore fully the character of these social relations; and, more particularly, the extent to which they themselves derive from, or are integral to, production and the characteristic social forms to which production itself gives rise.

Of course, Williams (1983) himself recognises the very preliminary nature of the analysis which he presents. And he is quite categorical in his statement of the need for more, rigorous, comparative investigations of the issues to which he draws attention. The papers presented in the remainder of this volume begin to fulfil this need.

The papers by Cooke (Chapter 2) and Cornish (Chapter 3) take as their focus the ways in which productive relations themselves develop in patterns differentiated over space and time and, hence, give rise to *contrasting* forms of political expression. Thus, both authors seek to trace out the political effects of given locations in the class structure which are *precisely* defined in terms of particular, spatially specific labour processes.

Cooke proceeds by means of a comparative analysis of three 'radical regions' – Emilia, Provence and South Wales. He argues that the characteristically militant and oppositional forms taken by both electoral and workplace politics in these areas may be understood by reference to three essential features of the social relations of production which developed there historically. First, and somewhat paradoxically, a close *interdependence* deriving from the relatively dense spatial forms taken by production in the three regions, combined with a high degree of *independence* of the direct producers, marking a low degree of subordination of labour to capital, to constitute a material basis for the development of relatively antagonistic class relations. Secondly, a key dimension of these antagonistic class relations related to the characteristic ways in which the *time structure* of the working day was shaped. Each of the regions exhibited time-disciplines which contrasted with other, neighbouring areas; moreover, these time-disciplines themselves constituted a resource in later class struggles. Thirdly, the three regions displayed acute forms of gender division of labour, with women being excluded altogether from paid work or confined to particular, secondary employment sectors.[3] Moreover, more recently, as – to use Massey's (1978) terminology – 'new rounds of investment' have come to penetrate each of the regions, this earlier gender division of labour has itself come to constitute an important precondition for the new development. In turn, the latter has generated new social conditions which have tended to undermine at least the established bases of 'radicalness'.

Cornish presents a detailed study of the ways in which typically *quiescent* political forms developed amongst a specific occupational grouping: the ironstone miners of east Cleveland. He emphasises the *vulnerability* of the miners which was structurally determined out of the particular conditions which characterised the industry's growth, most clearly in respect of the highly competitive markets for its products. However, what is distinctive is his stress upon the ways in which this vulnerability was perceived by the miners themselves. The *actual* relations of production which they experienced were filtered by the manner in which they were *socially constructed*. Hence, the asymmetry of power which exists ubiquitously between capital and labour and which defines capitalist social relations, came to be defined by this group of workers as constituting the basis for a necessary quiescence. Moreover, in marked contrast to the histories of other occupational groupings (for example, Francis and Smith, 1980), this quiescence became reinforced by the subservient positions occupied by the ironstone miners (relative to the local petite bourgeoisie) in the determination of the wider social and cultural conditions within their residential communities. In Cornish's own words, 'In sum, the ironstone miner had a peripheral status in a peripheral region': his quiescence was shaped both by the *external* relations of the industry in which he laboured and *internally*, within the localities which those relations shaped.

Cornish's use of the terminology of 'periphery' here is not without significance. A considerable part of the contemporary literature addressed to the relationships between social structure and spatial patterns has attempted to encapsulate such relationships by analogy with some variant of theories of dependency, originally developed in the context of imperialism and uneven development at the world scale (for excellent critical summaries, see Massey, 1978; Day, 1980). Further, the corollary in terms of the analysis of political behaviour has often involved the identification of the *cultural* specificities of such 'peripheral' areas as providing the necessary preconditions for the growth of 'regionalist' or 'nationalist' movements (for example, Hechter, 1975, presents an extreme statement of this view). Indeed, such movements have frequently been seen as the *characteristic* political expression of the economic and social particularities of these 'peripheries'.

Sacouman's paper (Chapter 4) provides a wide-ranging review of these issues. His principal concern is to argue the basis of 'regionalist' and 'nationalist' movements in the class conflicts which are integral to uneven capitalist development, not in some presumed cultural or ethnic distinctiveness. Hence, 'regionalism' and 'nationalism' are viewed as primarily *ideological* constructions of the 'region' or the 'nation' which are *made* by identifiable class groupings and used by them in the course of political struggles. This generalised perspective enables the critical evaluation of two of the major contributions to the theoretical literature, by Hechter (1975) and Nairn (1981) respectively. The former is deficient in its failure to address the real historical complexities of uneven development and class conflicts which have characterised 'national' development in the British Isles.[4] The latter is criticised not for *ignoring* these processes, but rather for providing only a partial account of them; more specifically, for its failure to encompass the structuring of uneven development as it manifests internally to Britain, by the latter's position within a *global* pattern of inequality, as has been depicted in the writings of Amin (for example, 1980). In like manner, the various empirical case studies in Britain and Canada which Sacouman reviews are judged to be – in varying degrees – inadequate, in that they fail to relate the necessary preconditions of 'regionalist' and 'nationalist' movements in uneven development to the actual political practice of these movements, in the particular international context of the current crisis. What is required, then, is further, concrete research which is able to accommodate these – extremely demanding – prerequisites.

This recommendation is taken up in Day and Suggett's analysis (Chapter 5). They are concerned with the particular manifestation of 'nationalism' in Wales, though not in the context of the contemporary crisis, but rather that of the nineteenth century. Here too, the emphasis is placed upon the ways in which the essentially ideological construction of 'nationalism' is a part of the continuing process of conflicts between class groupings. More specifically, they show the ways in which the chracteristic patterns of economic development in nineteenth-century Wales shaped the emergence of a new configuration of classes, exhibiting its own stresses and tensions. It was within this framework that an emergent middle class was able both to create a specific account of Wales as a 'nation' and to use this 'nationalism' as a powerful tool in the establishment of a significant class bloc, incorporating a diversity of class groupings, but within which the middle class was dominant. However, this class bloc was crucially dependent upon external conditions and its fragility was made apparent as it was swept away by the tide of economic change. Nevertheless, the particular account of the Welsh 'nation' which was created during this period has continued to exert an influence over subsequent 'nationalist' developments in Wales: an indication that the *resources* which are available in the construction of a 'nationalism' are not *infinitely* flexible. To revert to the terms of my earlier discussion, there is a major *interaction* between class location and other social relations in the determination of political forms.

The papers by Pickvance (Chapter 6) and O'Dowd

(Chapter 7) introduce a new – and essential – element into the discussion: the state. It is, of course, the case that patterns of economic and social development in the contemporary period are profoundly affected by the character of state intervention. Moreover, it is equally clear that the object of much political activity is precisely to shape such state intervention. Indeed, many of the issues which have been raised earlier derive from perceptions of the *failures* of particular forms of state activity ('labourist', 'centralist', etc.). It is thus not at all surprising that state policy and its determination provide a fruitful arena for the examination of some of the general themes which have been posed.

Pickvance makes an important contribution to ongoing debates in the fields of state theory and spatial policy (regional policy, inner cities policy and so forth). A powerful theme within this literature has been that the class character of the capitalist state is such that the prime determinants of state policies should be sought in the fulfilment of the interests of given fractions of capital. Indeed, Pickvance (1981) himself in earlier writings has given an account of the development of regional policy in Britain in essentially these terms; hence, the grants and incentives available under such policy have acted to subsidise capital restructuring, rather than to relieve unemployment or to achieve some other 'welfare' objective. Here, however, he seeks to extend and to qualify this analysis. Hence, the specific forms taken by state policies (for example, spatial as opposed to non-spatial; affecting certain areas, but not others) he relates to the pressures which are exerted upon the central state by what he terms 'spatial coalitions'. These are essentially *cross-class* alliances which take as their focus the representation of the supposed needs of the 'region' as a whole; and here, of course, there are clear echoes of the arguments presented in rather different contexts by Sacouman (Chapter 4) and Day and Suggett (Chapter 5). What perhaps is missing from Pickvance's analysis is some explication of the *internal* character of these 'coalitions'; the interaction between the *institutions* (political parties; trades unions; employers' organisations; local authorities) which play a part in them and the *social bases* or constituencies of these institutions remains relatively unexplored.

The significance of the latter point is, I think, brought home particularly clearly in O'Dowd's case study of the development of regional strategy in Northern Ireland. The latter is presented as a state response to the local (i.e. Northern Ireland) effects of global capital restructuring. However, what is crucial is that this response embodies the state's own *formulation* of the requirements of monopoly capital in the province. Hence, the strategy is constrained not simply by the changing conditions of global capital restructuring itself, but also by the specificities of Northern Ireland society. Hence, the attempts by the state to orchestrate necessary support ('regionalist consensus' in O'Dowd's terms) behind the various stages of regional strategy reflect the extremities of class and sectarian divisions within the province, as well as the forms (Stormont, Direct Rule) taken by the Northern Ireland statelet itself. Moreover, the instabilities and tensions which arise from these particularities have become heightened as the central, British state's strategies have changed ' under Mrs Thatcher's 'New Right' administrations. Again, then, the point is emphasised that the determination of state policy cannot be deduced from some form of general and abstract identification of class interests.

One of the specific features of the 'New Right' strategy to which O'Dowd refers is the switch of policy objectives from employment creation to the encouragement of small business growth. This theme is taken up by Gerry (Chapter 8), although in a rather different context. He is concerned by the crisis confronting the Left in the context of the rapidity and extent of contemporary capitalist restructuring. In effect, then, he presents an exploration of some of the implications of the breaking-up of those traditional, solidaristic communities to which Williams (1983) refers (in the quotation given earlier). Hence, to the extent that *past* conditions of uneven capitalist development generated contexts for the emergence of particular forms of political commitment and expression, what does present and future capitalist restructuring hold in store?

Gerry argues that *one* of the effects of current changes in economic organisation, especially under the pressures generated by recession, is the emergence of a greatly enlarged and enormously heterogeneous small enterprise sector. Whilst it is important to recognise the differences within this sector – between industries, forms of internal organisation, the 'legitimate' and 'black' economies, localities – Gerry suggests that it is a development which opens up a significant new terrain of class conflict. So much has been recognised already, as is indicated by the political and media prominence accorded to small businesses. Moreover, it would appear that the strategy of the Right in this context, centrally aimed at the resuscitation of capital both nationally and internationally, includes an important role for such small enterprises, both in direct economic terms (for example, in generating surplus, risk-bearing, etc.) and ideologically (for instance, in re-establishing a 'work ethic' of self-employment). The response of the Left, however, has been much less effective. Gerry suggests that attention has been focused overwhelmingly on the supposed 'disappearance of the working class': an analysis which is seriously defective. In particular, this preoccupation has distracted attention from the small enterprise sector and its contribution to the emergence of a wider phenomenon, 'the disguised proletariat', outside the mainstream of economic activity. Getting to grips with the latter, within an appropriate analytical framework, is an essential precondition for developing socialist strategy.

Redclift's concluding paper in this volume is also concerned with fundamental questions of Left thinking and strategy in the emergent conditions of the contemporary world, though the context for his discussion is radically different. His focus is the growth of the Green Movement in Europe and the challenge which it presents to traditional forms of Marxist analysis. This challenge is twofold. First, the Green critique seeks to problematise the model of economic growth which lies at the heart of industrial capitalism. Secondly, it brings to the centre of the stage the environmental consequences of such capitalist growth, not simply for the advanced economies themselves but also for the world 'periphery' of underdeveloped countries which are dependent upon the former. In this way, then, some of the implications of uneven development at the world scale are brought to bear on the analysis of political strategy in the 'centre'. Redclift proceeds by means of critical reviews of conventional Marxist treatments of the environment (such as they are); of the inadequate theoretical bases of much environmentalism; and of the failures of Marxist accounts of underdevelopment to encompass environmental issues. He appears to see in the writings of Rudolph Bahro (1982) some possible avenues of escape from the problems thus identified: in particular, his emphasis upon the indivisibility of personal lifestyles and political practices; his identification of the ecological crisis as the determining instance in contemporary society; and, perhaps most contentiously, his claim that class interests need to be displaced as a central analytical category by a wider conceptualisation of human needs. In much of this, of course, he shares the concerns of Williams (1983) which were sketched earlier. It is perhaps ironic, then, in the light of that earlier discussion that, having, as it were, removed class, the indispensable issue of the *agency* by which Bahro's and the Greens' ideology may be translated into effective political action remains unresolved.

The diversity of the concerns expressed in the papers presented here make any neat summary and conclusion difficult; the intention is to make available current work, rather than definitive conclusions. Nevertheless, each of the contributions has sought in its own way to expose the bland generalities of any simple identification of class position with given forms of political expression. Moreover, it does now begin to be possible to sketch out the elements of an analytical framework by which to guide *future* research and analysis. Certainly, the comprehension of political experience and activity, in whatever form, implies the unravelling of the complexities of the interactions of class, locality and ideology. For, to give Raymond Williams the final, introductory word: 'It is by working and living together, with some real place and common interest to identify with, and as free as may be from external ideological definitions, whether divisive or universalist, that real social identities are formed' (1983, p. 196).

NOTES

1. Many of the relevant issues here are addressed in the companion volume to this, *Restructuring Capital: Recession and Reorganisation in Industrial Society*.

2. Professor Williams made many of the arguments reviewed here in a paper presented directly to the conference at Cardiff. It was unfortunately not possible to include it in this volume, as it was already committed to appear in the form to which I refer here.
3. I have presented the argument in terms of the 'gender division of labour', although the author refers at times, rather confusingly perhaps, to 'patriarchy'.
4. Similar points were made by Professor Gwyn A. Williams in his paper to the Cardiff conference which also regrettably could not be included in this volume.

REFERENCES

Amin, S. (1980) *Class and Nation: Historically and in the Crisis* (New York: Monthly Review Press).

Bahro, R. (1982) *Socialism and Survival* (London: Heretic Books).

Day, G. (1980) 'Wales, the Regional Problem and Development', in G. Rees and T.L. Rees (eds) *Poverty and Social Inequality in Wales* (London: Croom Helm).

Dunleavy, P. (1979) 'The Urban Basis of Political Alignment: Social Class, Domestic Property Ownership and State Intervention in Consumption Processes', *British Journal of Political Science*, 9, pp. 409–43.

Dunleavy, P. (1980) 'The Urban Basis of Political Alignment: A Rejoinder to Harrop', *British Journal of Political Science*, 10, pp. 398–402.

Francis, H. and Smith, D. (1980) *The Fed: A History of the South Wales Miners in the Twentieth Century* (London: Lawrence and Wishart).

Gamarnikow, E., Morgan, D., Purvis, J. and Taylorson, D. (eds) (1983a) *Gender, Class and Work* (London: Heinemann).

Gamarnikow, E., Morgan, D., Purvis, J., and Taylorson, D. (eds) (1983b) *The Public and the Private* (London: Heinemann).

Gamble, A. (1981) *Britain in Decline* (London: Macmillan).

Gamble, A. (1983) 'The Impact of the SDP', in S. Hall and M. Jacques (eds) *The Politics of Thatcherism* (London: Lawrence and Wishart).

Giddens, A. (1979) *Central Problems in Social Theory* (London: Macmillan).

Gorz, A. (1982) *Farewell to the Working Class* (London: Pluto).

Hall, S. (1983) 'The Great Moving Right Show', in S. Hall and M. Jacques (eds), *The Politics of Thatcherism* (London: Lawrence and Wishart).

Harrop, M. (1980) 'The Urban Basis of Political Alignment: A Comment', *British Journal of Political Science*, 10, pp. 388–98.

Hechter, M. (1975) *Internal Colonialism: The Celtic Fringe in British National Development, 1536–1966* (London: RKP).

Hobsbawm, E. *et al.* (1981) *The Forward March of Labour Halted?*, (London: Verso).

Hobsbawm, E. (1983) 'Labour's Lost Millions', *Marxism Today*, October, pp. 7–13.

Massey, D. (1978) 'Regionalism: Some Current Issues', *Capital and Class*, 6, pp. 106–25.

Nairn, T. (1981) *The Break-Up of Britain* (2nd ed) (London: Verso).

Pickvance, C. (1981) 'Policies as Chameleons: An Interpretation of Regional Policy and Office Policy in Britain', in M. Dear and A. Scott (eds), *Urbanization and Urban Planning in Capitalist Society* (London: Methuen).

Siltanen, J. and Stanworth, M. (eds) (1984) *Women and the Public Sphere: A Critique of Sociology and Politics* (London: Hutchinson).

Sarlvik, B. and Crewe, I. (1983) *Decade of Dealignment: The Conservative Victory of 1979 and Electoral Trends in the 1970s* (Cambridge University Press).

Williams, R. (1983) *Towards 2000* (London: Chatto and Windus).

2 Radical Regions? Space, Time and Gender Relations in Emilia, Provence and South Wales

PHILIP COOKE[1]

Recent changes in the geography of production in advanced and formerly under-industrialised countries have resulted in some significant adjustments to the socio-spatial structures which became established in the 1950s and 1960s. Amongst the more noteworthy of these have been the growing involvement of women in the labour market, the loss of employment from large cities, especially in manufacturing, the increasing industrialisation of rural areas, and the substantial recomposition of the occupational patterns of workers in regions which were the earliest to industrialise and which became centres of heavy industry. To these could be added the continuing growth of the service industries as sources of employment, the possible move towards a self-service economy, as described by Gershuny (1978), the informal economy (Pahl, 1981) and, stimulated by the present high levels of unemployment, the prospect for many people of a workless state (Showler and Sinfield, 1981). Despite the importance of these tendencies for work to be developing away from manufacturing industry, even, in the face of the new international division of labour, in developing countries (Walton, 1981), this paper will not pay specific attention to non-manufacturing activity.

The reason for this industrial emphasis is tied in with the tasks which are set in the paper. These are twofold, and concern, first, an investigation into the reasons why some areas develop a tradition of highly developed proletarian consciousness and preparedness to resist the encroachments of capital and the state into their culture and society. Then, secondly, I want to examine the extent to which such regions become abandoned by capital, as predicted by many theorists of locational shift by capital, as, for example, is implicit in the following assertion:

> concentration of industry has created areas with the most experienced, skilled, well-organized, high cost, and militant labour force; as a result many industries, not only those which are labour intensive, have found it advantageous to seek out greener pastures in the suburbs, small towns, the south and beyond (Walker and Storper, 1981, p. 496).

THE MAKING OF RADICAL REGIONS

In order to achieve these twin objectives it is necessary first to identify some regions which are representative of the category of 'radical' and/or 'militant' in the political and industrial senses. This is a complicated matter because as well as having to justify radicalness, one is forced to justify the designation of region to particular formations. Moreover, having satisfied the criteria for achieving those tasks, it is desirable that the chosen, radical regions should have different geographical and historical traditions. This is necessary to exclude the possibility that such regions derive a large part of their character from national influences, or from the fact that they have similar historical origins.

Thus, for example, regions in Britain specialising in vehicle manufacture have displayed militant characteristics at various times, and these could be candidates for analysis, except that their histories are similar in being forged in the struggle against anti-unionism – a national characteristic of British car manufacturers up to the 1960s (Zeitlin, 1980) – or in a context of renewed automation and world competition afterwards, again a national-level influence (Elger, 1982). Equally, single-industry regions in different countries can be subject to similar pressures leading to industrial revolt, as occurred in the French, Italian and British motor industries between 1968 and 1972, or French and British steel districts between 1978 and 1980. However, these do not help us specify the deeper social and spatial interconnections which enable certain regions to display systematically non-conforming allegiances, which may erupt into militant opposition in the face of national pressures or the practices of other regions.

In the remainder of this introduction I will say briefly why I chose Emilia–Romagna in Italy, Provence in France, and South Wales in the UK as the regions to be investigated. Studies which have preceded this one (Cooke and Rees, 1982; Cooke, forthcoming) have led me to conclude, against some well-argued views to the contrary (Urry, 1981; Giddens, 1981), that regions are meaningful social categories in so far as they designate the spatial units within which class practices in the work-place and everyday life exist more or less homogeneously. Now, as I understand it, part of the critique of the usefulness of the notion of 'region' rests on the changes which have overtaken the geography of production in recent years. John Urry (1981) argues that the internationalisation of capital, the decline of older industries, and the effects of state intervention and/or regional competition for new jobs have resulted in the deconstruction of the old, homogeneous regions with the result that, often, the most meaningful spatial unit for workers and their families is now the locality, based on the local labour market. While this argument, and the more woolly and abstract notion of 'locale' which Giddens (1981) employs, point to an important base-point in a sea of change, it seems to me that both are unduly economistic. They overlook the degree to which a supra-local cultural form can outlast the economic base which may have been crucial to its formation, and indeed, the extent to which important regional practices may have little to do with production, past or contemporary, notably in such bases of collective identification as ethno-regionalism.

The argument for the notion of regions as spaces designating specific practices is constructed as follows. Due to the manner in which capitalist production develops unevenly, class relations will also be spatially unevenly developed. Different territories will give rise to different industrial specialisms. These, in turn, will be characterised by different labour processes and diverse forms of capital ownership depending upon the time at which development began, the preceding social and cultural relations predominating in that territory, and the spatial remoteness from each other of centres producing similar commodities. A good example of the latter are the profound social, political and cultural differences between the Great Northern Coalfield (Durham and Northumberland) and the South Wales coalfield, despite the fact that they were contemporary export coalfields, distinctions to which I will return later in the chapter (Daunton, 1980; 1981). These work-related practices are expressed in the differentiation of the social hierarchy in everyday life; in other words, within the confines of the general relations of production operating where production consists of commodities for the market, regionally specific class practices will exist. These will begin as regional practices because competition between producers is only limited by the extent of the exploitable resource and the space-time constraint upon connecting to relevant markets. They will remain as regional practices, even after the productive base has entered decline, to the extent that the regionally specific class practices actively involve developing institutions capable of defending valued elements and opposing counter-valuations of those practices through time.

Having argued for the validity of the notion 'region', it is now necessary to show why some become radical and others do not. Of key importance in measuring the degree of regional radicalism are, for example, such factors as the regional presence of a range of Left political parties, trades union and related organisations with large membership, discipline, etc., and, beyond these formal institutions, a range of informal structures such as educational, health, leisure and other communal facilities which are popular in origin rather than being state-funded or privately provided. The extent to which these are present will vary according to: the influence of previous production relations – particularly whether or not these gave rise to defensive institutions – and cultural specificities; the degree of differentiation and hierarchisation, or solidarity, egalitarianism and interdependence in regional social relations; the extent to which capital ownership involves abrasive or paternalistic industrial relations; whether labour organisation is incorporated or independent; and, finally, the nature of the productive base, the fluctuations in its markets, and the impact of these factors on the wages, conditions and moral sensibilities of the workforce.

Hence, the regions which were to be examined needed to satisfy the following criteria. First, they should demonstrate both a historically well-established level of productive homogeneity and a long tradition of regional radicalism, notably through Left-voting and control of government, militant trades unionism and supportive popular institutions. Secondly, they should be diverse in their productive character – ideally ranging from heavy industry, through mixed industrial/agricultural, to agricultural, so that the effects of sectoral world trade cycles could be minimised. Finally, they should be located in different countries to minimise the national effect upon regions located within the same national territory. The regions which fulfilled these criteria most closely were, first, Emilia–Romagna, a traditionally agricultural and artisanal region in what may be termed, after Wallerstein (1979), the Italian semi-periphery, between the power-house of the Milan–Turin–Genoa triangle and the backward Mezzogiorno. It is a region in which the Italian Communist Party (PCI) governs at all levels of the regional state hierarchy, assisted in places by the Socialists (PSI), and where the important metalworkers unions, *Federazione Italiana Operati Metallurgici* (FIOM) and *Federazione dei Lavoratori Metalmeccanici* (FLM) are fiercely loyal to the Left parties. It is also celebrated as a buoyant centre of Italian microcapitalism, a conjuncture of characteristics which appears bewildering but is of great interest to the project of this chapter.

The second region is Provence, again a traditionally agricultural, largely wine producing region which was one of the earliest and most loyal centres of French socialism (PSF). According to recent electoral results, the region is becoming more strongly socialist, and it also has substantial political, and especially trades union representation by the French

Communist Party (PCF). In recent years the population base of Provence's rural socialism has been severely eroded as agriculture has entered a steep decline and the region has become the recipient of one of the French state's planned, heavy industrial, growth complexes near Marseilles. The third region is South Wales, a classic heavy industry region based in coal-mining and steel production. Since the 1920s it has been a heartland of the British Labour Party, the latter having replaced the Liberals, and fought off the Communist Party (CPGB) during the 1930s and 1940s. The region has a militant reputation, largely due to the activities of the coal-mining, and, historically, the railway unions, although neither of these industries is now the most important employer. In the post-war era, largely under state guidance, the region has become an important centre of mechanical and electrical engineering, as external capital has established numerous branch-plants in the region. As with Emilia and Provence, therefore, we seem to have in South Wales the paradoxical situation of radical regions attracting rather than, as recent restructuring theory would have us believe, repelling new industrial development. It is also the case that Provence and South Wales have experienced massive growth in service sector employment, although Emilia has not grown so rapidly in this respect; space, however, does not permit any detailed analysis of this phenomenon.

In what follows I shall try to show how far these three regions conform to the theoretical criteria outlined above as indicators of regional radicalism. There will thus be five main sections dealing in sequence with the productive base, the labour processes, the ownership of capital, specific social relations, and the oppositional institutions of the three regions. At each stage, an attempt will be made to show what it was about the emergence of these spatially confined, resistant class formations which also makes them apparently quite attractive locations for new industrialisation. In explaining the nature of the hinge-points between opposition to control by capitalists and industrial development, I shall refer quite often to three fundamental categories of what Sack (1980) refers to as *a relational concept of space*. Where Sack refers to the three categories of Space, Time and Substance as being exhaustive in this respect, I shall put some flesh on the third category and focus, as far as possible, on the dualistic qualities of Space, Time and Gender in forming and reforming these radical regions.

THE PRODUCTIVE BASE

There were spatially very distinct boundaries to the productive bases of the three regions, governed by natural factors in the first, objective, instance and limiting the area over which specific class relations could develop. In the case of South Wales, the limits of exploitable coal resources within the constraints of existing technology were clearly determinate. In the case of the two agricultural regions, natural factors were almost as determinate. Provence specialised in the production of early fruit and vegetables for the metropolitan market and flowers either directly for the same market or indirectly as perfume. The limits of this agriculture coincided with the limits of the appropriate environmental and climatic conditions. These were found close to the sea. By the 1870s though, Provence was specialising massively in wine production, another industry with natural, spatial limits.

In Emilia, the radicalisation process began in the fertile Lower Po Valley where, after the unification (*Risorgimento*) two important occurrences enabled the extremely fertile soil to be exploited capitalistically. The first was the enormous expansion of the market for cash-crops caused by the establishment of the Italian national territory, especially bringing the Piedmont industrial cities into its sphere. The second was the forced sale of church and state land which was signified by the ascendancy of a liberal state. In Emilia, more than in any other Italian region, this land was bought and worked by city merchants as capitalist agriculture. Hence, a share-cropping peasantry was partly transformed into a tough, rural proletariat – *braccianti* – and Emilia become 'one of the earliest working-class conquests of the Socialist movement' (Williams, 1975, p. 16; see also Geary, 1981).

A second crucial spatial factor was the extreme concentration, especially in the agricultural regions, of population into small towns (Emilia) or big urbanised villages (Provence). Industrial South Wales, unlike some other mining districts, was characterised by very dense linear settlements occupying the valley bottoms of the upland coalfield. The fact that each region was well established into production for the market had important effects on the establishment of two kinds of heterogeneous time structures, where previously the population concerned would work, broadly, to a similar cyclical time discipline. In South Wales, for example, the coalfield was initially an upland, transhumant, pastoral area, and the vast bulk of the migrants who came into the coalfield from elsewhere in Wales in the early years of its development came from a similar productive background. The disjuncture was therefore between what Thompson (1982) refers to as a cyclical time discipline, governed by the natural cycle of animal birth, maturation and sale in the local, or often lowland England, livestock markets, and the linear time-discipline of the capitalist labour process, where one day is much like the rest, and the notions of work-time and free-time are key structural components of social life.

In Emilia and Provence, production for the market had different effects depending upon the product specialism. Where vegetables, flowers and fruit were produced for early, direct consumption as in Provence, or for later processing, as in the tomato, sugar beet and hemp industries of Emilia, rural proletarianisation occurred. This was because the necessary scale of production, investment and risk were greater than peasant producers were capable of meeting. In Emilia, this proletariat was largely male, in Provence it was female. Either way it involved members of the single family unit in different kinds of cyclical time-discipline. The Provencal male could easily work the small, mixed arable plots of the traditional peasant farm himself, while females were locked into the exploitative relations of capitalist agriculture – testified in their strike at Hyères in 1907 for an increase in wages and a reduction of hours from twelve to eight a day. In Emilia, the urbanised settlement pattern was augmented by sharecroppers leaving the countryside when wage-labour became available in the cash-crop industries. Women became increasingly involved in supplementing their husbands' often precarious incomes by working in the traditional handicrafts industries. However, where the specialisation was in wine production the family work-pattern remained within the same time-horizons because of the extremely labour-intensive nature of the work involved in tending vines, and the absence of alternative employment in these single-industry settlements.

Where temporal divisions were established between male and female work, it was normally the case that the porosity of the woman's working day was reduced to a greater extent than that of the male. And where, as was the case initially in the coal industry of South Wales, men and women worked underground together, it did not take long for women to be excluded from the male sphere, under the pretext of patriarchal propriety, but as Walby (1983) argues, supported strongly by male workers eager to discourage cheap labour from reducing their own opportunities for work and for negotiating a better wage for themselves.[2] Hence, by and large in these three regions, capitalist production was rapidly followed by a gender division of labour which was very different from the pattern under pre-industrialised or pre-capitalist production. Only in the Provence wine districts was the gender division of labour resisted, and it is interesting to note that it was in such districts that women were not discouraged from taking part in the public affairs of the villages, as they were in most of the rest of Europe (Agulhon, 1970; Loubere, 1974; Judt, 1979).

It seems, therefore, that if patriarchy is not necessarily confined to capitalism, as Eisenstein (1979) seems to argue, it nevertheless receives an immense shot in the arm, whether because of the precariousness of male work and the need for some supplementary income earned in a different time-structure and spatial location, or because of the male interest in removing sources of cheap labour, of whom women would be the principal, and ensuring that their often prodigious work-related needs were serviced by unwaged domestic labour. That women were not unsophisticated in their opposition to exploitative wage-relations is testified by the flower-women's strike in Provence, and their frequently attested rioting in the South Wales coalfield at the occasion of (male) industrial disputes long after they had ceased being employed themselves (Francis and Smith, 1980; Macintyre, 1980; Williams, forthcoming). The mystery is why this was not reproduced at home, although Macintyre (1980) may have one answer when he draws attention to the role of male violence as a means of enforcing patriarchy in the coalfield, as no doubt, elsewhere.

THE LABOUR PROCESS

In this section I want to trace the implications for contemporary labour processes of the space, time and gender structuring in production that was described in the previous section. The most interesting region of the three is Emilia because, unlike the others, its labour processes have been transformed by more directly political action, and it shows the greater extent of fluctuation in the degree of autonomy of the direct producer. The relatively high level of mechanisation of capitalist agriculture created conditions whereby strongly unionised agricultural workers had some degree of control, and indeed an enhanced skill-content, in the direct labour process. Nevertheless, the conceptual part of the process no longer belonged to them as it had, for all its mindless repetition, when they were small peasant proprietors or, to a lesser extent, sharecroppers. Emilia, as well as being an early centre of socialist politics, also saw the emergence of a land-based counterpolitics that grew into fascism in the 1920s. It was from this late period, unlike the cases of the South or North-East of Italy, that share-cropping became a major form of agricultural production; it was the result of the breaking up of the rural proletariat rather than its cause. Increased mechanisation also created a demand for agricultural machinery, the production of tools, adaptation of equipment and provision of repair services. This is the key to the early growth in Emilia of small, craft-based workshops in which these products and services were concentrated.

As fascism came to dominate the political life of the region and Italy itself from 1922, the scale of production and associated labour processes were massively transformed. There was a policy of rapid centralisation of production, especially in the engineering sector centred on Bologna, and diversion of production from agricultural machinery to armaments for the

Italian imperialist and war efforts. Clearly, under such circumstances any independence that the engineering worker might have enjoyed was thoroughly snuffed out as methods of supervision of the most extreme authoritarianism were introduced. Despite this real subordination of labour such large productive units obviously formed pools of highly class-conscious labour and, thereby, the basis for future organisation.

However, such was the perceived danger posed by such concentrations of democratically inclined factory workers that the Italian state, working to an Anglo-American reconstruction blueprint in which Marshall Aid was the principal incentive, rapidly broke up these large units, running them down, purging Left-wing workers and returning the Emilian economy to its pre-Fascist structure.

Four important points follow from these experiences which are of relevance to the contemporary pattern of labour processes found in Emilia. The first is the high level of political and industrial organisation exerted in the unionised plants. These tend to be the larger factories, although there are so many smaller units that it is normal for unionisation to reach down to plants of over thirty employees. In such plants workers are in a relationship of formal subordination to capital and management finds it difficult to dismiss or otherwise discipline them – this is seen as a union function. Secondly, the wide dispersal of skilled engineers who were also Left sympathisers has been the vital condition for the growth of the small-firm sector which is very large in Emilia by contrast with, for example, the Piedmont, or the Italian average (Sabel, 1982; Brusco, 1982; Solinas, 1982). But this growth has, thirdly, been assisted greatly by industrial relations difficulties in Piedmont in the late 1960s and early 1970s that led to a process of *productive decentralisation* of subcontracting to Emilia. Moreover, changes in consumer demand favouring customised products over standardised ones has enabled the small artisans to find competitive market niches. But, finally, it is the PCI with its strategy of an anti-monopoly alliance which depends on constructing links between workers and small businessmen for political expansion which has provided the necessary backing, in terms of legislative and financial aids, for the now buoyant microcapitalist sector.

The key irony deriving from this labour market dualism is that while predominantly male workers in the larger firm sector enjoy a reasonable degree of autonomy and union protection, the small firm sector, owned largely by PCI sympathisers, exploits female labour in the most aggressive way. Here, there are no shop floor union oranisations, legislation against unfair dismissal does not apply in firms employing less than fifteen employees, contracts are individually negotiated, workloads and hours fluctuate enormously, health and safety norms go unregarded, and homeworking, especially for older women, is an integral form of labour-intensive production.

Superficially, this dualisation of labour processes contrasts with the experience of Provence and South Wales, yet, in practice, gender restructuring (Walby, 1983) in combination with spatial and temporal bifurcation have occurred. The traditional radicalism of agricultural Provence has been eroded by rural depopulation, the growth of Marseilles as a state-planned manufacturing and services growth pole, and the continuing growth of the Côte d'Azur as a massive concentration of tertiary sector employment. Surprisingly, much of the latter is higher-order service sector employment with industrial R & D, managerial and technical occupations approaching, according to Lipietz (1980), Parisian levels.

The implantation of a massive, steel and chemicals complex near Marseilles has restructured the subregional labour market into three layers. There are, first, the large, 'Fordist' plants employing semi-skilled, disciplined male workers, often committed to consumerist, acquiescent working and everyday practices. Next, there are smaller marginalised factories comparable to the Emilian subcontractors, employing women and ethnic minorities under sweatshop conditions. Finally, there are the independent craft-workers, previously the vanguard of Marseilles socialism, employed as subcontractors in the shipyards, but who find themselves increasingly being assimilated to Taylorised labour processes as their industry declines and is mechanised. These labour-markets are spatially separate, with marginalised employment being found in smaller towns away from concentrations of industry. One effect of this is the growing pauperisation of labour by time as work-journeys lengthen (Bleitrach and Chenu, 1979; 1981; 1982).

Just as subcontracting has become an important activity in the two Mediterranean regions, it is being reproduced in a new form in the South Wales coalfield. The coal and steel industries were characterised from the outset by subcontracting, divided crucially between the *gang-work* system in the coal industry and the *craft-work* system in steel (Littler, 1982). However, unlike the gang-work system elsewhere, at least as described by Littler, the ganger was not prone to develop close, incorporated links with employers to justify his separate status. Rather, pursuing, against mighty odds, the model of craftsman – skilled at performing *all* the tasks of the job such as hewing, shotfiring, hauling and filling (unlike his aristocratic Durham counterpart (Daunton, 1981)) – he was likely to enjoy a highly conflictual relationship with managers and deputies. This was because of the need for constant negotiation over 'deadwork' enforced by the geological fragmentation of the coal-measures. The collier, as subcontractor, employing his own men, often from his family, was sufficiently powerful to resist the introduction of a double-shift system after the time-cutting 1908 Mines Regulation Act, arguing against the disruption of family life and sociability that such a new time-discipline would entail. It was not until the inter-war years, and the widespread mechanisation of colliery work, with supervision taken away from the skilled miner, that this independence of control over the labour process was seriously eroded.

However, the new time-discipline of three eight-hour shifts had important effects in habituating miners, and, more importantly, perhaps, their wives and families to a less porous daily pursuit of the capitalist clock. For, although solidarism in the coalfield was given a boost by the massification of the workforce, the faster work-tempo, and attendant increases in industrial injuries, it presaged the post-war development of the regional labour market as overwhelmingly semi-skilled. A good example of this is the way that motor vehicle manufacturing (including components) now employs more than either the coal or steel industries. Other new industries such as electrical engineering, petrochemicals and furniture-making have also taken the place of coal-mining, especially. Three features are of interest with regard to the motor industry: the first is the low-skill content of the occupations concerned; the second is the anomalously high proportion of women employed in the South Wales car plants – nearly twice the male share of British motor industry employees; and the third is the spatial dualism between five larger assembly plants in the coastal towns, with higher skill-content, better levels of unionisation and more male work, and the forty-five small subcontractors and minor branch-plants located in the old coalfield, less well unionised and employing a larger share of women. As Rhys (1982) puts it: 'with a relatively good industrial relations reputation, *and no real tradition of motor industry militancy*. . .the position is such that almost every industrial valley has a significant part of its workforce in the motor industry' (Rhys, 1982, p. 31, emphasis added).

Each region displays a marked similarity in the sense that modern employment has grown away from the original base of industrial and political radicalism. There is in each case the development of a segmental labour market structure with the kind of relative autonomy previously enjoyed by subcontracting craft-workers having been appropriated by the male trade unions. For women, by contrast, there is a concentration of economic activity in the small, sweatshop industries with generally worse wage and employment conditions. An increasing spatial fragmentation in employment has developed, a factor which further reduces the porosity of the working day by extending it; and there seems to be little opposition emerging to the kind of spatial, temporal and gender restructuring which has occurred in the labour processes of these regions.

CAPITAL OWNERSHIP

The three regions display contradictory tendencies in the development of capital ownership. Provence and South Wales have seen a massive decline in the proportion of internally controlled capital that is deployed in their industries, whereas Emilia–Romagna, while not bereft of multiregional or multinational capital (Plessey and FIAT are represented) has maintained a high level of internal capital ownership. This is a reflection of the continuation of a significant small and medium-sized firm sector that, in the nineteenth century, was focused upon agriculture, textiles and associated engineering industries, but which has now become more diversified. The most notable change in capital ownership in Emilia has been the growth, under PCI hegemony, of co-operative industries in engineering and, especially, agricultural production and food processing. But, in general, ownership can be divided into three functional scale-categories. There are, first, the larger, vertically integrated firms producing directly for the consumer in relatively self-contained labour and supplies markets. Secondly, there are subcontracting firms engaged in a single, intermediate stage of production on a small-scale, largely in-house basis. The final category is that of the small, innovative firm producing prototypes and customised products, often heavily reliant on homeworking, as in the case of the spatially specialist textile, clothing and footwear industries. This sector has begun developing 'internal colonies' in adjacent regions, and even in the South as labour enters short supply (Brusco and Sabel, 1981; Solinas, 1982).

Provence and South Wales have been heavily penetrated by external capital having, to a considerable extent, been regionally self-reliant in the nineteenth century. In Provence, the wine industry was small-scale with co-operative production methods being favoured at the manufacturing and distribution stages. And even though the perfume, soap and related cash-crop industries were in private hands Provence remained under-industrialised until the 1960s. Then under Gaullist state guidance Provence took off industrially, as an attack began to be made on southern European markets. Steel and chemicals' monopolies led this penetration, and, as we have seen, accrued around them smaller subcontracting industries, some of which overlapped with traditional small- and medium-sized craft-dominated firms.

Capital ownership in South Wales is now split between the established coal and steel industries which are state owned, and the still-growing number of, initially mainly UK multiregional and American branch-plants, and more recently, European and Japanese-owned branch-plants. As in the case of Provence and Emilia, it is in the traditional, rather than the newer industries that the strongest adherence to conscious industrial organisation and action is found. This is undoubtedly an expression of the profound separation that can be found between the spatial locations of the older and newer sectors and the gender divisions in employment between the larger, male-dominated industries and the smaller female-dominated firms. The tendency, which used to be pronounced, for family recruitment to the main industry to occur, has been reversed as labour markets have become fragmented and employers are able to pick and choose their employees.

SPECIFIC SOCIAL RELATIONS

Within the general social relations of production under capitalism it is likely that certain spatially specific social cleavages, alliances or antagonisms will underpin regional radicalism. The best example of a combination of specific social relations is found in the South Wales coalfield. Here, the early rural migrants were largely from a Welsh countryside already characterised by turbulence and antagonism between the landed aristocracy, and the smallholding farmers and tenants. This antagonism arose from the exploitative property relations operated by rack-renting absentee landlords. The structuring of the opposition between agrarian classes was threefold: in linguistic terms there was a clear divide between Welsh-speaking smallholders and English-speaking (though actually Welsh) landlords; this was expressed in a religious division between Anglican landlords and Nonconformist tenantry who, importantly, developed egalitarian forms of religious observance; and, finally, these divisions were expressed in political cleavage between Tory landlords and Liberal smallholders (Cooke, forthcoming).

When this radical class migrated in large numbers to the coalfield it was a confident, democratic and self-sufficient force, capable of reproducing its opposition to exploitation in the new, industrial context. This egalitarianism is revealed in the difference, for example, between the work habits of South Wales miners as compared with miners in the physically similar Great Northern coalfield centred on Durham. The skilled miner in South Wales took pride in his versatility, while his northern counterpart did so in his exclusivity. The result was a more hierarchised occupational structure, and a similarly hierarchised social structure in the Great Northern region, whereas both were less differentiated in South Wales. Indeed, industrial conflict only begins in earnest in the coalfield in South Wales from the period when market fluctuations brought widening differentials between skilled coal-hewers and unskilled hauliers (Daunton, 1981). Finally, as we have seen already, the spatially concentrated nature of residence and work-place, the extreme consciousness of the miner regarding the distribution of work-time and free-time, and his capacity to enforce patriarchal relations inside and outside work contributed massively to the capacity of the region to reproduce its specific social relations. It was the loss of control over time with the onset of mechanisation that triggered the miner's loss of control over spatial and gender relations, and, subsequently, his loss of control over the new forms of production which were to penetrate the region.

In Provence, the ethno-regional factor cannot be excluded since the region had enjoyed autonomy as a distant province of France until the later Middle Ages. But the socialism which became so powerful and relatively advanced there owed its origins to the structure of property relations and the interdependencies to which these subsequently gave rise when production of wine, in particular, for a fluctuating marketplace became widespread. Property took the *allodial* form whereby, from the Middle Ages, rather than the Revolution as elsewhere in France, the estate was held in absolute ownership by the peasant. Though small, these properties enabled individual proprietors to be unusually independent, but it also encouraged a high level of communal interdependence, especially given the spatial concentration of settlements. These factors combined to produce the unique blend of personal, commercial and political openness which is referred to as Provencal *sociability* – a communal, democratic spirit (Loubere, 1974; Judt, 1979; Brustein, 1981). As Bleitrach and Chenu (1981) make clear, this aspect of Midi culture was reproduced in the transition from agrarian to industrial, urban settlement and production in the Marseilles (and it might be added, Toulon) shipyards, though its strength is under attack from regional development planning at present.

Finally, perhaps the most unusual, or at least, extreme, specific social relations are those of Emilia–Romagna. We have seen how capitalist agriculture led to the early formation of a tough, rural proletariat and the establishment of the socialist movement in the region, and heralded the fascist backlash. Then, in the inter-war years, share-croppers were dragooned into the armaments factories, and afterwards their potentially oppositional workforces were broken up and purged by the supposedly liberal post-war state. It would be surprising if, after such experiences in which only the relative strength of, first, the PSI and, later the PCI, offered any sort of clandestine protection or assistance to the worker, Left political and industrial organisations had *not* received such widespread support. However, the oddest social relations in contemporary Emilia are undoubtedly those by which the PCI assists micro-capitalism at the expense of women's exploitation, while encouraging 'responsible' bargaining with the larger union-ised employers. This appears to be a 'historic compromise' with a vengeance!

To conclude this section, each region has noteworthy speci-ficities to the historic and contemporary social relations be-tween its major classes. They are, however, different in kind, being property-derived in Provence, politically-derived in Emilia, and economically-derived with ethno-regional overtones in South Wales. The connecting link is that in each case the main producers retained a degree of independence in work and everyday life that was out of the ordinary, yet, paradoxi-cally that independence did not result in exclusivity between male classes, only between males and females.

OPPOSITIONAL INSTITUTIONS

Clearly, if particular regions which, for reasons discussed in the preceding sections, develop the capacity to oppose un-wanted changes but fail to sustain that capacity, then they will be unexceptional in the terms of this chapter. The key factor in sustaining that capacity is the ability of such regions to reproduce it institutionally. In this respect, each of the regions under discussion here is remarkably similar, something which is rather surprising given their diverse locations and specific histories. Each region fulfils the rigorous requirements set at the outset of this paper in displaying, first, a range of Left political parties in control of the various levels of local government; secondly, a well-organised trade union presence; and thirdly, a base of informal institutions upon which such formal apparatuses could be constructed.

In Emilia, for example, large parts of the region are controlled by the PCI, the rest by the PSI. These roles have changed over the present century as it was the PSI which was historically the stronger and older party. In the period leading up to 1922, the PSI helped to organise the anarchic, communal and intensely local labour unions typical of the region, and became more popular than the Italian Anarchist Union and the Italian Syndicalist Union in the process. The PCI entered the field in 1921 as one result of a split within the PSI but shortly afterwards Mussolini came to power, creating a Left-vacuum until the post-war period.[3] At the level of trade unionism the post-war years were crucial in rebuilding the shattered labour movement, but this was a period of massive disputes which saw the appearance of three separate trade union confederations, *Confederazione Generale Italiana del Lavoro* (CGIL) associated with PCI and PSI, *Confederazione Italiana Sindacati Lavoratori* (CISL) associated with the Christian Democrats, and *Unione Italiana del Lavoro* (UIL) associated with the Republican and Social Democratic parties.

The dominant unions, FIOM and FLM, are representative of the largest industries, mechanical engineering and metal working, each closely affiliated with the political Left. More surprising, yet typical of the anti-monopoly alliance, is the strength of National Confederation of Artisans which represents 55 per cent of registered Italian artisan enterprises, and in Reggio Emilia, Bologna and Modena, the main engineering centres of Emilia, the average was 66 per cent in 1980. The Confederation is itself closely affiliated to the PCI and PSI (Sabel, 1982). The popular antecedents of this network were the locality-based *camera del lavoro*, which was a community-based focus for workers' organisations, co-operatives, savings schemes and, most of all, a worker-controlled labour exchange.

It would be housed in the *casa del popolo* (as in Spain; see Shubert, 1982) which was the educational and recreational centre of most sizeable settlements. These early institutions sustained a basis of working-class culture upon which the more formal and wide-reaching institutions of the present were constructed.

In Provence, a similar pattern prevailed with the locally important, traditional *chambrée populaire* performing the same function as the *casa del popolo* in Emilia. This would be a key focus for sustaining the sociability of Provencal community life. From this base, first the Radical Alliance and then the Socialist Party were formed in the region, the latter affiliating to the PSF by 1905. Syndicalism in Provence emerged, as elsewhere in France, with the concern of workers to control mutual aid funds and improve wages and conditions, especially in urban centres such as Toulon, followed later by agricultural syndicates. The Anarchist movement was weak in rural Provence, partly because of their antipathy to organisation which was disapproved of in the sophisticated wine villages (Judt, 1979). Although the PCF has been active since the 1920s it has not replaced the political hegemony of the PSF, unlike the position in Emilia. The PCF is heavily involved in trades union activity through the CGT (*Confédération Générale de Travail*), a union which is suffering somewhat from the growth of neo-Fordism in French industrial relations, as in the celebrated case of Aérospatiale helicopters near Marseilles where reformist unions have been replacing CGT as the principal representative of labour (Ardagh, 1982).

Finally, in South Wales there is a similar history of wide-ranging Left political activity including Syndicalism in the early years of the present century, a choice of Labour parties (the Independent Labour Party and the Labour Party) until the early 1970s, and the Communist Party which came within less than a thousand votes of winning a parliamentary seat in 1945. Labour, in its numerous forms, had replaced Liberalism by 1924. The most important trade union until recently has been the coalminers union which has usually been heavily influenced by the CPGB, although led by Labour Party members as well as Communists in the post-war years. In the form of the South Wales Miners Federation, the mining union was responsible for building on the pre-industrial, egalitarian cultural forms of the mining communities, and South Wales until the 1950s was unique in the range of popularly available educational, recreational and health services, many of which pre-figured and influenced the Welfare State services, many of which were established throughout Great Britain from 1945.

CONCLUSIONS

This paper set out to answer the question of how it was that the regions under study developed their radical, combative and oppositional character, and what was it about such regions that, far from discouraging renewed capital accumulation, seems to have resulted in important conditions of production being present. The answers to these questions emerge as the two sides of three conceptual coins.

The first of these is that each region displays an initially high degree of what Sack (1980) refers to as 'action by contact'. That is, they were marked by intense *spatial* interdependence in the sphere of work either through subcontracting or co-operative production. But intermingled with interdependence, each region demonstrates a high level of independence on the part of the direct producer whether as craftsman, peasant-producer or artisan. This independence marked a relatively low degree of subordination of labour to capital and, in a context of wide-ranging markets prone to fluctuation, could easily lead to fairly antagonistic class relations being established, even where, as in the case of Emilian agricultural labourers, working conditions were notably exploitative. But this spatial knot between work and everyday life with its widespread sociability was vulnerable to labour process changes, especially mechanisation – and the effects of political representation within the state which in all three cases has been influential in introducing new industrial systems.

Secondly, perhaps the strongest area of control exerted by these relatively powerful associational or unionised groupings was that which could be exerted over the *time* structure of the working day. The regions were separated from others close-by by being slotted into different, non-local, time-cycles or even different time patterns (cycles versus linear). Well-organised workers were able to resist the imposition of new time-disciplines, using as arguments the disruption of the sociability which was itself a space opened up by the splitting up of the day into work-time and free-time. Finally, male workers quickly entered different time-scales from females either by extruding them from the labour market or subordinating women's working conditions to the advantage of their own. The failure to resist the temporal restructuring of the working day and the habituation of women to that time-structure, in a context where the porosity of the female working day was likely to be markedly less than that of the male, constituted crucially important conditions of production for new industries in the post-war era.

Lastly, the most notable feature shared in common by the three supposedly radical regions which I have examined is the ubiquity of patriarchy and the generally reactionary character of *gender* relations present within them. In each case, women, who had worked side by side with men in the earlier stages of the region's development, had, by the later stages, been relegated to distinctly secondary positions. This was not accidental, at least in the cases of South Wales and Emilia; even in Provence where separate labour markets developed, women got their employment in the least attractive occupations. Interestingly, only in the parts of Provence where women remained peasant-proprietors, working in wine production with their husbands, did they also enjoy rights of equality in the spheres of politics and civil society (Judt, 1979). Patriarchy seems, from the evidence of the important role which women are taking in the growing industrial sectors in these three regions, the most valuable condition of production which an oppositional culture can yield up to private industry in a context of declining profits, severe international competition and the perceived need for wage–cost reductions.

NOTES

1. I would like to thank the following for their help in producing this paper: Fergus Murray, Roger Penn, John Urry and Sylvia Walby.

2. It is important to stress the role of patriarchy in helping to structure the gender division of labour, especially in the South Wales context. Male workers and managers were able to exert dominance over female workers, first, to exclude them from underground work, then to exclude them from surface work in order to strengthen their own bargaining position *vis-à-vis* management. Because of the lack of alternative waged work for women, the latter were thus confined to domestic labour. The argument that legislation excluding women from underground mining was a result of pressures mainly from above rather than below is clearly inadequate on this point.

3. Plainly, Emilia–Romagna was not a homogeneously Leftward leaning region in the inter-war years as its accommodation to fascism shows. It is the case, however, that the authoritarian backlash was provoked, at least in part, by the early development of solidarism amongst agricultural workers engaged in capitalist farming. And, of course, attachment to traditional social relations regarding 'the soil' and so on, was a central element of Italian fascism. The support for fascism in the region came from some disaffected and opportunistic former socialists such as Mussolini, elements of the petty bourgeoisie, and landed capital. The radical tradition was submerged but in no sense terminated by the fascist interlude.

REFERENCES

Agulhon, M. (1970) *La République au Vallage* (Paris: Libraire Plon).
Ardagh, J. (1982) *France in the 1980s* (Harmondsworth: Penguin Books).
Bleitrach, D. and Chenu, A. (1979) *L'Usine et la Vie: Luttes Régionales*, (Paris: Maspero).
Bleitrach, D. and Chenu, A. (1981) 'Modes of Domination and Everyday Life: Some Notes on Recent Research', in M. Harloe and E. Lebas (eds) *City, Class and Capital* (London: Edward Arnold).
Bleitrach, D. and Chenu, A. (1982) 'Regional Planning – Regulation or Deepening of Social Contradictions?', in R. Hudson and J. Lewis (eds) *Regional Planning in Europe* (London: Pion).
Brusco, S. (1982) 'The Emilian Model: Productive Decentralisation and Social Integration', *Cambridge Journal of Economics*, 6, pp. 167–84.
Brusco, S. and Sabel, C. (1981) 'Artisan Production and Economic Growth', in F. Wilkinson (ed.) *The Dynamics of Labour Market Segmentation* (London: Academic Press).
Brustein, W. (1981) 'A Regional Mode-of-Production Analysis of Political Behaviour: the Cases of Western and Mediterranean France', *Politics and Society*, 10, pp. 355–98.
Cooke, P. (forthcoming) 'Class Practices as Regional Markers: A Contribution to Labour Geography', in D. Gregory and J. Urry (eds), *Social Relations and Spatial Structures* (London: Macmillan).
Cooke, P. and Rees, G. (1982) 'The Social Democratic State in a Radical

Region, paper presented at I.S.A. Xth World Congress of Sociology, Mexico City, August.

Daunton, M. (1980) 'Miners' Houses: South Wales and the Great Northern Coalfield, 1980–1914', *International Review of Social History*, 25, pp. 143–75.

Daunton, M. (1981) 'Down the Pit: Work in the Great Northern and South Wales Coalfields, 1870–1914', *Economic History Review*, 34, pp. 578–97.

Eisenstein Z. (1979) *Capitalist Patriarchy and Socialist Feminism* (New York).

Elger, T. (1982) 'Braverman, Capital Accumulation and Deskilling', in S. Wood (ed.), *The Degradation of Work?* (London: Hutchinson).

Francis, H. and Smith, D. (1980) *The Fed: A History of the South Wales Miners in the Twentieth Century* (London: Lawrence and Wishart).

Geary, R. (1981) *European Labour Protest* (London: Croom Helm).

Gershuny, J. (1978) *After Industrial Society* (London: Macmillan).

Giddens, A. (1981) *A Contemporary Critique of Historical Materialism* (London: Macmillan).

Judt, T. (1979) *Socialism in Provence, 1871–1914* (Cambridge University Press).

Lipietz, A. (1980) 'Inter-regional Polarisation and the Tertiarisation of Society', *Papers of the Regional Science Association*, 44, pp. 3–18.

Littler, C. (1982) 'Deskilling and Changing Structures of Control', in S. Wood (ed.), *The Degradation of Work?* (London: Hutchinson).

Loubere, L. (1974), *Radicalism in Mediterranean France* (Albany: State University of New York Press).

Macintyre, S. (1980), *Little Moscows* (London: Croom Helm).

Pahl, R. (1981) 'Employment, Work and the Domestic Division of Labour', in M. Harloe and E. Lebas (eds), *City, Class and Capital* (London: Edward Arnold).

Rhys, G. (1982) 'The Motor Industry in Wales', *Agenda*, 1, pp. 18–37.

Sabel, C. (1982) *Work and Politics: The Division of Labour in Industry*, (Cambridge University Press).

Sack, R. (1980) *Conceptions of Space in Social Thought* (London: Macmillan).

Showler, B. and Sinfield, A. (1981) *The Workless State* (Oxford: Martin Robertson).

Shubert, A. (1982) 'Revolution in Self-Defence: the Radicalization of the Asturian Coal-miners, 1921–34', *Social History*, 7, pp. 265–82.

Solinas, G. (1982) 'Labour Market Segmentation and Workers' Careers: The case of the Italian Knitwear Industry', *Cambridge Journal of Economics*, 6, pp. 321–52.

Thompson, E.P. (1982) 'Time, Work-discipline and Industrial Capitalism', in A. Giddens and D. Held (eds), *Classes, Power and Conflict* (London: Macmillan, first published 1967).

Urry, J. (1981) 'Localities, Regions and Social Class', *International Journal of Urban and Regional Research*, 5, pp. 455–74.

Walby, S. (1983), 'Women's Unemployment: Some Spatial and Historical Variations', paper presented at Urban Change and Conflict Conference, Clacton, January.

Wallerstein, I. (1979) *The Capitalist World Economy* (Cambridge University Press).

Walker, R. and Storper, M. (1981) 'Capital and Industrial Location', *Progress in Human Geography*, 5, pp. 473–509.

Walton, J. (1981) 'The New Urban Sociology', *International Social Science Journal*, 33, pp. 376–90.

Williams, G. (1975) *Proletarian Order* (London: Pluto).

Williams, G. (forthcoming), 'Women Workers in Contemporary Wales', *Welsh History Review*, 16.

Zeitlin, J. (1980) 'The British Car Industry: The Emergence of Shop Steward Organisation and Job Control', *History Workshop*, 10, pp. 119–37.

3 Powerlessness in Peripheral Regions: The Case of the Non-militant Miner

STEVE CORNISH

The creation and maintenance of peripheral status and the attendant feature of dependency is due not only to the rise and fall of economic fortune, the depletion of resources or the ebb and flow of technological development; it is due also to the dialectical relations between individual and group and between consciousness and economic power. In the context of peripheral regions within a capitalist economy, the analysis of such relations necessarily focuses on both temporal and spatial dimensions of the formation and maintenance of the labour force in a condition that best suits the requirements of dominant forces in the national and international economies. One crucial characteristic of the labour force in a peripheral region is that consciousness seldom develops to the extent that dependency relations can be severed. Powerlessness is created and maintained in the labour force by the existence and use of power relationships involving an 'engineering of consent' and hegemonic aspects. These particular uses of power are applicable to populations on the periphery of industrial society but still contained within a single political unit, the nation-state.

Analyses of the use of power to mould the labour force into a dependent relationship with the centre are relatively numerous in the context of the sociology of development (e.g., Memmi 1967; Freire 1972). Little research of this type has been undertaken in the peripheral regions of the dominant capitalist powers; of note, however, is the work of Gaventa (1980) on

Appalachia. The more popular approach by far has been to assume that no significant difference exists between the working class of internal peripheral regions and the working class of the centre; that both are subject to similar, if not the same effects of the use of power. Urry (1981) has pointed to the limitations of any approach that ignores the significance of spatial factors as determinants of class action.[1] Such factors include the local pattern of income, occupational and class mobility and the organisation of the local labour market, its sectoral, occupational and gender changes; and the dominant forms of class struggle (Urry 1981, p. 463). In considering the commodification of space, attention can be profitably focused on the ways in which historically some localities become peripheral and dependent. Sociologically, the concern is with how local class structures emerge in these areas and what the characteristics of such local class structures may be. This is not to consign such issues solely to the comparative safety of historical analysis for, as Urry suggests, in contemporary capitalist relations, such local class structures are in fact of increasing importance.

This paper will consider one aspect of the development of local class structures in peripheral regions, that is the capacity to utilise power and how such capacity can be subject to strategies of containment in part derived from the circumstances, both historical and spatial, in which the local class structure has emerged. It will then be argued that part of the explanation of the continuation of a 'regional problem' has to do with the patterns of activity undertaken by local class structures, constrained by strategies similar to those involved in the recent past but now pursued by different agents. The outcome being the same; the pattern of uneven development continues and peripheral areas and their populations retain their dependent status. It is necessary first to deal with some of the theoretical context to these issues.

THE PERIPHERY, UNEVEN DEVELOPMENT AND DEPENDENCY

Capitalism structures a spatial division of labour in the process of ensuring efficiency and economy in technical processes geared to the maximisation of profit. Thus, in a market economy certain regions within a country will experience economic peaks and troughs in response to technological changes, depletion of resources and market fluctuations. Associated with this pattern of development is a transfer of surplus value from the region at the periphery to the centre. Such unequal exchanges have been analysed both in the context of the underdevelopment of the Third World (Emmanuel, 1972) and for the peripheral regions within the dominant capitalist nations (see, for example, Malizia, 1973). The result of such transfers of surplus value is to retard the development of certain regions and to accumulate capital at the centre.

The historical process of capital accumulation and the contradictory development of the capitalist mode of production is comprehensively analysed by Marx in *Capital*, but regional imbalances were not a major concern of his unless allied to the issue of slavery or colonisation.[2] In a Marxian framework, development is structural, involving changes both in the forces of production and the relations of production; it also involves improvement in labour productivity centrally. These elements are crucial to the accumulation process in capitalism. Regional inequalities therefore appear to derive from the uneven accumulation of capital caused by the spatial relationships of production as they undergo developments.[3]

The application of dependency theory (e.g., Amin, 1974; Wallerstein, 1976) to regional disparities within the countries of the centre conjures up the image of internal peripheries or internal colonies. Amin encouraged such an application in stating that 'each developed country has created its own underdeveloped country within its own borders' (quoted in Edel *et al*, 1978, p. 6). Despite this there have been few attempts to apply dependency theory to internal development in developed countries. It has been argued that dependency theory suggests that internal peripheries, if they exist, are not analogous to the world periphery.[4] Internal peripheries are subject to a different process of exploitation, a process that paradoxically may include the establishment of political rights, trade unionism and substantial social improvements. In using the logic of dependency theory, any analysis of peripheral regions should focus on the conditions which allow such regions to exist and on how divisions within the working class are maintained on a spatial basis.

Relating class action to the external forces that act on regions requires a further analysis of how consciousness emerges in a regional and peripheral context. This interplay of regional and class consciousness is not often systematically studied, but John Gaventa (1980) and Raymond Williams (1973) are examples of differing but effective studies in this vein. Essentially such analyses are pointing to the spatial implications of capital maintaining the social relations of production. Involved in this is the structuring of authority relationships between the capitalist class and the working class, with the ideological role of identification with a region acting to hinder the development of working-class consciousness. The necessity of capitalists organising the labour process so as to establish and maintain particular relationships is now widely recognised by Marxist economists. Braverman (1974) and Marglin (1974) have shown how capitalist development has been historically associated with the degradation of work and the monopoly of the capitalist class over the information needed for the management of the production process. In both these cases there is a spatial dimension that needs to be clearly defined.

Having briefly discussed some aspects of uneven development and drawn attention to potential effects on local class structures and consciousness, it remains now to elucidate the process by which the working class fails to exploit any potential power, constrained by the use of power by external forces and their local agents. Central to the understanding of this process is a clear categorisation of the nature of power involved in the maintenance of the social relations of production.

POWER AND POWERLESSNESS

For the purposes of the present paper, elements of the sociology of power dealing with the impact of power on the relatively powerless will be applied to the case study of Cleveland miners. Much of the following discussion relies on Gaventa's work on the coal-mining population of Appalachia, which in turn rests on the application of Lukes' three-dimensional approach to the concept of power (1974). The use of Gaventa's work has the added benefit that he is dealing with a mining population and as such there are some interesting parallels with the case study discussed later in this paper.

Much of the power debate revolves around the problem of the political inactivity of the working class, whose acquiescence, in spite of the persistent inequalities which define their position, has been variously attributed to apathy, hegemony, cultural deficiency, low socio-economic status, or even to the notion that the inequalities are not perceived as such by the disadvantaged classes, hence they are not 'real' (Gaventa 1980, p. 4). In part, such explanations rely too heavily upon the subjective aspect of the definitions of working-class interests, as Saunders has pointed out (1979, p. 40). Whether those interests can only be defined in terms of objective evidence, or whether we must rely upon the disadvantaged actually perceiving their position before we can credit their inactivity to apathy, cynicism or consensus, is one important point in the discussion. One other issue concerns the mechanisms of power, mainly in decision-making, which reduce the options of the relatively powerless while enhancing the position of the more powerful. Since it is clear that delayed decisions, decisionless decisions and a range of sanctions, threats and force invoked in lieu of decisions (or, non-decisions) can achieve the same result as decisions, the question of where to draw the line arises. Which acts are to be included and which are not relevant in explaining the excercise of power? How can the non-events which some of these entail be taken into account? These questions, and the answers to them have important implications for the analysis of local class activity in peripheral regions.

It would appear that for the present discussion the crucial aspect of Gaventa's application of Luke's work concerns the awareness of grievances and the problems of assessing the use of power where no awareness of grievances either on the part of the powerful or the powerless is present. In this examination of power, importance is attached to the many ways in which potential issues are kept out of politics, whether through the operation of social forces and institutional practices or through the individual's decisions. Given this, it would appear that an approach of this sort is particularly suitable for researching issues of power among populations that exist in states of dependency in internal peripheries, where such expressions of power may well be characteristic.

The mechanisms by which power is used in Lukes' three-dimensional approach are admittedly wide-ranging and complex. A full analysis would necessarily have to study language, myths and symbols, particularly with respect to the communication of information, and the socialisation process. The aim of this would be, as Gaventa puts it, 'to focus upon the means by which social legitimations are developed around the dominant and instilled as beliefs and roles in the dominated' (1980, p. 15). It is through these mechanisms that change in power orientation would occur as the local class structure, economic, political and spatial relationships of a region change over time. Lukes sees the nature of human action as both contingent and creative; people exist within 'a web of possibilities' and 'make choices and pursue strategies within given limits', and also in consequence these limits 'expand and contract over time' (1977, p. 29). No doubt this accounts for differences between populations in superficially similar areas with respect to their use of, and response to, power.

The nature of the psychological effects of powerlessness on deprived populations have been documented by Haggstrom (1965) and the effects he reports are not dissimilar to the kinds of adaptations noted by Gaventa. The first of these is characterised as an 'adaptive response to continual defeat': *A* has repeated victories over *B* so that eventually *B* comes to anticipate *A*'s reaction and success and therefore ceases to challenge *A*. This calculated withdrawal becomes an unconscious pattern maintained not by fear of *A*'s power but by *B*'s own sense of powerlessness 'regardless of *A*'s condition' (1980, p. 17). Having thus internalised the values and beliefs imposed by the powerful, 'a means of escaping the subjective sense of powerlessness' is found (1980, p. 17). Allied to this process is the effect of exclusion from means of controlling conditions of social existence. If this denial prevents the growth of political consciousness then it is unlikely that any steps will be taken to redress inequalities. In support of these indirect mechanisms of power Gaventa uses the work of Freire (1972), Mueller (1973) and Gramsci (1957). It is perhaps significant for a discussion of power in internal peripheries that Freire writes in the context of the closed societies of the Third World. Freire acknowledges that a 'culture of silence' develops from the inequality of political experience, a context in which the development of consciousness is stunted. The silence of the powerless then becomes a legitimation of the powerful interests. Mueller writes in a similar vein stressing that attempts to break the silence are necessarily poorly oriented and ineffective and tend to reinforce patterns of withdrawal to a point of quiescence. Gramsci sees such a state of 'moral and political passivity' deriving from 'the point where the contradiction of conscience will not permit any decision, any choice' (1957, pp. 66–7).

The variable of the context in which consciousness develops is a crucial factor in two senses. First, consciousness itself may develop in contradictory and ambiguous ways, so that in specific instances it is not of assistance to the powerless because it is rendered neutral by the activities of the powerful in using the third dimension of power. Secondly, as such consciousness emerges it is malleable, especially vulnerable to the power field around it. In particular, the use of myths and symbols, through which the powerful manage the emergence of beliefs and actions in one context in contradiction to those expressed in other contexts, is to be observed (Gaventa, 1980, p. 19). Such an account of the third dimension of power and the mechanisms by which it operates demonstrates how power is intimately and inherently related to inequality, in the sense that the dynamics of power relationships tend to maintain and even exacerbate social and political inequalities.

THE NORTH-EAST, AN INTERNAL PERIPHERY

The initial industrial development of the North-East was in terms of the extraction of coal, dominated largely by an essentially pre-capitalist class of landowners who rapidly recognised the opportunities of realising surplus value vastly in excess of that obtained from ground rents. The market for the coal was outside the North-East, in London initially, and then in other emerging industrial areas. As coal-mining moved

away from the Tyne to the concealed coalfields of Durham
and Northumberland, the amount of capital required for deep
mining rose sharply and reduced the rate of profit and bit into
the already accumulated capital.

In this early period there were many interacting variables
tending to fragment the labour force (e.g., size of pit, demographic mix, technology employed, methods of payment, etc.).
The collection of papers edited by Harrison (1978) amply
qualifies this point. Allen (1981) provides an account of the
miners' struggle for higher wages and better conditions,
pointing out that the coal-owners had to attack labour costs as
these constituted two-thirds of the total costs of production
(1981, p. 17).

The early ineffectiveness of the unions (largely regionally
based) had not only an effect in terms of organisation but must
have had an effect, specific to each region, in terms of promoting or retarding class action based on notions of the classes'
power or powerlessness. What is explored here, in an application of the power theory described above, are the reasons
why such differences occur.

Late nineteenth-century economic transformations were
paralleled by changes in ownership and a trend towards
vertical integration of coal, iron ore, iron and steel production.
'Rationalisation' in the major industries steadily pushed out
labour during periods of recession. In the first decade of the
century 33 000 left and 141 000 in the second. The competitive position of the North-East was further undermined by the
advances in production by other regions and industrialising
countries. The finance capital necessary to revitalise North-
East industry was going into the industries in other regions or
being exported for use in the colonies (Bowden and Gibb, 1967).

After the First World War had temporarily averted a collapse of the North-East's economy, the relatively inefficient
firms of the North-East were amongst the first to collapse
during the depression of the 1930s. The reduction in investment and export demand particularly affected the North-East
as a region, producing investment goods for home and foreign
markets. The human toll was in unemployment of 13 percent
rising to 35 percent and a consequent decline in working-class
living conditions, not matched by other regions (see Aldcroft

and Richardson, 1969). State intervention became a regular feature in order to retard, as far as possible, the falling rate of profit. Such intervention, however, becomes less effective under modern conditions as the reputation of the region becomes a self-fulfilling prophecy and as the underdevelopment of the region and its population make it less and less equipped to take up new technology (see Gibbs, Edwards and Thwaites, 1982). A further aspect is that the attempt to maintain and expand the manufacturing sector in the North-East has led to a growth in the proportion of such employment that is externally controlled. Seventy-three percent of this employment, largely in British and American multinationals, was externally controlled in 1973. These new plants were more integrated into their respective corporations than into the regional economy (Austrin and Beynon, 1979).

It is contended, as stated above, that this process of underdevelopment of the region has had specific effects on the use of, and responses to, the power of the population in the region. Yet these effects are not uniform but vary according to the differing experience of local communities. Some communities will feel and act in a more powerless way than others, depending on their experience of powerful groups and of conflict involving them. The following case study is an attempt to trace the development of a relatively powerless section of the working class in the North-East, the ironstone miners of Cleveland.

A CASE STUDY: THE CLEVELAND IRONSTONE MINERS

The emergence of Teesside as an iron-making region in the 1850s coincided with the displacement of home demand by export markets. Apart from the North-East itself, the natural outlets for Teesside's low-cost pig-iron were overseas and in some of the coastal districts of Britain.

During this early period of expansion, so great was the demand for iron ore (known locally as ironstone) on Teesside and elsewhere in the North-East that the Cleveland mines could not meet it and ore had to be imported. This led to a search for cheap sources of richer ore elsewhere and during the 1870s Spanish haematite began to arrive on Teesside in large and increasing quantities. Local companies began to play a part in the development of mines in northern Spain as interest grew in making steel by the Bessemer process, for which purpose Cleveland ore was then unsuitable. Despite the invention of the Gilchrist–Thomas process in 1879 which made it possible to make basic steel from Cleveland pig-iron, and therefore enabled mines to find a market for their ore, the inroads made by the availability overseas of cheaper and purer ores remained a potent bargaining factor in negotiations between mine-owners and miners.

The development of ironstone mining parallels in a number of ways the development of coal-mining in Durham and Northumberland. Indeed, much of the technical knowledge used in ironstone mining was derived from coal-mining experience. The early stages of development involved drift mines (Eston, Upleatham) where large quantities of ore could be obtained at relatively little cost and requiring little mining skill. As these mines could not cope with Teesside's burgeoning demands, more speculative and costly mines were sunk to get at concealed seams in East Cleveland. This required the expenditure of much more capital, a skilled mining labour force and a belief in the continuing strength of the market for iron and steel. The first two requirements were met while the third created continual fluctuations in the fortunes of mines, miners and communities.

The new mining communities of East Cleveland were a mixture of new settlements purpose-built for mining and expanded agricultural settlements. These settlements developed rapidly in the late 1860s and 1870s and within a decade the area was producing more than a million tons of ironstone yearly. By 1881 thirty-one mines were producing 6, 500, 000 tons and Teesside was providing 27 per cent of the United Kingdom's pig-iron (Bullock, 1974, p. 85). Most of the mines were part of a highly integrated production process, the ironmasters having control over limestone quarries, coal and ironstone mines, smelting plants and blast-furnaces. The labour force for the new mines came largely from the surrounding agricultural areas, from Lincolnshire, Norfolk and the more established mining areas of Northumberland, Durham, Cornwall and Wales.

Ironstone was linked directly to the main consuming industries on Teesside, for all but a short initial period, and its profitability had always been greatest as part of a vertically integrated process. As such, any interruption in the production process, and also the vagaries of the market, affected the mines: stoppages, short-time working and lock–outs were commonplace.

The working conditions of the ironstone mines were primitive; the mechanisation of ironstone mining took an extremely long time and was only effectively achieved in the last two decades before closure. Much of the working was by hand, the miners and the 'fillers' working in teams serviced by 'drivers' (generally younger men) of horse-drawn 'tubs'. Injury was frequent, deaths were not unusual, both partly due to the lax attitude to safety regulations, but mainly because of the inherently dangerous nature of the work. Payment was on a piece-work basis with fines for contaminating clean stone with shale or other impurities. There were thirteen other deductions possible from a miner's wage, not including income tax. It is of some significance that house rent, fuel and explosives could all be deducted from wages by the mining companies. This indicates in a small way how the mine-owners controlled not only the conditions of work but also much outside of work that was essential to the miner. The phenomenon of the company town did not occur fully in East Cleveland, due in part to the decreasing willingness of the owners to invest extensively in ventures outside the increasingly financially precarious mining operations and also to difficulties in purchasing land from local landowners in some areas. Most of the communities did, however, have a proportion of the housing stock provided and controlled by the company (usually for key workers) and the more paternalistically inclined owners provided for miners' institutes, chapels and churches.

Output reached peaks of over 6 million tons in 1875–7, 1880–3, 1906–11 and 1913; thereafter there is a steady decline to the closure of the last mine in 1964. At its peak the industry employed 8 500 men and was without doubt the dominant occupation in East Cleveland and the basis on which the prosperity of the communities rested.

There are a number of differences between these communities and the ideal type mining community as depicted by Bulmer (1975). Three features in particular are worthy of comment: the separation between mine-owners and land-owners, the lack of any significant emigration when mines closed for long periods and the conspicuous lack of militancy coupled with a conciliatory stance on the part of miners and their union towards the owners (for further details see Cornish, 1982; 1984). East Cleveland was distant enough from the growing urban centres of population on Teesside, so that few, if any, of the inhabitants seriously considered employment on Teesside as a realistic proposition until the advent of public transport and widespread car ownership. For most of their existence these communities have had little day-to-day contact with the urban areas. The method of working in the ironstone mines created closely knit and well-integrated work teams. Work was experienced as a group activity that was to a high degree under the daily control of the miner, in that it was impossible to supervise closely widely dispersed work teams operating a piece-work system.

Central to any analysis of reactions to, and use of, power must be the incidence and character of economic and political conflict. The structure of industrial relations in the ironstone mines basically consisted of associations formed to protect the interests of mine-owners and miners, and although objectively these interests were opposed, the record of negotiations between the associations are interwoven with expressions of mutual interest and conciliation. For example, in 1923 the Pease and Partners Annual Report stated: 'the cost of manufacture is more accentuated in the case of Cleveland iron. Having regard, however, to the reasonable way in which the Cleveland men have met us I feel it is our duty to draw the maximum quantity we possibly can.' Without doubt the miner was aware that the mine-owner through his overall control of the work and his strong influence in the community had the upper hand, but this did not encapsulate the miner in a world of no choice. There was considerable movement between the mines owned by the different companies and although there is evidence of collusion between mine managers to exclude certain miners, such a black-list was ineffective as the competition between mining companies kept the door open for the skilled and experienced miner. Choice was therefore limited; the parameters of the miner's economic existence and a large part of his social existence were fixed by the mining companies.[5]

In interviewing elderly miners[6] it was remarkable how frequently, when questioned about militancy, the retort 'There was never a strike in the Cleveland mines!' was repeated. The remark was accurate for these men, but ignores the one strike beyond their recall. In 1874, in response to the downward trend of prices, and following wage reductions of 10 per cent for coal-miners and blast-furnacemen, the ironstone mining companies imposed a 12 per cent cut in the ironstone miners' wages. The strike lasted for seven weeks in May and June, and demonstrated the dependence of the iron manufacturers on local ore. Attempts were made to import ores from elsewhere but technical problems and cost made this prohibitive. Despite this power of the labour force the strike was broken and the men returned for 12 per cent less wages and short-time working. Throughout the rest of the history of these mines there were only minor examples of industrial unrest involving single mines. These outbursts were generally dealt with by negotiations between the union and local management. All other stoppages (1879 – six weeks; 1892 – three months; 1912 – five weeks; 1921 – three months; 1926 – seven months) were due to industrial action taken by coal-miners.

> I can't remember Cleveland miners having a strike on their own. Only time they were out of work was when they were brought out either with coal or railways. I think they were pleased to have a job to go to. (Interview with E.B., 84-year-old miner).

Despite these examples of fellow miners taking action, the Cleveland miners never initiated any industrial action sympathetic to the coal-miners; they passively waited for the notices of the lock-outs to go up on the pit-yard gates.

Wage reductions were a constant feature of union and owners' negotiations from the 1870s to 1920s. In most cases the union accepted the reductions and were suitably acknowledged for their good sense and loyalty to the owners. The miners' high reputation for loyalty was recognised by an outside body, the Labour Commission of 1891–2, and such recognition was emphasised by the owners consistently through to the 1930s. For example,

> May I also pay a tribute to the attitude and conduct of the miners, who were in our service and whom we hope to again employ, whose behaviour during this cessation of work was beyond reproach. (Lord Gainford, Pease and Partners Chairman, Company Annual Report 1926.)

Adding these reductions, non-payment for travelling and other 'dead' time, and fines for unclean stone, it is clear that the owners had a ready means of increasing profit margins. Simon (1980) analyses the effect of wage reductions on surplus value in conditions similar to those that existed in the Cleveland mines. The popularity of this method among owners was due to their inability to increase the length of the working day and their unwillingness to invest further in increasing the productivity of labour.

> A cut in wages, whether time or piece wages, is like an absolute increase in surplus value in that productivity is not increased. A cut in wages does not revolutionise the techniques of production. A cut in wages, like absolute surplus value, does not decrease the amount of labour time necessary to produce a commodity and does not free labour for employment elsewhere (Simon, 1980, p. 49).

Often in negotiations the union would draw attention to their inferior wages and conditions when compared to the coal-miners of Durham (see, for example, Cleveland Miners' Association minutes, 6 August 1892, 10 October 1895. County Archives U/S/259). This point can be further endorsed by accounts given by those interviewed, of attempts to employ Durham miners in Cleveland. Most of the Durham men left after short periods, blaming poor conditions and the heavier nature of the work.

It is worth reiterating at this stage that the above case presents us with a clear contradiction between those exercising power (the owners) and the real interests of the excluded group (the miners). Yet the early attempts to resist and the consequent defeat presage a period of acceptance of the inequalities and those that are responsible for them.

In the course of interviewing miners, attempts were made to explore the role of the union, the Cleveland Miners' Association (amalgamated with the GMWU in 1932). This proved to be difficult as most of the responses indicated very low interest in the union. For example,

> It doesn't do to say what some of them thought about the union. . .a lot wasn't in the union, they had the idea it was no good. They didn't fight then, same as they do now, for the men. (Interview with W.J., 75-year-old miner.)
> That's the sort of union we had, mate. They wouldn't do nothin' for you, everything you asked them you were ignored. They never fought a case yet. (Interview with J.W., 67-year-old miner.)

Prolonged discussion proved impossible despite the use of probes, prompts and the rest of the interviewer's armoury of techniques. A certain amount of information can be gleaned from documentary sources.[7] This indicates that the union, under the guidance of two very long-serving agents (Joseph Toyn 1875–1911; Harry Dack 1911–36), developed into little more than a conciliation apparatus between men and owners. The records of the union are dominated by routine, well-mannered and deferential meetings with representatives of the owners bound together in the Cleveland Mine-owners' Association. As the union developed oligarchic features, compensation cases and administrative matters became the daily staple of union business, as it ceased to challenge for better wages and conditions. The ritual of the annual Demonstration Day declined into a holiday rather than an expression of solidarity. The union officials were responsive to the owners' views and as such became incorporated into a system of man management, but not totally. Cousins and Davis (1974), writing about the Northumberland coalfield of the 1870s, see union action entailing the following contradictions:

> Outright oppositional policies risk the collapse of the organizational means of opposition so painstakingly built up; outright integrative policies mean the acceptance of unacceptably large cuts in pay which it is one of the main purposes of the organization to resist. Economism implies the attempt to regulate and socially control market forces; the coalowners attempt to 'incorporate' and 'dis-incorporate' the union according to their own economic exigencies. To the extent that the proponents of the incorporation thesis do seize upon historical events. . . they fail to see the double meanings inherent in their growth – the means of resistance are themselves dependent; and the means of dependence are not unconditional and can generate opposition (1974, p. 293).

The generation of opposition may have occurred in Northumberland through the use of the political system but this was not the case in Cleveland, where it can be argued the dependent position of the union deflected working-class attention away from the political structure, because of the interchangeability of the personnel involved in the union and in the Labour Party.

Applying Lukes' and Gaventa's ideas about power's third dimension, the attitude of the Cleveland Miners' Association can be seen as having developed as a response to a perception of the power of the owners, anticipation of their reaction and a calculated withdrawal from conflict with the owners. This no doubt was a reflection of the majority feeling among the miners, who therefore came to view the union as inconsequential. Other factors need to be taken into account to support this contention of a development of powerlessness.

The majority of migrants into Cleveland during the opening up of the mines were from an agricultural background and their experience of the power 'field' developing along with mining operations has many features similar to that which would have been experienced in agriculture. The isolated and closed world of the agricultural labourer associated with deferential attitudes and behaviour is ideally malleable from the employers' point of view. Much of this attitude and behaviour would not be radically altered by the experience of employment in the Cleveland mines. The work pattern of ironstone mining isolated miner from miner and through the piece-work system men competed for the best places and were acutely aware of their relationships with the overmen and undermanagers who decided their daily conditions of work. Different systems of payments within and between mines, different allowances and variable geological conditions created and reinforced differences between workers. This, together with the rivalry, based originally on the different origins of migrants, between communities, presented barriers to the creation of group consciousness. These differences were also supported by the behaviour and attitudes of the local landowners and the individual mining companies.

The owners engaged in attempts to impose on the miners the idea that ironstone mining was largely unskilled work and could be undertaken by the simplest agricultural labourer of which there was a good supply. This idea was in fact contradicted by the owners' need to bring in skilled miners who passed on their skills to others, particularly when the shaft mines were sunk (Nicholson, 1982). The perceptions of miners were shaped in other ways too. The dominant religious force in the area was Methodism but this did not act as a training ground for union leaders, instead its ideological content was mediated by the local petite bourgeoisie (local shopkeepers, mines' engineers, skilled workers acting as local landlords). The potential for Methodism to act as Moore (1974) reports for Durham miners existed, but the social forms in which beliefs existed in the community affected the way in which those beliefs took effect. This is strongly reflected in the interview material gathered from elderly people when asked about their attitudes to owners, managers and local landowners. A great deal of difficulty is evident from those interviewed in terms of discussing these aspects of the power structure. Such elements are percieved as remote and not directly part of everyday life. Notions like Freire's 'culture of silence' in which the position of those in power is legitimised seem well suited to this population and to similar internal peripheries.

In many senses the mining population inhabited a restricted world where the flow of both material and cultural capital was controlled to a very large extent by those that derived, directly and indirectly, profit from the mining industry. In the present research one community has been closely examined in terms of possible responses to this structure (Cornish, 1984). One feature of interest that emerges is the widespread involvement in every institution and organisation in the community of the small group of petite bourgeoisie. They occupy all the influential positions in the community and this bloc precludes any significant working-class participation. Such a denial not only lessens the development of consciousness but also retains the powerless in highly dependent relationships. The extent to which this obtains has been explored in the case of the supposedly unconstrained world of the informal economy, but even here the parameters of involvement and the structure of activities are delimited by the powerful (Cornish, 1982).

CONCLUSION

This account of powerlessness among miners has emphasised the constraints and influences on action in the industrial context, the nature of this context being defined by economic, spatial and historical factors. The miners' reactions to such an unequal struggle are conditioned by their experience of the day-to-day working conditions and the sporadic attempts made by them and their organisations to improve such conditions.

A significant part of such a quiescent reaction, I would argue, is the miner's acceptance of his position as dependent on the vagaries of market competition, the owners' decisions (seen as contingent on their relative assessment of the value of domestic ironstone supplies compared to foreign imports, among other factors), and indeed the actions of other more powerful groups of workers in connected industries (primarily coal-miners). In sum, the ironstone miner had a peripheral status in a peripheral region. His reaction to, and use of, power was limited by an acceptance of such status.

The control of factors determining the miner's attitude to political and industrial action extended beyond work into almost every facet of his social life. Institutional practices in the mining communities were dominated by the petite bourgeoisie whose ideological stance, allied to the mine-owners' world view, severely limited the opportunities for an alternative consciousness to develop. The exercise of power was directly against the interests of the miner, whose acceptance of this was engineered through 'influencing, shaping or determining his very wants' (Lukes, 1974, p. 23).

There is no doubt a temptation to designate the above analysis as both historical and spatially specific, not generalisable to the contemporary situation or to other peripheral regions. I would contend that such an extension of the above findings is possible. Urry (1981, p. 464) emphasises how changes in contemporary capitalism have heightened the economic, social and political significance of locality. In the context of Cleveland and the North-East this can be clearly seen as determined by the continuing external control exercised by the key industries, whether multinational or nationalised. In Cleveland, the attitude to labour on the part of both ICI and the British Steel Corporation is all but indistinguishable. The growth of state expenditure and to a lesser extent employment again represents external control, but is dependent not on market forces but on the ability of localities to affect the allocation apparatus of the state. If, as has been indicated in the case study, this ability never develops or develops in a weak form, then little more than is necessary to maintain stability will be allocated by the state. The increasingly footloose nature of capital in a sense creates a power vacuum in the peripheral region, a vacuum not readily or effectively filled by a population in which powerlessness has been nurtured.

NOTES

1. See Urry's comment on the extent of the neglect of local effects (1981, p. 470), and his reference (p. 464) to Foster's historical work on spatial variations in local class structure (Foster, 1974).

2. An exception to this is the examination of the decline and depopulation of Lincolnshire, but this is presented as a refutation of Malthus rather than a thorough analysis of the reasons for regional decline (*Capital*, vol. II, ch. 25). Interestingly, it is from Lincolnshire that many of the immigrants to the Cleveland mines in the nineteenth century originally came (Lamballe, 1969).

3. A more detailed account of this process, particularly with respect to the extraction of surplus value can be found in Simon (1980, pp. 48–50). This type of analysis could be replicated in precisely the same way for Cleveland miners.

4. Such an argument and a further expansion of this point can be found in Edel *et al.*, 1978.

5. The only viable employment opportunities other than mining were in very low paid agricultural work, a few low paid local authority jobs and at the nearest steel plant at Skinningrove. However, miners had extreme difficulty in getting employment at any iron and steel plant, the owners requiring miners to remain miners.

6. In the course of the research, the results of which are found in Cornish (1984), extended interviews were carried out with a sample of elderly miners and other inhabitants in the community that was the focus of the research. Full details of the research methods employed and documentary sources can be found in Cornish (1984).

7. These are primarily the minutes of both the Cleveland Miners' Association and the Cleveland Mineowners' Association, and other documents relating to these associations.

REFERENCES

Aldcroft, D.H. and Richardson, H.W. (1969) *The British Economy* (London: Macmillan).

Allen, V.L. (1981) *The Militancy of British Miners* (Shipley: The Moor Press).

Amin, S. (1974) *Accumulation on a World Scale* (New York: Monthly Review Press).

Austrin, T. and Beynon, H. 'Global Outpost: The Working-Class Experience of Big Business in the North East of England, 1964–79'. Discussion document, Department of Sociology, University of Durham.

Bowden, P.J. and Gibb, A.A. (1967) *Economic Growth in the North East of England* (Business Research Unit, University of Durham).

Braverman, H. (1974) *Labour and Monopoly Capital: The Degradation of Work in the Twentieth Century* (New York: Monthly Review Press).

Bullock, I. (1974) 'The Origins of Economic Growth on Teesside', *Northern History*, vol. 9, pp. 79–95.

Bulmer, M. (1975) 'Sociological Models of the Mining Community', *The Sociological Review*, 23, pp. 61–92.

Cleveland Miners' Association and Mineowners' Association minutes, Cleveland County Archives U/S/259.

Cornish, S. (1982) 'The Structuring of the Informal Economy in East Cleveland Mining Communities', *North East Local Studies*, vol. 1, no. 2, pp. 39–57.

Cornish, S. (1984) 'The Social Consequences of Industrial Decline: A Case-study of an East Cleveland Mining Community'. (Unpublished Ph.D. dissertation, University of Hull).

Cousins, J. and Davis, R.L. (1974) 'Working-Class Incorporation – A Historical Approach With Reference to the Mining Communities of S.E. Northumberland 1849–1890', in Parkin, F. (ed.) *The Social Analysis of Class Structure* (London: Tavistock).

Edel, C.K., Edel, M., Fox, K., *et al.*, (1978) 'Uneven Regional Development: An Introduction to This Issue', *Review of Radical Political Economics*, 10 (3).

Emmanuel, A. (1972) *Unequal Exchange* (London: New Left Books).

Foster, J. (1974) *Class Struggle and the Industrial Revolution* (London: Methuen).

Freire, P. (1972) *Cultural Action for Freedom* (Harmondsworth: Penguin Books).

Gaventa, J. (1980) *Power and Powerlessness: Quiescence and Rebellion in an Appalachian Valley* (Oxford: Clarendon Press).

Gibbs, D., Edwards, T. and Thwaites, A. (1982) 'The Diffusion of New Technology and the Northern Region', *Northern Economic Review*, no. 5, pp. 22–8.

Gramsci, A., trans. by Lewis Marks (1957) *The Modern Prince and Other Writings* (New York: International Publishers).

Haggstrom, K. (1965) 'The Power of the Poor', in L. Ferman, J. Kornbuth, C. Haber (eds), *Poverty in America* (Ann Arbor: University of Michigan Press).

Harrison, R. (ed.) (1978) *Independent Collier: The Coalminer as Archetypal Proletarian Reconsidered* (London: Harvester Press).

Lamballe, L.J. (1969) 'The Origin of the Cleveland Ironstone Mines from the 1861 Census', *Bulletin of the Cleveland and Teesside Local History Society*, no. 7, pp. 14–16.

Lukes, S. (1974) *Power: a Radical View* (London: Macmillan).

Lukes, S. (1977) *Essays in Social Theory* (London: Macmillan).

Malizia, E. (1973) 'Economic Imperialism: An Interpretation of Appalachian Underdevelopment', *Appalachian Journal* , I, pp. 130–7.

Marglin, S. (1974) 'What Do Bosses Do?' *Review of Radical Political Economics*, Summer, 1974.

Marx, K. (1976) *Capital*, vol. 1 (Harmondsworth: Penguin Books).

Memmi, A. (1967) *The Colonizer and the Colonized* (Boston: Beacon Press).

Moore, R. (1974) *Pit-Man, Preacher and Politics* (London: Cambridge University Press).

Mueller, C. (1973) *The Politics of Communication: A Study in the Political Sociology of Language, Socialization and Legitimation* (New York: Oxford University Press).

Nicholson, A. (1982) 'The Growth of Trades Unionism Among the Cleveland Ironstone Miners 1850–1876' (Unpublished M.A. thesis, Teesside Polytechnic).

Saunders, P. (1979) *Urban Politics, A Sociological Interpretation* (Harmondsworth: Penguin Books).

Simon, R.M. (1980) 'The Labour Process and Uneven Development: The Appalachian Coalfields 1880–1930', *International Journal of Urban and Regional Research*, vol. 4, no. 1, pp. 46–71.

Urry, J. (1981) 'Localities, Regions and Social Class', *International Journal of Urban and Regional Research*, vol. 5, no. 4, pp. 455–75.

Wallerstein, I. (1976) *The Modern World System* (New York: Academic Press).

Williams, R. (1973) *The County and the City* (London: Oxford University Press).

4 Broken-up Canada and Breaking-up Britain: Some Comparative Lessons in Uneven Development, Regionalism and Nationalism During the Current Crisis

R. JAMES SACOUMAN

The unevenness of capitalism never ceases to amaze and confuse. The central unevenness is, of course, the immense wealth and control of the very few, the capitalist class, that is systematically expropriated from the combined labour power of the very many, the working class. Yet this fundamental and structured class-conflictual contradiction in capitalist social relations of production, the sytematic appropriation in social production of the surplus value created by the combined labour power of the many, never occurs straightforwardly. Systematic class exploitation is always *actually* mixed in with other systematic unevennesses: for example, by 'gender', by 'race', by 'region'. No worker, no capitalist, no petty producer, no unemployed person is free from gender, race and region; is unaffected by their impacts.

This amazing unevenness of capitalism leads to a number of common confusions in many everyday and social scientific

attempts to make sense of any one unevenness, such as regional inequality. These confusions tend to break down into
three major types: (i) the idealist confusion, the denial of the
importance of social relations of production in favour of
free-floating cultural–psychological traits; (ii) the economistic
confusion, the reduction of all unevenness to the strictly
economic aspect of a capitalism that is viewed as a machine;
and (iii) the reformist confusion, the assertion, by combining
the first two confusions, that what will solve unequal regionalisation is better programmes, policies and politicians, without radical change.[1]

If anything, nationalism and regionalism are even more
confusing. On the one hand, for example, we are confronted
with the *popular* spectacle of all those heroes (Gurkhas, Welsh,
Scottish, protectors of Northern Ireland, *et al.*) steaming off to
the South Atlantic to save the Great British nation from the
external threat of the barbarian; Britain-on-the-rocks, we are
assured, remains whole and free. On the other hand, the
current crisis has, since the late 1960s, encompassed an immense upsurge of regionalist and nationalist movements in the
relatively advanced capitalist states: movements which apparently run the range of being reactionary (such as Albertan
Western Canadian separatism?), liberal (Scottish National
Party?), social democratic (*Parti Quebecois? Plaid Cymru?* Scottish Labour Party? The Waffle?) and socialist (*le Mouvement
Socialiste?*); and which occur both in the relatively better-off
areas, such as Alberta, and in the relatively less well-off areas,
such as the Scottish Highlands and Islands.

How can we better understand these contemporary events
in all their historical, social, and political diversity? Can
anything be gained from comparisons between two countries
which, on the surface at least, appear vastly different? To
anthropomorphise, Canada is big, Britain much smaller;
Britain was the great mother empire, Canada is the paid
junior partner, the whore of shifting empires; and so on. Can
we learn some comparative lessons for Marxist analysis/
practice concerning the specific social-historical origins, mobilisation processes and outcomes of current nationalist and
regionalist movements? Can we learn these lessons by critically examining the literature in one of the most regionalised

nation-states in the world, Canada, and one of the most centralised, Britain?

This paper aims at one further step towards the adequate Marxist analysis of nationalism and regionalism in contemporary advanced capitalist states, particularly those of the middle power variety. A first section introduces a heuristic framework, extracted directly from a prior critical evaluation of the classical Marxist literature on nationalism and of recent contributions to the analysis of the advanced capitalist states and contemporary class cultures (see Sacouman, 1983a); which was itself derived partly from an earlier review and reformulation of the Canadian literature on regionalism (1983b); and a prior summing up of lessons learned from many concrete historical analyses by Marxists in the Maritimes and Newfoundland of worker and petty producer struggles (Sacouman, 1981; see also Brym and Sacouman, 1979; Sacouman and Grady, forthcoming).

In a second section I use this heuristic guide as a short, critical evaluation of what are surely the two most wideranging, state-wide attempts to make sense of nationalism and regionalism in Britain, the books by Hechter (1975) and Nairn (1981). In a third part, I review a selection of recent strong, within-region Marxist analyses of 'regionalisation' in Canada and Britain with a view to learning from these concrete cases while showing differences, similarities and shared deficiences. In a fourth section, I propose a more inclusive and incisive theorectical approach to historical materialist analyses of specific nationalist–regionalist movements in contemporary Britain and Canada – their origins, mobilisation processes, outcomes.[2]

AN INITIAL HEURISTIC FRAMEWORK[3]

This section outlines key aspects of an adequate historical materialist inquiry of nationalism/regionalism in advanced capitalism during the era of imperialism (that is, roughly the last century). The central feature of this heuristic framework is its focus throughout on struggle generally and class struggle, in all its uneven complexity, specifically. Thus, it *can* begin to provide a theoretical basis not only for insightful, substantive Marxist analyses, but also for clear socialist evaluations of particular nationalisms/regionalisms. Hence, understanding nationalist–regionalist movements is the key to understanding nationalism/regionalism, which is the key to understanding nations/regions as national–regional social formations.

All social movements are both part of and more than *the* social movement in capitalism: the structured, unequal and dynamic capitalist–working-class conflict for state supremacy/ hegemony, for renewed capitalism or for socialism. The 'essential' class struggle never occurs purely, but is always linked to the formation of class blocs between and within the fundamental classes and is always embedded in other movements that are across-class, but not beyond-class, struggles, such as nationalism/regionalism. *Nationalist movements* are organised struggles to define or redefine spatially and socioculturally a nation and to seize formal independence of a nation-state in the name of 'the people', spatially and socially (re)defined. Thus, all socialist movements are in fact nationalist, but not all nationalist movements are, by any means, socialist. *Regionalist movements* are organised struggles to define or redefine spatially and socio-culturally a region and to seize some (often further) relative autonomy within or between existing state areas in the name of 'the people', spatially and socially (re)defined.

Understanding regionalisation in the capitalist system – by class AND at global, inter-state and intra-state levels – is the key to understanding nationalist – regionalist movements, nationalism/regionalism and nations/regions as changing social formations. *Regionalisation* is the social class and political–juridical–spatial dimension of unequal or uneven development (as differentiated from the purely class-in-itself 'forces of production – logic of capital' dimension and from other dimensions of inequality, such as the social class and political-juridical-sexual dimensions). Regionalisation in any chosen period within the capitalist epoch is, then, a resultant of both the prior unequal reproduction of the forces of production and of former struggles of class blocs organised spatially. As such, regionalisation provides both the principal social bases for, and the central content of, nationalist–regionalist (and, indeed, socialist) struggles. All such movements attempt to alter or supplant prior regionalisation.

Nationalism/regionalism is an ideology, or system of 'habits, behaviour, beliefs, representations' (Legaré, 1982, p. 50) of a class or class bloc concerning the content and direction of 'the nation'/'the region'. The specific content (e.g., 'language', 'ethnicity', 'conditions of struggle') is often systematised by intellectuals and varies tremendously between and within regionalisms and nationalisms. No particular item (e.g., language, religion) is a necessary component. Nationalisms/ regionalisms are commonly best developed by dominant state blocs *or* by nationalist–regionalist movements, themselves the emergent (i.e., relatively creative) resultants of regionalisation.

On the other hand, regionalisation by class, globally and between and within states, provides the historical–material basis for *regionalised class culture*, lived and spatially distributed differences, by class, in habits, behaviours, beliefs and representations. These regionalised class cultures and beliefs are themselves the 'bottom-up' bases for the differences upon which conflicting nationalisms and regionalisms are formed and upon which nationalist and regionalist movements mobilise. Indeed, they set the 'internal' conditions of successful mobilisation in national–regional formations. Thus, through nationalist–regionalist movements and through varying class cultures, capitalist regionalisation provides the central, but never fully determinate, conditions for the origins and the content of alternative nationalisms/regionalisms and for the successful mobilisation of movements.

Any adequate analysis of regionalism/nationalism in central capitalism during the current imperialist era must further differentiate between states and between types of state regime, in order to specify further conditions for nationalist–regionalist growth and containment. Whereas Amin's treatment of unequal development rightly differentiates between central and peripheral capitalist states in the era of imperialism (e.g., 1976; 1980), his central argument concerning the centrality of the global periphery gets in the way of an adequate differentiation between *central-power central states*, that is, imperialist states like the USA, and *middle-power central states*, or 'junior partners' dependent upon imperialist states, like Canada and recent Britain. This differentiation is crucial to clarify relations between central states, but also to theorise and evaluate regionalisms/nationalisms from a Marxist perspective. State-wide nationalisms in imperialist states that are not in fact anti-nationalist (i.e., anti-imperialist) and fully socialist are necessarily reactionary in the case of central powers. Nationalisms and regionalisms in middle powers may or may not be socialist, depending, as in the global periphery, on their anti-imperialism and actual programme. The imperialist state is the theoretical and practical limit to nationalist–regionalist movements. Such movements in the middle powers, as in the periphery, *may* facilitate socialist change. Furthermore, any adequate approach to the problem of nationalism/regionalism in advanced capitalism must differentiate between the limitations and advantages to nationalism/regionalism (and to socialism) of historically developed *forms of state regime* (e.g., specific forms of democracy, degree of centralism–federalism, degree of direct state involvement in capitalist enterprise).

Finally, any analysis of contemporary nationalism and regionalism in central states must situate all of the above (regionalisation, movements, -isms, and state types) in the context of the current social crisis of capitalism and its states. Tall orders indeed.

DUES AND ADIEUS TO TWO GROUND-BREAKING OVERVIEWS

In many respects, Michael Hechter's *Internal Colonialism: The Celtic Fringe in British National Development, 1536–1966* (1975) can be seen as the 'efficient cause', by negative example, of the wealth of recent Marxist studies of regionalisation in Britain. The volume has taken a proper beating by Marxists, on both theoretical and historical–empirical grounds (e.g., Lovering, 1978; Nairn, 1981: esp. p. 65n and pp. 199–207; G. Williams, 1981).[4] Its central argument may be simplified, for both Nairn's and our purposes, as: 'British capitalist development produced a set of "internal colonies" in its Celtic fringe, for basically the same reasons as it created external colonization all over the globe. It is the contradictory nature of capitalist growth to do so. After external decolonization the liberation movements of the interior colonies have begun', based upon a cultural (ethnic) reaction to the imposed 'cultural division of labour' (Nairn, 1981, p. 201). Nationalist–regionalist movements in Britain are seen, then, as democratic, popular reactions to English dominance, rooted in an unequal and systematically *cultural* division of labour.

This theory has, for instance, rightly been criticised as 'over-abstract', 'insufficiently historical, and misses too many of the specifics', for overstressing 'cultural identity and cultural oppressions' (Nairn, 1981, pp. 65n, 199), and for being supportive of bourgeois nationalism (see G. Williams, 1981, pp. 279). The common core of these criticisms is, again as in the more general underdevelopment literature, the use of a primarily *spatial* core–periphery analogy. Nairn stresses Hechter's too simplistic linking of Britain's non-English regions to Britain's former external colonialism; Britain's external colonialism enabled 'real integrative tendencies to outweigh those of "uneven development" for a prolonged period' and even allowed relative 'over-development' in some British regions, 'Protestant Ulster and Scotland' (1981, pp. 65n, 202). Williams stresses 'the inadequacy of his treatment of internal variations that derives from an overemphasis on the spatial dimension of inequality' (1981, p. 280).

From the perspective of the preceding heuristic framework, Hechter's stance is at least equally as deficient. Internal colonialism virtually ignores changing class relations and forces of production; ignores the class alliances across regions; overly 'nation'-alises the so-called Celtic peoples; treats social movements as merely reactive to external exigencies; *de facto* justifies bourgeois nationalist–regionalist ideologies; declasses class cultures; ignores an understanding of the advanced central state; and ignores the impact of capitalist crises within that central state.

What does need to be retained (in the sense of going beyond) is an important emphasis on the common viciousness of the imperialist central state externally, *vis-à-vis* 'non-whites' especially, and *therefore* its more uneven viciousness within 'the United Kingdom' (most apparently in Northern Ireland). Hechter's central error was, then, in not proceeding towards a thoroughgoing Marxist class analysis of uneven British development, such as Amin has done for uneven global development. His error, it needs to be said again and again to all centrist Marxists who apparently stopped reading the uneven development literature with Emmanuel's and Frank's first volumes, was *not* that he pursued uneven development but that he did so merely spatially and culturally, without class analysis.

Tom Nairn's *The Break-up of Britain: Crisis and Neo-Nationalism* (1981, first published in 1977) remains, despite its inconsistencies and theoretical and empirical deficiencies, a landmark attempt at the proper treatment of the particular features of the national and regional question in one advanced capitalist state. In the 1977 version, Nairn examines nationalism as a relatively creative, though predominantly bourgeois response to the historical and current peculiarities of the British multinational state: its peculiarly 'patrician' (p. 19) and 'archaic' (p. 22) imperialism that is 'moribund' (p. 77) and increasingly dependent on US imperialism, and its singularly incorporated 'intellectual class' and 'labourist' alternative (p. 33). His central argument, in the 1977 version, may be simplified as: (i) 'uneven development (in Britain as a whole) "generates these given facts" of imperialism and nationalism for the contemporary era (*c.* 1750–2000), not vice-versa' (p. 21n); (ii) 'for most of the period (of imperialism) the leaner, marginal countries around England were associated with the act' (p. 41); (iii) but 'peripheral bourgeois nationalism has today become the grave-digger rather than the intelligentsia or the proletariat' (p. 80).

Nairn's 1977 contributions have been criticised most ably by Nairn in his 'Into Political Emergency: A Retrospect from the Eighties' (1981, pp. 365–404; see also Johnson, 1980, pp. 68 and 69; and, from a Stalinist stance, Blaut, 1980, 1982). The focus of Nairn's self-criticism and reformulation is his over-stressing of peripheral bourgeois nationalism as the grave-digger. The real crisis, he now claims, is a much more general, political, state-wide crisis based on the 'internationalization of the UK economy' between 1900 and the present (p. 382) and the consequent 'general class and territorial disequilibrium of UK state' (p. 387) due to Southern

City (i.e. financial capital's and British mega-multinationals') hegemony of the British State:

> a structural 'North–South' divide quite inseparable from the special historical form of the existing state. The under-lying trajectory of the state is towards the eversion of the British political economy. The metropolitan heartland com-plex will become even more of a service-zone to inter-national capital – the conveniently offshore location for investment or reinvestment, assurance and speculation, guaranteed by both public and private institutions and underwritten by a famous social stability. Unnecessary to offshore success, the industries and populations of the Northern river valleys will eventually be shut down or sold off. There is no possibility of 'reviving' such an old, chron-ically deprived industrial sector on a scale capable of sup-porting UK capitalism's top heavy metropolis; however, a significant manufacturing presence and significant employ-ment prospects can be returned by turning over the North directly to foreign capital. To make the river valleys as-sembly stages or branch-units of American, German, Japanese (and eventually Korean and Brazilian?) enter-prises is the ideal complement to the main City–Southern strategy (p. 388).

Britain, in other words, is, in its peculiar way, joining Canada as a middle-power central state in crisis.

Much is insightful from the perspective of our heuristic framework. But Nairn proceeds to gut his topic and his argument by concluding with a call to return to a renewed Britain-wide Socialism, based on a federalised Alternative Economic Strategy after the 'phoney war' (p. 393) of nation-alist struggles in the 1970s. And this despite his own admis-sion that:

> The chances of such enlightenment appear pretty small when set against England's indurate metropolitanism – that hege-monic arrogance which such long experience has turned into daily bread. But there is a question: can a new English socialism shed its political backwardness in time? Having

gone so far, is it really incapable of breaking with the shame and defect of British Socialism? (p. 404).

Why, theoretically, this shift to dependence on English social-ism instead of developing a committed analysis of the con-ditions, processes and outcomes of socialist movements that are nationalist–regionalist in 'the North'?

From the perspective of our heuristic framework, the short answer is his failure to take seriously the most recent contri-butions of Marxist analysts/activists in the global literature on uneven (unequal) development, in particular the work of Samir Amin (1976–80). This thoroughly common failure takes its theoretical justification from Marx's general model of the *abstract* capitalist mode of production (*as if* 'primitive accumulation' had been totally superseded by and only by 'expanded reproduction' even within the classic exemplar, Britain). It neglects one hundred years of world history, wherein the central struggles have been on the peripheries. It systematically excludes, even from vigorous critique, what has been surely the central historical materialist contribution in the last decade, Amin's (with others') Marxist theorisation of necessarily unequal capitalist development, based on the prob-lematic of formal and real capitalist domination and of class and nation in the era of imperialism.[5]

In the light of our framework, then, Nairn's analysis of Britain would have been substantially more apposite had he been able and willing to incorporate, critically, Amin's latest writings (especially, 1977; 1978; 1980) into his approach. Some of his substantive errors would not have been made: for example, his admitted 'ultra-Europeanist outlook' (p. 396) and his unadmitted *de facto* support for Thatcherite rolling devolution in Northern Ireland. His class analysis would have been strengthened by a consideration of regional variations in both formal and real subordination to capital. His 1977 sup-port for bourgeois nationalism would have been tempered with an understanding of other, actually broken-up middle-powers, like Canada. He would have focused his analysis of nationalism and regionalism on the formation and refor-mation of class blocs in the state and on nationalist–regional-ist social movements, in order to counteract his sometimes psychologistic treatment of nationalist ideologies.

A COMPARISON OF CASE STUDIES OF
REGIONALISATION IN BRITAIN AND CANADA

In this section I review and compare the approaches of
Marxist case studies of uneven regional development by analysts in the North-East of England, Wales, Scotland, the
Maritimes, Newfoundland and the Prairies in Canada,
Quebec, and Northern Ireland, with a view to building upon
them, where appropriate, in the light of heuristic framework.[6]
The literature in regionally rooted cases of uneven regional
development in advanced capitalism has, of course, recently
mushroomed, following the rise in nationalist–regionalist
movements during the current crisis and the prior theorisation
of such movements in 'peripheral' capitalism on a global
scale. And, as in the analysis of global capitalism, Marxist
analyses have taken the lead in this bountiful growth (see,
e.g., Lebas, 1982).

However, there has been very little theoretical and substantive cross-fertilisation, in the cases considered, when judged at
least by references. This is so not only between cases in
Canada and the UK, but also even between cases within these
states. In good part, this lack of a comparative dimension is
simply because the examples have all been very recent.
Hence, the central concern in all cases has so far been – and
must necessarily have been – the initial capturing of the
historical specificity of uneven regional development. But, at
least in some part and ironically enough, the lack of comparisons has been tied ideologically to state hegemony concerning
'uniqueness': two telling cases of this being state and
academic insulation of Northern Ireland from British comparisons (O'Dowd, Rolston and Tomlinson, 1980, p. 208);
and the insulation of Quebec regionalisation from comparison
with the rest of Canada (as in Sacouman, 1983b). Presum-
ably, then, comparisons are vital at this point in our development.

In the North-East of England, Carney et al. (e.g., 1976;
1977; 1981) have attempted to situate their region within a
general approach to regionalisation which views Britain, like
France, as a highly centralised 'declining imperialist', 'late
capitalist' society increasingly under the shadow of other
imperial countries; both Britain and France are 'attempting to

internalise their lost empires by the importation of alien labour and regional underdevelopment; both heavily dependent on the State as an economic and social regulator; both with oversized capitals performing an important hegemonic role' (1976, p. 12). For these authors, exploitation, imperialism and underdevelopment through super-exploitation are rightly key concepts. They sketch the early rise of the industrial North-East through single commodity (coal) and single market (London) dependence; the reproduction of a relative surplus population through, especially, attempts by the coal combines to increase the absolute rate of exploitation; the decline of coal and the growth of diversified dependence on Empire after 1880 (iron, steel, shipbuilding, arms); the internal crisis of Empire and the growth of state intervention for capitalism from the Second World War onward in shipbuilding and arms and in Department II (consumer goods) industries. The authors suggest the validity of their approach for other British regions, such as Wales and Scotland.

A People and a Proletariat (Smith, 1980) and *Poverty and Social Inequality in Wales* (Rees and Rees, 1980) are both preliminary attempts to grapple with the complexity of Welsh regionalisation; the first is primarily concerned with nineteenth century, the second with post-1945 Wales. Both volumes include a diversity of stances though both are against the vulgar metropolis–hinterland perspective.

Merfyn Jones' fine contribution to the 'historical' volume, 'Notes from the Margin: Class and Society in Nineteenth Century Gwynedd' (1980, pp. 199–214) stresses, against the tide of backwardness approaches, the early impact of capitalist industrialisation in, particularly, the copper and slate industries in the region and their links to the burgeoning English economy. He empirically differentiates (though undertheorises) the fully fledged proletarianisation of some workers, the semi-proletarianisation (this is not his term) of others, and the persistence of a class of poor tenant farmers and smallholders in the region, and thus sites the maintenance of Welsh as a popular, that is, across productive classes and fragments, although dominated medium.

Rees and Rees (1980, p. 21) attribute the rise of regionalised nationalism in Wales since the late 1960s to the uneven and necessary failures of the interventionist capitalist state to deliver its region-wide commitments, a position Gareth Rees (pp. 185–205) develops in more detail for industrial South Wales. Glyn Williams (pp. 168–84) stresses the spatial, class and cultural polarisation of post-1945 rural Wales due to a state subsidised and state-led growth pole or enclave strategy, which creates and recreates a diversity of 'marginalised' class fragments in the non-enclaves and heightens the dependence of those marginalised fragments on Welsh and Welshness.

The heterogeneity of the low income groups in the marginalized sector, together with the false sense of economic opportunity associated with self-employment, militates against the development of any proletarian consciousness amongst marginalized workers. The economic arrangements characteristic of marginalized areas tend to individualize the problems of making a living. These circumstances make class-based action difficult. It is also evident to many that the policies of the state, in collusion with external capitals, are, in part at least, responsible for the very process of marginalization. Hence, the 'adversary' can only be defined as a capitalism imported to the area and controlled by 'foreigners'. However, the class group which makes this definition is itself restricted to a marginal position. Therefore, class struggle cannot be characterized as embodying 'progress', as class struggle appears to be directed against the means of attaining that progress – foreign capital. It is in this situation that the tendency to align along ethnic lines, in opposition to a 'foreign master', arises. (Williams, 1980, p. 182)

As Tony Dickson's edited volume, *Scottish Capitalism: Class, State and Nation from before the Union to the Present* (1980) exemplifies, Marxist analyses are only beginning to make sense of uneven regional development in Scotland. This volume in general, and John Foster's contribution in particular (pp. 21–61; see Kerevan, 1981) eternalises 'the nation' as something formed in feudal times and kept alive until today. Because of this reification, in part, the contributors fail to treat the 'internal' regionalisation of Scotland in any depth, too often focusing on the Clyde subregion as representative. The contributors develop a notion of 'client capitalism' or 'junior partnership' that is 'complementary' to an English-led capitalist economy and Empire. They document Scottish capitalism's early extraversion both in terms of goods and money and discuss its limiting implications for uneven development, for working-class responses and for cultural assimilation within Britain. With the post-war crisis of Empire, they note the continuing flight of Scottish capital, stress the increasingly 'supplicant' status of Scotland and the ongoing deindustrialisation of imperial industries in the current crisis. Scott and Hughes (1980) add that the process had been one of junior partnership that has moved from (unequal) interdependence to integration, especially with the post-1945 'Anglicisation', 'Americanisation' and nationalisation of the economy.

In the Scottish case, fortunately, 'subregional' rural studies such as James Hunter's *The Making of the Crofting Community* (1976) and Ian Carter's *Farm Life in Northeast Scotland, 1840–1914* (1979) allow important specificity and theoretical advance. In particular, against any posited fully fledged or real capitalist penetration of petty primary production, Hunter and Carter document the persistence and maintenance up to the First World War at least, through struggle (especially Hunter) *and* because of direct and middle-term benefits to capitalism (especially Carter), of various forms of petty producer and semi-proletarianised class cultures in huge swathes of Scotland.

Somewhat similar emphases on junior partnerships and on *varieties* of petty production have informed some of the Canadian positions on uneven regional development. And rightly so, given Canadian capitalism and its state's prior relationship to the old British Empire and current relationships to ongoing US imperialism; given also, historically and currently, the 'Quebec problem'; and given the huge swathes of petty and non-petty primary production that is all but a very small space of Canada.

One 'early' quasi-Marxist, dependency approach to Canada's junior partnership with the US, similar in many respects to Dickson *et al.*'s (1980) general approach, was Robert Laxer's edited volume *(Canada) Ltd.: The Political*

Economy of Dependency (1973). In the intervening decade, an extensive debate has occurred during which numerous Marxist critiques of vulgar dependency theory and its Canadian non-Marxist roots have been developed (see the entire issue of *Studies in Political Economy*, no. 6, 1981). These critiques share an emphasis on inter-class analysis for the adequate understanding of the Canadian state but disagree, often and strongly, on the very nature of Canadian capital and its state. There is as yet no adequate Marxist analysis of Canada *vis-à-vis* its imperialist senior partners and the rest of the world – just as there is none of the UK.

The distinction between quasi-Marxist or reformist studies of regional uneven development in Canada and Marxist analyses is evident also in regionally rooted analyses. A strong example of the former is John Richards and Larry Pratt's *Prairie Capitalism: Power and Influence in the New West* (1979). *Underdevelopment and Social Movements in Atlantic Canada* (Brym and Sacouman, 1979; but see also Sacouman and Grady, forthcoming) can be taken as an attempt to initiate the second approach.

A quite subtle reformism, based on the combined confusion of economism and idealism, is entailed in *Prairie Capitalism*. The authors trace the economic development of the new staples of potash, oil and natural gas in Saskatchewan and Alberta and document their impact on the former agricultural base, class and political, of these two provinces. Their central argument is that a move away from 'dependent capitalism' has been engineered by an emerging 'new middle class' of provincial state officials and bureaucrats, in concert with a rising indigenous corporate élite. The authors support what they see to be a growth in the 'relative autonomy' of the provincial state fragment from American and central Canadian monopoly capital, both in its social democratic guise in Saskatchewan and its Tory dress in Alberta. Their reformism is problematic for a number of scholarly reasons: (i) it discredits the degree of economic power of multinational, monopoly capital, while overcrediting the importance of provincial political will – a position which the secondary author has himself criticised in a prior work (Pratt, 1976); (ii) it neglects the class relations of exploitation expanded upon by

the provincial state fragment in concert with both multinational and indigenous capital; and (iii) it provides a merely
political solution to a profoundly political, economic, social
and cultural process of uneven capitalist development.[7]

Underdevelopment and Social Movements in Atlantic Canada attempts to link the normal unevenness of state-wide capitalist
development to analyses of concrete, regionalised class struggles in an area that has been relatively underdeveloped
throughout this century. To do so, most contributors have
stressed the high variation in class fragment formations and,
thus, struggles in the region. Whether we looked at the life of
an individual semi-proletarian or semi-proletarian households
(see Sacouman, 1980) or the reproduction of a relative surplus
population in the region as a whole (Veltmeyer, 1979), our
findings can be summarised in the following manner:

> If the production of marketable items for private gain, of
> exchange-values or commodities, has been the fundamental
> dynamic in regions of capitalist development, the pro-
> duction of marketable raw materials and semi-processed
> goods, of primary products (staples) has tended to be a *more
> restricted* dynamic in regions of capitalist underdevelopment
> at least until very recently. If the social relationship of
> working class exploitation through capitalist production is
> basic to an understanding of class conflict under the capi-
> talist mode of production in general, social relationships of
> production tend to be *more variegated* in regions of capitalist
> underdevelopment. Producers in underdeveloped regions
> become distributed and maintained not only in capitalist-
> working class relationships of exploitation but also in
> capitalist-petty producer social relations in which surplus
> labour of petty commodity producer units is appropriated
> by large capital. As an integral part of the production and
> reproduction of surplus value and surplus labour pools
> within the underdeveloped regions, capitalist development
> maintains a significant percentage of petty primary pro-
> ducers in pre-capitalist or primary forms of production. . . .
> Thus, precisely because capital accumulation *per se* is un-
> even, underdeveloped regions are particularly character-
> ized by a *variety* of class conflictural relations. All of these

relations need to be specified in order to understand regional formations and the national-regional configuration. For example, 'semi-proletarianization' (i.e., a combination of wage labour and petty production based on an incomplete separation of the direct producers from the means of production) was the key process in the Maritimes from 1900 to 1940. This process structured both the large subregional pockets of surplus labour power and the major class conflicts in the region in that period (Sacouman, 1981, pp. 142 and 143).

A number of extended critical evaluations of this initiating volume have appeared (Barrett, 1980; Bickerton, 1982; Clow, 1983); the rational kernel of these evaluations rightly argues against our economism.

The literature on 'the Quebec–Canada problem' is, as would be expected, immense. S. B. Ryerson's *Unequal Union* (1975; see also Kealey, 1982a; 1982b) perhaps best exemplifies the standard Marxist view of the problem: a deeply historical reality of two founding settler nations in one state; a conquered Quebec nation in an unequal alliance with a conquering English–Canadian nation, held together by force and capitalist interest against the interest of the popular classes (see also Crean and Rioux, 1983). This approach combines an *a priori* definition of 'nations' (see Sacouman, 1983a) with a simplified analysis of the formation of class blocs within Quebec and within Canada. Certainly, it tends to beg both the question of the *construction* of nationality through the dominant state bloc and through nationalist movements (see, e.g., Monière, 1979; Guindon, 1978; Denis, 1979) and the question of the regionalisation of Quebec itself (e.g., Gagnon and Montcalm, 1982; *Interventions Economiques*, 1982).

An alternative historical materialist approach to the examination of Quebec society has been developed by Linteau, Durocher and Robert (1983). This approach, drawing upon some of Ryerson's best insights, stresses class formations and class blocs within Quebec in order to examine Quebec holistically. It begins to view social relations within Quebec in a North American context and thus is a landmark enterprise.

Yet, if a prize were to be awarded for the most adequate Marxist analysis of uneven regional development yet produced in the regions considered for the period of the current crisis, *Northern Ireland: Between Civil Rights and Civil War* (O'Dowd, Rolston and Tomlinson, 1980) should, from our perspective, receive it – despite its admitted lack of an analysis of the full Irish context and of the encompassing global context.[8] *Northern Ireland* develops a clear anti-imperialist stance, *against* the 'anti-anti-imperialist' stance on the question of Northern Ireland by such as Nairn (1981) and the Labour Party and *beyond* the merely all-Ireland nationalist stance of many others (see Martin, 1982).

O'Dowd *et al.* show the continuity, through changing appearances, of British capital and the British state's creation and reproduction, in alliance with the local bloc of Protestant bourgeoisie, officials and working class, of a sectarian statelet from partition through the 'reforms' to the current 'authoritarian populism' (for an updating, see O'Dowd *et al.*, 1982). On the one hand, the authors stress the social reproduction of sectarian class relations by the dominant class bloc and its state, demonstrating both religious sectarianism and class fragmentation to be closely linked, but not subsumed, historical–material relations. On the other hand, the authors argue the profound continuity of British capitalist state policy, whichever party has governed, with the Northern Ireland bloc of Protestant bourgeoisie, officers and workers: a (self-contradictory) policy of 'insulation' or 'containment' of the Northern Ireland question from home island affairs. Thus, the state has effected and secured a fundamental split of 'economics' from 'politics', of class from other social factors, and of reform from repression within the 'United' Kingdom of uneven regional development. These splits are further secured even in most Marxist analyses of regional uneven development in Britain (and in Canada).

Nothern Ireland and Northern Ireland, the statelet, are of crucial importance to the development of regionally rooted Marxist analysis *not* because Northern Ireland is the same as, or even very similar to, Scotland and the Maritimes. Sound, concrete, historical materialist work remains the creative task. They are important precisely because they demand all of us to take *variations* in imperialism and its specific impact on working-class fragmentation and alliances into central account in our analyses, just as Amin's work demands this from a global perspective. In reasserting the unity of political economy, of politics and economics, they force us to rectify our own economistic/idealist reliance on the mechanism of capitalism, as if capitalism actually existed as a pure mode of production, or our own reformist reliance on purely political reshuffling of marked decks. They force us to deny our too characteristic division of class and cultural matters (e.g., working-class struggle versus airy-fairy nationalism) and begin to clarify their materialist bases in conditioned struggles. They require us to examine repression and reform. These very requisites are the most serious deficiencies in the current analyses of uneven regional development considered here.

But, if we do have a best-yet example of regionally rooted Marxist analyses of uneven regional development in Canada and Britain (despite its being in the UK), we have *no* extended Marxist analysis in any region or in either state which has actually linked the conditions for nationalist–regionalist movements – i.e., capitalist uneven regional development – to the mobilisation and success/failure of these movements in the era of imperialism and in this current crisis. And if we have not done this, we cannot understand nationalism/regionalism in any but an idealist or economistic manner.

TOWARDS A MORE ADEQUATE THEORETICAL APPROACH: REQUISITE CONSIDERATIONS

In the light of our heuristic framework and our reading of the foregoing examples of regionally rooted Marxist analyses of uneven regional development in Canada and Britain, we can conclude by outlining a more adequate historical materialist understanding of our chosen cases in the contemporary period.

Capitalist Unequal Development (Uneven Regionalisation) as the Principal Social Basis for the Dominant State Bloc and Regionalised Class Cultures

Unequal development occurs on global, inter-state and intra-state scales. While virtually all of the preceding analyses were concerned, quite rightly, with thoroughly understanding the intra-state level of analysis, Amin's analysis suggests that the intra-state level can only be itself understood in the context of a global and interstate reality. Understanding unequal development on a global scale in the era of imperialism (1880 onward) entails an at least general understanding of global class formation, deformation and reformation through a focus on class struggle and the forces and relations or production and reproduction on a global scale. Understanding inter-state unequal development entails some solid situating of the capitalist state's relationships with other advanced capitalist states of both the central power and middle power varieties and with peripheral capitalist states – including, in all comparisons, inter-state relationships within the global working class and the global capitalist class.

Both the dominant state bloc and regionalised class cultural blocs can *then* be best understood by a focus on unequal development within the state and by period of boom and bust during the era of imperialism. Central considerations in terms of the dominant state bloc are: (i) the prior unequal development of its forces and relations of production within and, increasingly, by the capitalist state; (ii) the prior formation of a state bloc of regionalised and nationalised class fragments dominated by the monopoly capitalist class; and (iii) the direction of the state bloc during the current crisis (1967–now). Central considerations in terms of regionalised class cultures, given an understanding of the formation and direction of the dominant state bloc are: (i) the inter-class and intra-class bases for regionalised fragmentation within the nation-state; (ii) the inter-class and intra-class bases for regionalised or nationalised unity; and (iii) other social-cultural bases for regionalised fragmentation and/or regionalised and nationalised unity, by gender, religion, language, and 'ethnicity'; (iv) the links between other social bases and inter-class and intra-class bases for fragmentation and unity; and (v) the direction of regionalised fragmentation and unity during the current crisis. With the above we can attain a better historical materialist understanding of both the dominant state bloc (and its form of régime) and of the real bases for the formation, deformation and reformation of alternative regionalised and nationalised class cultural blocs.

The Dominant State Bloc and Regionalised Class-cultural Blocs as Principal Bases for the Mobilisation of Nationalist and/or Regionalist Movements

Both the dominant state bloc and alternative regionalised/ nationalised class cultural blocs can and do mobilise for 'nation' and/or 'region' building. Mobilisation by the dominant state bloc is, of course, for capitalism. Mobilisation processes here include: (i) Active state formation and reformation of the dominant state bloc of class fragments dominated by the monopoly capitalist class (including its own state capitalist fragment); and (ii) active state formation, deformation and reformation of means of co-optation and repression of alternative, dominated regionalised or nationalised class blocs. Alternative regionalist and nationalist movements 'proact' to their class cultural bases and 'react' to.the state's co-optation and repression. The crucial question for movement mobilisation becomes, therefore, its degree of fit in terms of (a) leadership, (b) ideology, and (c) programme with the basic class cultural bloc against the dominant state bloc's mobilisations. The social (and socialist) context of the movement depends on its fit with the underlying solidary bloc.

The Struggle Between Alternative Nationalist–Regionalist Movements and the Dominant State Bloc for Nationalism/Regionalism, for the 'Nation' or 'Region'

The dominant state bloc formulates and reformulates in struggle a state-wide ideology of 'nation'-building and of 'region'-building and uses its control over and access to means of official and unofficial communication to build and rebuild a state nationalism and regionalism: an institionalisation of 'nation' and 'region'. In contrast, the alternative movements shape, reshape and communicate their ideologies, programmes and leaderships in struggle with both the state's necessarily 'big capitalist' position and the positions of other movements (nationalist, regionalist, internationalist). Nationalism/ regionalism, the 'true nation' and the 'true region', are real constructs of the relative success of these struggles between class blocs at any given moment.

This theoretical approach is, of course, a first formulation based on an intensive and relatively extensive period of reading and rethinking that followed a period of much more concrete work in the Maritimes. The framework may or may not make sense of the real world of nationalist and regionalist movements and of nationalism and regionalism. Theoretically and comparatively, it should make better sense, or so I have argued. Whether it does or not depends upon further and varied concrete studies, one of which I am pursuing for the case of one middle power during the current crisis: Canada, 1967-present. Others in Canada and Britain may and perhaps even should take up the approach and alter it as found necessary and appropriate.

NOTES

The original version of this paper was prepared with partial Social Sciences and Humanities Research Council of Canada funding while on sabbatical leave from Acadia University at the Centre of Canadian Studies, University of Edinburgh. Thanks to all these organisations for their encouragement. David Nock made some helpful initial suggestions, despite the fact that he must view this paper as a theoreticist diversion from more concrete work. All inadequacies remain my own.

1. For a review of these three confusions in the anglophone Canadian literature concerning regional inequalities, see Sacouman (1983b).
2. I have moved – haltingly and unevenly, and with the opposite criticism of other socialists in Canada – from concrete cases of struggle to abstract theorising. I am now finally on my way back to the concrete by pursuing a book-length manuscript on 'nationalism and regionalism in a middle power during the current crisis: Canada, 1967-present'. For a *general* justification of this long-term methodology, concrete-to-abstract-to-concrete, see Johnson (1982).
3. Key sources for developing this heuristic were Marx (especially 1976) and Amin (1976; 1977; 1978; 1980).
4. Hechter himself saw his model as a 'painfully preliminary' (1975: 6) and has somewhat modified his views *vis-a-vis* Scotland (in *Cencrastus*, 1982).
5. I make this point more rigorously in Sacouman (1983a) and (1983b).
6. I do *not* attempt here to situate historically, socially and politically the diverse Marxist positions taken. Such an enterprise is no doubt both

instructive and crucial (see, e.g., Johnson *et. al.*, 1982), especially because some of the analysts considered come close to denying their own positioning with claims to disciplinary objectivity (e.g., Smith, 1980, p. 238).

7. For the argument against reformist analyses in Newfoundland, see Overton (1979; forthcoming).

8. Any adequate analysis of the whole of Ireland must take into account James Connolly's path-breaking revolutionary analyses (e.g., 1973), their being systematically ignored in Britain and other places, *and* the use and misuse of Connolly's work inside Ireland. One non-Marxist writes: 'No fewer than twenty-three such communist, socialist and left-wing groups exist in Ireland, according to a list appearing in the 23 June 1972 issue of *Hibernia*. These organizations represent various trends in national and international politics, but all, without exception, lay claim to James Connolly as their model and inspiration' (Levenson, 1973, p. 339).

REFERENCES

Amin, Samir (1976) *Unequal Development* (New York: Monthly Review Press).

Amin, Samir (1977) *Imperialism and Unequal Development* (New York: Monthly Review Press).

Amin, Samir (1978) *The Law of Value and Historical Materialism* (New York: Monthly Review Press).

Amin, Samir (1980) *Class and Nation: Historically and in the Current Crisis* (New York: Monthly Review Press).

Barrett, L. Gene (1980) 'Perspectives on Dependency and Underdevelopment in the Atlantic Region', *Canadian Review of Sociology and Anthropology*, 17 (3), pp. 273–86.

Bickerton, James (1982) 'Underdevelopment and Social Movements in Atlantic Canada: A Critique', *Studies in Political Economy: A Socialist Review*, no. 9, pp. 191–202.

Blaut, J. M. (1980) 'Nairn on Nationalism', *Antipode: A Radical Journal of Geography*, 12 (3), pp. 1–17.

Blaut, J. M. (1982) 'Nationalism as an Autonomous Force', *Science and Society*, 44 (1), pp. 1–23.

Brym, Robert J. and Sacouman, R. James (eds) (1979) *Underdevelopment and Social Movements in Atlantic Canada* (Toronto: New Hogtown Press).

Carney, J., Hudson R., Ive, G. and Lewis, J. (1976) 'Regional Underdevelopment in late Capitalism: A Study of the Northeast of England', in I. Masser (ed.), *Theory and Practice in Regional Science* (London: Pion Ltd.) London Papers in Regional Science, 6, pp. 11–29.

Carney, J., Hudson R., and Lewis, J. (eds) (1981) *Regions in Crisis* (London: Croom Helm).

Carney, J., Lewis J., and Hudson, R. (1977) 'Coal Combines and Interregional Uneven Development in the UK', in D.B. Massey and P.W.J. Batey (eds), *Alternative Frameworks for Analysis* (London: Pion Ltd.) London Papers in Regional Science, 7, pp. 52–67.

Carter, Ian (1979) *Farm Life in Northeast Scotland, 1840–1914* (Edinburgh: John Donald).

Cencrastus (1982) 'Symposium', no. 10.

Clow, Michael (1983) 'Politics and Uneven Capitalist Development: The Maritime Challenge to the Study of Canadian Political Economy'. Paper presented to the annual meeting of the Canadian Sociology and Anthropology Association, UBC. Forthcoming in *Studies in Political Economy: A Socialist Review.*

Connolly, James (1973) *Selected Writings* (P. Barresford Ellis (ed.)) (Harmondsworth, Penguin Books).

Crean, Susan and Rioux, Marcel (1983) *Two Nations* (Toronto: James Lorimer).

Denis, Roch (1979) *Luttes des classes et question nationale au Quebec, 1948–1968* (Montreal: PUQ).

Dickson, Tony (ed.) (1980) *Scottish Capitalism.: Class, State and Nation from Before the Union to the Present* (London: Lawrence and Wishart).

Foster, John (1980) 'Scottish Nationality and the Origins of Capitalism', in Dickson (ed.), pp. 21–61.

Gagnon, Alain G. and Montcalm, Mary Beth (1982) 'Economic Peripheralization and Quebec Unrest', *Journal of Canadian Studies*, 17 (2), pp. 32–42.

Guindon, Hubert (1978) 'The Modernization of Quebec and the Legitimacy of the Canadian State', in D. Glenday *et al.* (eds), *Modernization and the Canadian State* (Toronto: Macmillan of Canada), pp. 212–76.

Hechter, Michael (1975) *Internal Colonialism: The Celtic Fringe in British National Development, 1536–1966* (London: Routledge and Kegan Paul).

Hunter, James (1976) *The Making of the Crofting Community* (Edinburgh: John Donald).

Interventions Economiques (1982) No. 8, Special Issue on 'La question régionale'.

Johnson, Richard (1980) 'Barrington Moore, Perry Anderson and English Social Development', in S. Hall *et al.* (eds) *Culture, Media and Lanaguage: Working Papers in Cultural Studies, 1972–79* (London: Hutchinson), pp. 48–70.

Johnson, Richard (1982) 'Reading for the Best Marx: History-Writing and Historical Abstractions', in R. Johnson, G. McLennan, B. Schwarz, and D. Sutton (eds), *Making Histories: Studies in History-Writing and Politics* (London: Hutchinson), pp. 153–201.

Jones, Merfyn (1980) 'Notes from the Margin: Class and Society in Nineteenth Century Gwynedd', in Smith (ed.), pp. 199–215.

Kealey, Gregory S. (1982a) 'Stanley Brehaut Ryerson: Canadian Revolutionary Intellectual', *Studies in Political Economy: A Socialist Review*, no. 9, pp. 103–131.

Kealey, Gregory S. (1982b) 'Stanley Brehaut Ryerson: Marxist Historian', *Studies in Political Economy: A Socialist Review* no. 9, pp. 133–70.

Kerevan, George (1981) 'Arguments Within Scottish Marxism', *Bulletin of Scottish Politics*, no. 2, pp. 111–33.

Laxer, Robert (ed.) (1973) *(Canada) Ltd.: The Political Economy of Dependency* (Toronto: McClelland and Stewart).

Lebas, Elizabeth (1982) 'Urban and Regional Sociology in Advanced Industrial Societies: A Decade of Marxist and Critical Perspectives', *Current Sociology*, 30 (1), pp. 7–234.

Legaré, Anne (1982) 'Towards a Marxian Theory of Canadian Federalism', *Studies in Political Economy: A Socialist Review*, no. 8, pp. 37–58.

Levenson, Samuel (1973) *James Connolly: A Biography* (London: Martin Brian and O'Keefe).

Linteau, Paul-André, Durocher, R. and Robert, J.C. (1983) *Quebec: A History, 1867–1929* (Toronto: James Lorimer and Company). First published as *Histoire du Quebec Enterporain de la Confederation à la Crise* (Montreal: Boreal Express).

Lovering, John (1978) 'Theory of the "Internal Colony" and the Political Economy of Wales', *Review of Radical Political Economics*, no. 10, pp. 55–67.

Martin, John (1982) 'The Conflict in Northern Ireland: Marxist Interpretations', *Capital and Class*, no. 18, pp. 56–71.

Marx, Karl (1976) *Capital*, Vol. I (Harmondsworth: Penguin Books).

Monière, Denis (1979) *Le developpement des ideologies au Quebec* (Montreal: Quebec/Amerique).

Nairn, Tom (1981 1977) *The Break-up of Britain: Crisis and Neo-Nationalism* 2nd edit. (London: Verso).

O'Dowd, L. Rolston, W. and Tomlinson, M. (1980) *Northern Ireland: Between Civil Rights and Civil War* (London: CSE Books).

O'Dowd, L., Rolston, W. and Tomlinson, M. (1982) 'From Labour to the Tories: The Ideology of Containment in Northern Ireland', *Capital and Class*, no. 18, pp.72–90.

Overton, James (1979) 'Towards a Critical Analysis of Neo-Nationalism in Newfoundland', in Brym and Sacouman (eds), pp. 219–49.

Overton, James (forthcoming) 'Crisis and Regional Policy in Canada', in Sacouman and Grady (eds).

Pratt, Larry (1976) *The Tar Sands: Syncrude and the Politics of Oil* (Toronto: McClelland and Stewart).

Rees, Gareth (1980) 'Uneven Development, State Intervention and the Generation of Inequality: The Case of Industrial South Wales', in Rees and Rees (eds), pp. 185–205.

Rees, Gareth and Teresa L. Rees (eds) (1980) *Poverty and Social Inequality in Wales* (London: Croom Helm).

Richards, John and Larry Pratt (1979) *Prairie Capitalism: Power and Influence in the New West* (Toronto: McClelland and Stewart).

Ryerson, Stanley Brehaut (1975) *Unequal Union: Confederation and the Roots of Conflict in the Canadas, 1815–1873* (Toronto: Progress Books).

Sacouman, R. James (1980) 'Semi-Proletarianization and Rural Underdevelopment in the Maritimes', *Canadian Review of Sociology and Anthropology*, 17 (3), pp. 232–45.

Sacouman, R. James (1981) 'The "Peripheral" Maritimes and Canada-Wide Marxist Political Economy', *Studies in Political Economy: A Socialist Review*, no. 6, pp. 135–50.

Sacouman, R. James (1983a) 'Nationalism and Regionalism in Capitalist

Democratic States: A Renewed Marxist Approach', Paper presented at the Conference on the Structure of the Canadian Capitalist Class, University of Toronto.

Sacouman, R. James (1983b) 'Uneven Development, Regionalism and Struggle', in J. Paul Grayson (ed.), *Introduction to Sociology: An Alternate Approach* (Toronto: Gage), pp. 149–69.

Sacouman, R. James and Donald J. Grady (eds) (forthcoiming) *Labour, Capital and the State in Atlantic Canada* (Toronto: New Hogtown Press).

Scott, John and Michael Hughes (1980) *The Anatomy of Scottish Capital: Scottish Companies and Scottish Capital, 1900–1979* (London: Croom Helm).

Smith, David (ed.) (1980) *A People and a Proletariat: Essays in the History of Wales, 1780–1980* (London: Pluto).

Studies in Political Economy: A Socialist Review (1981) No. 6. A special issue on 'Rethinking Canadian Political Economy'.

Veltmeyer, Henry (1979) 'The Underdevelopment of Atlantic Canada', in Brym and Sacouman (eds), pp. 17–35.

Williams, Glyn (1980) 'Industrialization, Inequality and Deprivation in Rural Wales', in Rees and Rees (eds), pp. 168–204.

Williams, Glyn (1981) 'Economic Development, Social Structure and Contemporary Nationalism in Wales', *Review*, 5 (2), pp. 275–310.

5 Conceptions of Wales and Welshness: Aspects of Nationalism in Nineteenth-Century Wales

GRAHAM DAY AND RICHARD SUGGETT

Wales exists because nationalism says that it exists . . . In this sense, Wales becomes a process rather than a place, and thus a fit subject of history. (R.M. Jones, 1982, p. 20)

What we propose to do in this paper is to identify some questions concerning nationalism that should interest sociologists, and provide an indication of how they might be tackled, through brief examinations of particular aspects of nationalism in nineteenth-century Wales. Our remarks are preliminary since much basic research remains to be done on the social and political movements of modern Wales.

A pertinent starting point is provided by a recent combative essay by Isabel Emmett (1982) which recognises that the theoretical constitution of Wales is a proper scholarly task for sociologists, but warns that an excessively analytical or conceptual approach can suggest only that 'the term "Wales" refers to a figment of some imaginations which a few people calling themselves Welsh may be tricking the British government into making a reality', a possibility she counters by an appeal to what could be termed the 'obvious' Wales, a real thing, grounded in ordinary people's conceptions of Wales. She makes the crucial assertion that

Wales has a history of its own . . . there is within Wales a pervasive nationalism . . . perhaps the majority of the Welsh regard the territorial frontier as meaningfully containing what they call Wales because the frontier is part of its history and of the distinctive political and administrative arrangements; and see the economic basis of Wales as the land, water, livestock, labour power and brains within that frontier (Emmett, 1982, p. 170).

While these claims are indisputable, Emmett's own discussion shows quite clearly that they do not settle the matter. In keeping with the prevailing view of ethnicity, and national identity, as an affiliation that must be produced and reproduced, she emphasises that while consciousness of national identity saturates life in Wales (North Wales in particular), there are *competing* definitions of what constitutes Wales and Welshness. Although Emmett asserts that the situational use of these alternatives causes little confusion, nevertheless she admits that the retention and creation of a distinctive identity is a practical problem for many Welsh people, and that any realistic nationalist movement must seek to reconcile these diverse meanings.

Such considerations pose the problem: in what sense should 'Wales' enter as a category into sociology? We cannot settle this by recourse to the meanings of actors themselves if there is no more than provisional or limited consensus among them, and when indeed the key terms are in dispute. Rather it is our contention that close attention must be paid to just those variations and discrepancies in meaning. After all, we might say with equal accuracy that actors' consciousness is suffused with a sense of class, yet be unable to look to the contents of that consciousness for a definition of what class *is*. Normally, we might turn here to the uncovering of some relevant 'objective' reality, supposing that classes are there whether or not people seem to act upon them. In the case of nations, or nationalities, it is less apparent what the objective underpinning might be: we are brought on to the difficult terrain of the relationship between cultural representations and the economic and social relationships which underlie them.

NATIONALITY AND HISTORIANS

The complexities involved in unpacking different versions of national identity and relating them to economic and social structures are well displayed in the work of certain historians. For example, Terence Brown (1981) has shown how, following independence, Irish identity was organised around the idea of religious distinctiveness and the imagery of a traditional rural Gaelic-speaking folk. The Irish example is of great interest in showing how a conservative conception of an organic nationality can emerge after the establishment of a nation-state. The success of this dominant conception rested in the end on the ability of the state to provide a focus for national identity, constructing an authoritative version through its deployment of key myths and symbols. This process of building-up a system of shared identifications involved the suppression or muting of alternative conceptions, especially those held by the labour movement and the Protestant minority in the south, and the exclusion of certain groups – Protestants and the newly defined Anglo-Irish – as non-Irish. Popular mobilisation around the key symbols, and identification with a rural national tradition, required the bracketing-off of much contemporary social reality: a task made easier by the partition which separated the main industrial region (Ulster) from the rest of Ireland.

The difficulties surrounding the idea of a common and distinctive Welshness are identified with characteristic clarity by Raymond Williams (1981). He takes the results of the devolution referendum, which have been described elsewhere in an illuminating phrase as 'the rejection of "Wales" by the Welsh' (G. Williams, 1982, p. 183), as signifying a crisis of Welsh identity, a dividing rather than unifying issue, and goes on to suggest some of the components of this crisis:

Some early phases of nationalism . . . supposed Welshness to be in effect genetic or, more plausibly, linguistic, when the actual cultural formation had been a prolonged interaction between always diverse native elements and the both dominant and alternative effects of an occupying power . . .

this long and intricate history had diverse potentials (that have) developed but also confronted each other. Neither relative prosperity nor absolute economic depression brought them more than temporarily together (R. Williams, 1981).

The success of an organic Irish nationalist ideology, and the weaknesses of a comparable Welsh ideology, is reflected in the respective historiographical traditions. Republican historiography, according to Brown (1981), consisted of the successful presentation of 'an indestructible, historic, predestinate nation that had achieved its apotheosis in the 1916 Rising', 'a myth of the seamless garment of Irish historical continuity' (Brown, 1981, pp. 287, 290). By contrast, the dominant strain of Welsh nationalist historiography has been a deeply pessimistic threnody organised around a series of key dates and events (1282 – the death of Llewelyn; 1485 – the Tudor ascendancy; 1536 – the Act of Union; 1959 – the drowning of Tryweryn) taken to represent successive, cumulative woundings of the Welsh nation through attacks on the inherited features of Welsh identity, especially language. This tradition extends well into the post-war period.

Bobi Jones' article 'The Roots of Inferiority' (1974) may be taken as a representative example. By taking the language as the 'central point in the Welsh character', he can argue that 'the legal or objective inferiority conferred on the Welsh languange in the sixteenth century (by the Act of Union) produced a subjective sense of inferiority in the Welshman regarding his own identity and character': a chronic inferiority complex is the lasting consequence of the relationship between the English and the Welsh. Despite the weaknesses of Jones' psychologising, he is pointing to an aspect of the sociology of power which is of great interest: the process through which the values of a dominant group/society are legitimised as superior and those of a subordinate group/society defined as inferior: a process which may involve the 'internalization of alien norms among dependent societies' (cf. the argument of Gaventa, 1980). Notions of internal colonisation have some relevance here. While this crucial process is hinted at within nationalist history, we would suggest it cannot be given adequate attention in the light of

the underlying image of the groups involved as simply separate (one oppressing the other) rather than as related and
interpenetrating, and developing *together* through a shared
history.

Given dominant interpretations of Welsh nationality, recent explorations of the artificial or manufactured nature of
many features of 'traditional' cultural identity in late
eighteenth- and early nineteenth-century Wales are especially
important (see P. Morgan, 1981 and G.A. Williams, 1980).
We can readily discern the correspondence between the
emergence of a Welsh identity in this period and the elabor-
ation of national culture among 'buried nationalities' elsewhere in Europe, and the links between this process and
subsequent demands for cultural autonomy. As Eley puts it,
'culture was the terrain upon which the category of the nation
was first elaborated, and in this sense nationality is best
conceived as a complex, uneven, and unpredictable process,
forged from an interaction of cultural coalescence and specific
political intervention, which cannot be reduced to static criteria
of language, territory, ethnicity or culture' (1981, p. 91).

SOCIOLOGY AND NATIONALISM

These considerations highlight the dangers touched on by
Merfyn Jones when criticising those historians who admit
concepts of nation and national identity as uninterrogated
terms within their work, treating them as serious analytical
categories. Instead, he argues, 'nationalisms should be located
as the objects of research and analysis, rather than admitted
as organizing concepts in themselves' (1982).

So far as nationalism in general is concerned, it is possible
to make some fundamental sociological points. Nationalism is
first and foremost an ideological phenomenon, a matter of
ideas and conceptions adhered to by certain individuals and
groups. This has been stressed by Zubaida, who argues that
'from the point of view of the sociologist or any social theorist,
there cannot be any systematic way of designating a "nation" '
(Zubaida, 1977, p. 53). He cites Lenin (1920, 1967) to similar
effect – 'it is not a problem for Marxist theory to define a

"nation" – it is not a theoretical problem, but one of political practice'. This orientation, to nationalism as a phenomenon of political practice and ideological discourse, is helpful: it means that the question we ought to address is not that of the real 'nation' or national identity which lies behind concepts employed in political life, but that of the formation, articulation, and propagation of the concepts themselves. Nationalist ideas, myths and definitions have to be deconstructed. This means that we need to treat 'Wales' as it has figured in successive, and rival, discourses, and consider the question 'How many Wales?' or 'How many ways of being Welsh?'

Confusions undoubtedly arise among sociologists from the tendency to adopt, as an authoritative criterion, some particular version of nationalism – usually, nationalism is equated with the project of creating a nation *state* of the typically self-contained nineteenth-century European variety. Because this is often the implicit standard of 'proper' nationalism, we find the generation of new terms to designate nationalist ideologies which fall short of it ('ethnonationalisms', 'ethnoregionalism', 'peripheral subnationalism', etc.). It may be, however, that the concept of nation-state was appropriate only for a particular historical phase and no longer carries weight as a plausible goal (at least in the First World) for movements which designate themselves as 'nationalist'.

In fact, nationalism is widely seen as an *exceptionally* flexible ideological field: A.D. Smith, for instance, equates nationalism with 'historicism', the creation of consciousness through a cult of national characteristics, and allows that nationalism is peculiarly vague and plastic. His reason for this is that 'of all ideologies it is one of the most remote from immediate social and economic consciousness and so can embrace many groups with conflicting goals within its fold' (1976, p.26). The appeal to an everyday consciousness of nationality effectively denies the first part of this statement: as we have already noted, Emmett (1982) sees immediate social and economic awareness in North Wales as full of nationalism: she contends that the most evident structural reality for local people is 'ruling England'. Similarly the North Wales quarrymen 'wore their Welsh identity like their working clothes' (R.M. Jones, 1982,

p. 56). It is not 'remoteness' which gives nationality its flexibility, but its inchoateness, the necessity for some means of articulation which sharpens and interprets it, to give it direction. Smith's second point is central here: within movements for nationalism there are always quite distinctive streams and directions whose positions overlap and diverge in complex ways. Given that different tendencies are to be found 'within' nationalism, their struggles must be fought out ideologically as well as politically.

This is sometimes lost sight of within sociological discussion. A common form of analysis has been to look for shared features of nationalism, regardless of time and place, to produce generalised descriptions, and then search for underlying causes. This methodology is used by Smith (1976), who comes up with 'bureaucratization' as the master process, and the intelligentsia or 'professional classes in the widest sense' as the most significant social base or bearers of nationalism. But although intellectuals are always prominent – for reasons that need discussion – the social bases for nationalism show a breathtaking diversity that includes landowning nobilities, 'national' bourgeoisies, petit bourgeoisies, and peasants (Kiernan, 1976). The interplay of highly varied social groups and collectivities emerges very clearly as a theme in the record of nationalist movements in Scotland (MacIver, 1982) and Ireland (Boyce, 1982), and Wales is no exception. This confirms the importance of seeing nationalism as an evolving matrix of shifting definitions and competing constructions. It is preferable to adopt a perspective which firmly situates nationalism in its time, place, and stage of development (Orridge, 1982). It hardly needs saying that nationalism is not a 'merely' ideological issue: the changing conceptions are grounded in real, extra-discursive, social formations. As Emmett (1982, p. 169) rightly notes, the contents of Welshness 'are neither trivial nor arbitrary but rooted in the specific historical experiences of people living in a specific part of the world': we have to look for the correspondence between ideas of Wales, and the changing reality of material existence for Welsh people.

Our central question therefore concerns the ways in which nationalism is *constructed* and given political expression. A 'nation' can be regarded as a particular variant of 'community'; ideas of the communal, of identity and difference, of who belongs and who does not, are integral to nationalist concepts. Just as at the immediate level of daily life, ethnicity is a label that can be situationally deployed, so at the political level nationality has to be worked on according to circumstances and objectives. Nationalist ideologies are formulated, we submit, in order to gain and retain hegemony; like other forms of political ideology, they serve to bring together social alliances containing a variety of different elements, including especially classes or class fractions, which mobilise to secure political and cultural ends. We would emphasise the importance of seeing this in terms of alliances: the 'job' of nationalism is to hold together, if possible, some combination of potentially disparate elements, which might easily be drawn apart into quite different forms of political alignment, and to do so within a particular relation that situates them in positions of domination and subordination. 'Hegemony' is the process which reproduces the relations between leaders and followers through an organisation of consent (Gray, 1977). Since this relationship is always subject to tension, it cannot remain static: hegemony is not fixed, but a moving relation which has to be constantly refurbished, i.e. 'renewed, recreated, defended and modified' (R. Williams, 1977, p. 112). The changing nature of the ideological discourse which results is usefully pinpointed by Mouffe (1979) who indicates the subtle and gradual rolling over of ideas which is likely to go on.

This implies that we should reject a conception of nationalism as a simple or rigid bloc of ideas that corresponds directly to a given social class, or even to a given ethnic collectivity, and the type of labelling that goes along with it ('Nationalism is a petit bourgeois ideology' etc.). Nationalism provides one of the (continually present?) ideological forms through which men and women may become conscious of, or try to make sense of, their social existence as it is transformed over time. It may still need saying, to those whose views are formed only at the 'centre', that for this reason it is not possible to dismiss nationalism as an 'antique' or reactionary phenomenon.

In the remainder of this paper, we intend to examine two

strands from the complicated tangle of nineteenth-century Welsh nationalism – the land question and the debate around education. We preface this with a very brief indication of the social context in which they occurred, a context that has been discussed more fully elsewhere (Day, 1984).

WELSH SOCIETY IN THE NINETEENTH CENTURY

The period witnessed the transformation of Wales from a predominantly agrarian society with a distinctive social character into a grotesquely unevenly developed economic and social formation dominated by industrial South Wales. In 1800, power was virtually monopolised by a highly concentrated landowning class, who exercised almost exclusive control over legal and military authority and political representation. The bulk of the rural population were tenant farmers, and holdings were mostly insufficient to yield much beyond subsistence returns. By the end of the century, power had been usurped by new social interests: a capitalist class of imperial pretensions, centred in South Wales but inextricably connected to wider British capitalism (G.A. Williams, 1982, pp. 171–87) and a significant indigenous middle class. It was the latter which successfully hijacked Welsh national identity and made it their own, harnessing institutions and ideology into the formidable construct of Liberal nonconformity. These were the 'halcyon days' (K.O. Morgan, 1981, p. 410) when for a brief moment rural and industrial Wales were held together within a framework of common values and shared leadership which has deeply inflected subsequent nationalist development. No sooner was this achieved than it was broken apart by the unstoppable momentum of economic development.

THE LAND QUESTION

The struggle over the Welsh land question clearly illustrates the battle for hegemony. An idea of nationality formed the focal point of an oppositional movement designed to effect the redistribution of power and resources through the creation of a 'Radical' class alliance. The failure of the landlords to reproduce their hegemony was clearly seen in the way in which the land question erupted on to the political stage in the 1880s; yet the grievances around which agitation revolved and which the Land Commission (1896) investigated – security of tenure, fair rent, the game laws, and so on – had existed for most of the century. What was new was that these grievances were incorporated into a coherent whole, along with other issues – payment of tithes, the burial question, disestablishment – which together constituted the ideological platform of Welsh Liberal nonconformity. This was articulated by an increasingly self-reproducing stratum, composed of ministers, teachers, journalists and other 'intellectuals' who allied with a commercial and professional middle class to man the Liberal party machine. This combination can be seen taking shape at local level, and increasing in strength with the expansion of new urban centres (see, for example, I.G. Jones, 1981, ch. 3).

There was a dual thrust to their campaign: upwards, against the landowners in the name of Welsh nationality, and downwards to embrace the various elements of the rural peasantry and urban working class:

> During the 1880s and 1890s the middle-class nonconformist elite, through the agencies of chapel and press, re-defined the idea of Wales in its own image, deftly excluding its opponents and *sometimes also its supporters*. The myth of the *gwerin*, of a classless or one-class Welsh democracy, was its main ideological achievement (R.M. Jones, 1981, p. 55; our italics).

The emergence of this alliance was presented as the natural outcome of 'years of silent but none the less sure and swift national growth' during which 'the Welsh talking their own language and reading their own newspapers . . . have been living their own life' (Hughes 1887b, p. 3). The ideology operated through a simple inversion of political and cultural characteristics, which counterposed a Welsh-speaking nonconformist Liberal tenantry to an alien (English) class of Tory landlords. A prominent radical journalist presented the contrast in this way:

Nearly the whole of the people of Wales . . . are Non-
conformists. The landlords alone are 'Church' folk. Here,
then, is one possible link of sympathy between the Welsh
landlord and tenant gone. Again, nine-tenths of the Welsh
landlords are Conservatives. The Welsh tenantry are radical to the core . . . There is no mutuality, but hostility of
political and religious creed between landlord and tenant.
Socially the disparities become limitless when we recall that
in Wales the landlord and the tenant do not even converse
in the same language. The one moves in a completely
English atmosphere and is usually anti-Welsh; the other
lives in a world in which Welsh is the language of the field
and the hearth and the place of worship. What is said of the
landlord is as true, and frequently more true of the land
agent. So you see the Welsh landlord and tenant are at
political extremes – are opposed to each other in a political
sense – and there is an utter absence of national kinship.
These things have an inexpressible force and meaning in
Wales where the people are intensely national (Hughes,
1887b, p. 7).

This powerful construction involved a sharpening and simpli-
fying of boundaries through the symbolic transfer of certain
elements across the divide. The categories were by no means
exclusive, yet were made to appear natural and consistent.
Thus in Merioneth most landlords were resident, Welsh-
speaking and had until quite recently been regarded with
some respect or even affection (I.G. Jones, 1981, pp. 99–104);
while in Gwynedd a loyalist middle class and a small section
of the working class, almost entirely Welsh-speaking but
supporting the Tory cause, were 'ideologically excluded from
being Welsh by the definitions of radicalism' (R.M. Jones,
1981, p. 54).

The social and religious boundaries within which the politics of the land question were fought were rigorously defined
and reinforced by attacks on those who confounded or con-
fused categories. Particular anathema was pronounced upon
'proselytes' (converts to Anglicanism from Nonconformity)
and *cynffonwyr* or informers who put their own interests before
those of their neighbours. Although their behaviour might be

explained as a response to the pressures of landlordism, those who betrayed their class or religion were denounced in the most violent language as social outcasts, more like animals than men, who forfeited their Welsh nationality. These practices highlight some of the mechanics of exclusion and inclusion surrounding the new social alliance, and also indicate the components of community, as articulated by the nationalism of the period.

One theme of the attack on the existing power structure was that there had been a failure of 'natural' leadership. The new Liberal nonconformist leaders could see themselves as filling the resulting vacuum. Similarly, it was a frequently rehearsed view that the Welsh people had turned to dissent as a reaction to neglect by Anglican clergy who were indifferent to the need to minister in Welsh. After 1850 fewer complaints were made against the 'younger sons of the aristocracy', unqualified for their livings by their lack of Welsh who 'like ignorant blacksmiths' tried 'to fit the hoof to the shoe by burning the foot of their horse' (Anon, 1849, p. 4). Instead Nonconformist polemics concentrated on an apparently increasing number of Welsh-speaking clergy recruited from the rural tenantry, and the occasional convert from the Nonconformist ministry. Dissenting ministers presented themselves as men of superior ability, better qualified and better educated than the Anglican clergy. Particular venom was reserved for the few seceders from the ministry who were regarded as men of inferior ability and defective character. Nevertheless, since Wales was a nonconformist nation, these Welsh-speaking clergy had to be 'the sons or grandsons of Nonconformist preachers, deacons and members' (R.H. Morgan, 1888, p. 39). In nonconformist rhetoric, proselytism involved severing the fabric of family and community relations – a seamless garment woven from different strands of dissent – and defectors were contemptuously satirised:

Behold one of them clad in canonicals, standing up at the desk on a fine Sunday morning, and addressing the empty seats as his 'Dearly Beloved Brethren'. . . His heart swells with pride, and he blesses his soul that he is not as other men are; he is not an Independent like his wife's father, nor a Baptist like one of the Churchwardens, nor a Wesleyan as the Sexton is, nor a Calvinistic Methodist like his own father (R.H. Morgan, 1888, p. 40).

Such clergymen, having betrayed their religion and identified with the Church and the landed class, were depicted as fomentors of mischief in the countryside, who 'naturally took up an attitude of antagonism towards the people who decline their ministrations' (R.H. Morgan, 1888, p. 16) Anglican parsons might act as intermediaries between landlord and *cynffonwyr*, passing on messages from those who would inform on the derelictions, and political and religious sympathies, of their neighbours for the sake of a tenancy (R.A. Jones, 1887, pp. 65–6).

The term *cynffonwyr* expressed 'the extremity of loathing and contempt' and it was applied both to those in the countryside who intrigued and ingratiated themselves into tenancies, and to blacklegs in the quarries. The term strictly meant 'flatterer' deriving from the Welsh for tail (*cynffon*). The *cynffonwyr* were both tail-bearers and tale-bearers who revealed their animal or devilish nature (exposed their tails) by informing on neighbours. Poets, politicians and preachers abused them as social pariahs to be excluded, socially and commercially, from their communities whose Christian values they subverted:

> They fully deserve expulsion from every society. Farmers ought to ignore them at fairs, ought to refuse to buy their produce, ought to let their produce rot in the fields, and their animals die from want of buyers. Let no one enter their service (Hughes, 1887a, p. 31).

Land reformers affected to believe that a spy system operated in the countryside to inhibit the solidarity of the tenantry (cf. R.A. Jones, 1887, pp. 60–4) although reality was more pathetic: letters from informers preserved in estate archives reveal the competition for tenancies fuelled by land hunger (Howell, 1978, *passim*). Something approaching a spy system was, however, developed in the slate quarries by the quarryowners' agents. 'Traitors' once identified were satirised as subhuman freaks and their appearance on the streets was greeted with hoots and mimicry of animal noises. *Cynffonwyr* were stripped of their nationality, as quarrymen were exhorted 'not to allow one of them, or any of their sons, to marry a Welsh woman. Let their descendants be forever foreigners to our land and to our language' (R.M. Jones, 1981, p. 71).

As a hegemonic struggle, the land question generated opposing historical conceptions. Alongside the notion of a 'failure' of natural leadership, and often within the same text, there appeared the image of landlords as an alien race who had dispossessed the Welsh people and progressively excluded them from the management of their own affairs: 'within less than three hundred years ago all the land belonged to the people, but by this time it has been usurped by a class of men who call themselves the lords of the land, which is hideous unrighteousness' (*Y Genedl*, 1886, quoted by Vincent, 1896, p. 14). A land nationaliser explained how 'the land was taken at first by sheer treachery and rapine . . . and the snatchers framed laws for their own protection'. He proposed that land should be transferred to the state, and compensation paid only to those who could show their ancestors had purchased estates with 'the then coin of the realm' (E.P. Jones, n.d., p. 182). Little further needed to be said to make the connection between the past and present political action, or to convince the slate workers of North Wales that the very mountains had been stolen from them (R.M. Jones, 1981, p. 104).

By contrast, the landlords' historical justification of their position was detailed and sophisticated, yet showed they had been compelled to fight on ground chosen by their opponents. Publication of lists of sheriffs was used to show that native owners, identified by 'endless series of Cymric names', were never dispossessed, an argument supported by analysis of the 1873 land return; the 'great preponderance of Welsh names among the owners of property in the various Welsh counties' was pointed out to the Land Commission (Vincent, 1896, p. 5–6). This argument was, however, easily brushed aside: 'it must be remembered that many even of our county families bearing good Welsh names, have hardly more Welsh blood in their veins than there is of the blood of Owen Tudor in the present Royal family, while many of the best estates have, either by purchase or marriage, fallen into the hands of aliens'

(R.A. Jones, 1887, p. 52). Nevertheless, numerous accounts of the 'ancient landed families' were published in the last quarter of the century (see Cardiff Catalogue, 1898, *Passim*). While these works may have largely been inspired by genuine anti-quarian curiosity, the terms of the research – the devolution of estates and the Welsh pedigrees of the landed families – were closely related to the interests of the landed class. In the event, the hegemony of the landlords was largely ended by the political defeats of the 1880s and 1890s, although the estates were not broken up until the following decades when land prices rose. H.M. Vaughan in *The South Wales Squires* (1926, Chapter 9) provides a memorable picture of an increasingly eccentric class deprived of its social and political significance.

The preceding discussion has been mainly concerned with the more explicit exclusionary devices of nineteenth-century na-tionalism, the means of policing the frontiers of identity. Implicit distinctions were, however, equally significant: in providing a statement of what characterised Welsh nationality (nonconformity, radicalism, classlessness and individualism) dominant conceptions simultaneously indicated what it was not (secular, collectivist, labourist).

The Welsh case provides a particularly developed version of a wider process whereby popular radicalism was channelled against the 'aristocracy' so as to benefit Liberal interests (Gray, 1977). For a time the resultant ideology successfully concealed the potential divergence of concerns between rural tenants and industrial workers, and drew a veil over the connections between landed capital and the 'new men' of the industrial economy. The industrial working class were sym-pathetic to the land question as it affected tenant farmers: a campaign for the reform of leases was in the interests of cottager and tenant farmer alike. Many colliers were recent migrants from the countryside, and understood the need for radical land reform. But the specific concerns of industrial workers found little echo within dominant conceptions of nationality; the realities of industrial life, and the communities it supported, were marginal to a Liberal order whose sources have been adequately described as 'the social structure of a small isolated, nonconformist and essentially rural culture'

(Parry, 1970, p. 15). Thus the intense struggle of the quarry-men was perceived not as a battle for the rights of labour against capital, waged by workers, but as a Liberal and religious contest against an alien employer. The quarrymen themselves had to break through a narrow conception of politics to develop their own notions of nationality that would challenge the grip of the Liberal leadership, both locally and nationally (R.M. Jones, 1981, pp. 66–70).

Such leadership was provided by a relatively small, com-pact and highly articulate middle class which by the latter part of the century appears as a hugely self-confident, thrust-ing force, firmly in control of a whole range of vital institutions and media of communication, through which it expounded its special vision of Welsh society and lauded its own character-istics and virtues as peculiarly Welsh. During the 1880s and 1890s it could claim, with little fear of opposition, to speak for Wales. Viewed with hindsight, its attitudes to Welshness were not without ambivalence, and it bequeathed a troubled heri-tage, as can be seen if we examine the significance attached to education.

EDUCATION

The latent nationalism expressed in the 'story' of education in Wales is still frequently reflected in official and professional attitudes towards educational policy. A recent history of the University College of Wales, Aberystwyth, one of the crown-ing achievements of the educational movement of the nine-teenth century, opens with the words 'the struggle for Welsh national identity and the striving for educational opportunity have almost always gone hand in hand' (Ellis, 1972, p. 1). We will now examine some of the ambiguities of that remark.

The movement is an almost unrivalled example of the steady, determined, cumulative creation of institutions upon which a class might base itself. It was seen as a process of political and educational evolution which gave rise to a kind of national saga, replete with its own heroes, that stressed an innate Welsh enthusiasm for learning, and a capacity for achieving academic success through the perfect machinery of the Welsh school system. The lives of many educationalists provided exemplary material: the son of an upland village shoemaker who became Professor of Moral Philosophy at Glasgow was said, for example, to symbolise for his people 'a victor in the struggle for knowledge', and he left his memoirs as encouragement and inspiration for Welsh and Scottish youth (H. Jones, 1923); as late as 1934 a memorial fund was created to purchase and maintain his birthplace (DWB, p. 466).

An event in the sphere of education, more celebrated than any other single incident in the entire history of Welshness, the Report of the Educational Commissioners in 1847, is widely held to have 'stung Welsh nationalism awake' (Coupland, 1954, p. 195). Important though the findings and assertions of the Commission were, they acted as a catalyst within an already active discussion: the unfortunate lawyers who compiled the Report were caught up in a situation primed for controversy. What was devastating was that they 'pilloried (Wales) before the world for its unusual immorality' (Coupland, 1954, p. 144). This attack threatened to undercut the attainments of the new type of Welsh leaders, who took pride in the fact that they came from humble origins but wanted to be fully entitled to take their place alongside their English peers: the emergent middle class wanted to ensure that Welshness was understood as a respectable identity. The 'treason' of the Blue Books (*Brad y Llyfrau Gleision*) stimulated the calculated drive to provide Wales with what were later referred to as the necessary 'educational appliances' (Davies, 1977, p. 95).

The entire project had the tone of something done for the people by a group which was its leaders, and betters. Welsh educationalists proceeded on two related fronts: to secure elementary education for the poor, as a source of social stability, and to consolidate the middle class. Whereas the campaign for elementary education was bedevilled by denominational conflict, the movement for middle-class education was distinguished by a unity of aim: the objective was a system of secular higher education, based on recognition of Welsh nationality by the state. The movement was sponsored by a revealing coalition of successful Welsh politicians, journalists and civil servants, aided by representatives from the dissenting academies, and a group of expatriate clergymen.

The prominence of the London Welsh and other exiles in Manchester and Liverpool is noteworthy. These were men who had won considerable social advancement, usually through the professions. For them education was a means of social mobility, and of reproducing and strengthening a social class; it had nothing to do with reinforcing a way of life, or upholding a specifically Welsh culture. They worked through an outer circle of respectable Welshmen, and their mode of operation involved frequent, planned use of the press, direct access to influential positions, and the formation of local groups and committees. Their themes were enunciated with monotonous regularity: Wales was a settled and peaceful country, loyal to Britain, whose middle class deserved support for higher education at least equal to that given to Ireland and Scotland. Comparisons were made with the disturbed state of Ireland, and the benefits this seemed to bring the Irish; while the recognition given to Scottish nationality was taken as a model for Wales.

The proposed Welsh colleges were to be non-sectarian with a teaching emphasis on practical instruction in 'useful knowledge', particularly civil engineering, agriculture, and the sciences that would provide access to 'a thousand lines of honourable employment and promotion' ranging from mining and manufacturing to the Civil and Indian services (1864; Report, 1871, pp. 7–13) and, in short, 'fit the young men of Wales for better stations in the mercantile world' (Ellis, 1972, p. 50).

The failure of the state to respond to claims for distinctive Welsh institutions of higher education compelled educationalists to turn to the people, in the name of Welsh nationality. The lines of an inter-class alliance were clearly drawn in 1870. The landed interest having failed to aid the middle class, support was enlisted from tenant farmers, quarryworkers, and colliers: hence 'the matter has been brought before the quarrymen of Caernarvonshire and Merionethshire, who have manifested much enthusiasm in the establishment of a national college, and among whom committees have been formed, for the purpose of canvassing the several localities'. Collecting cards were issued which mapped the lines of a popular Liberal alliance: to the labour aristocracy, through the lodges of the Oddfellows of Wales; to three hundred schoolmasters; to banking institutions; to the business communities of Liverpool and Manchester; and to nearly 1700 religious congregations (Conference, 1870, pp. 28–31). The most significant contributions were actually received from industrial capital.

Nationality was used to express judgements on this work: the activists were both praised as 'energetic patriots' and abused as 'half Welshmen', an *emigré* plutocracy for whom Wales was 'a good place to come from' (Sherrington, 1980, pp. 135–6). These influential figures took a fairly instrumental view of Welshness: thus English was used virtually throughout the Welsh educational system because for many leaders of Welsh society at the time, English was 'the language of self-advancement and material success' (Davies, 1977, p. 39). A prominent Welsh-speaking MP observed that 'the Welsh who (have) succeeded have done so by knowledge of English, and their assimilation to Englishmen: mere knowledge of the Welsh language has made none among them clerks and useful mechanics'. It was well known 'that the educated Welsh leave their country . . . and forgo all pretensions to Welshmanship save on Sundays'. Thus he found himself 'pretty well convinced that the extermination of the Welsh language would be the greatest possible blessing to Wales' (Salisbury, 1849, pp. 6–7). Among the resident middle class similar sentiments were expressed: Gruffydd Rhisiart suggested in 1851 that 'it would be an unspeakable advantage to both Welshmen and Englishmen if the Welsh language . . . were to cease to exist before tomorrow morning and the Welsh nation made as one with the English nation' (W.R. Jones, 1967, p. 45). The use of English among such people indicated their social class 'which is why they enjoyed using English when writing privately to each other, and . . . multiplied the social and public occasions in which its use might seem to be prescribed' (I.G. Jones, 1980, p. 59). The virtues of English were proclaimed, in typically vulgar fashion by David Davies, the 'self-made' industrialist:

If you wish to continue to eat black bread and to lie on straw beds, carry on shouting 'May the Welsh language live for ever!' But if you wish to eat white bread and roast beef, you must learn English (I.G. Jones, 1980, p. 62).

In the circumstances of the times, there was little anxiety about the fate of Welsh; it was taken for granted that it would remain the normal speech of the common people. Nevertheless, these statements show how little positive significance was attached by many middle-class people to the Welsh language. The position of the National Eisteddfod, modernised by the same Welsh educationalists, serves as an index of the pragmatic attitude adopted towards the language. The Eisteddfod Council, in 1866, distanced themselves from national 'self-glorification' and from the objective of 'the shutting out of the English language from Wales': 'Our great objective is SOCIAL PROGRESS . . . (to) elevate and refine a thriving and most orderly people', 'a more complete fusion of the Welsh and English peoples (is) the desired result' (National Eisteddfod, 1866, p. 3, 8). Similarly the proposed University was not to have the effect of fostering a 'merely Welsh nationality': instead the barriers to progress in Wales were to be removed, through the diffusion of English (Report, 1871: p. 8).

Welshness, as conceived by the education movement, was completely compatible with Britishness. The aspiration was that Wales should have an educational system as good as any in the Empire, whereby Welshmen would take their place in the administration and development of Imperial power. The Welsh language would have to take its chances in competition with English: when fully enlightened about their interests the people would decide how far they valued 'the perpetuation of the vernacular and other peculiarities of the nation' (Report, 1871, p. 8). With admirable Liberal rationality, it was asked:

Why must the Welsh language be given protection any more than the Welsh farmers? Let free trade be granted to the languages of the world, like other things; and if Welsh shall thus survive, let it survive; and if it shall die, let it die (W.R. Jones, 1967, p. 45).

For the duration of the campaign to achieve a Welsh educational system, the middle class were buttressed by a coherent evolutionist and progressivist ideology. Yet as soon as their goals had been achieved, a striking inversion of these ideas took place: the achievement is reinterpreted as an expression of the innate qualities of the Welsh. The Welsh countryman, previously the very epitome of stagnation, was now the guardian of moral values essential to the progress of the Welsh people. Above all, the Welsh language was no longer a fetter, but something to be promoted (*Cymmrodorion*, 1887,). This complete reversal of attitude found concrete expression in the Society for Utilising the Welsh Language which was established at the Eisteddfod in 1885. Membership of the society was largely composed of teachers, school board members, and other educationalists. Its aim was to promote the Welsh language as an instrument of education in Wales and Monmouthshire through mobilisation of public opinion, submission of reports and memoranda to local and central government, and the preparation of suitable textbooks (Evans, 1885). The progress of the Society was marked by the confessions and recantations of those who had formerly supported a policy of anglicisation in Welsh schools. According to the secretary of the movement 'the systematic ignoring of the Welsh language in schools . . . had a debasing influence on the character of the nation and tended to implant habits or self-doubt, servility and possibly deceit' (*Cymmrodorion*, 1887, p. 17). The bilingual movement shows in a particularly transparent way the linkages between class interests, attitudes to language, and ideas of nationality. If Wales was beginning to produce a surplus of intellectuals, bilingualism could ensure appropriate employment for those with the necessary linguistic competence; that the process of social closure could extend into other professions was shown by the suggestion that 'all parents in Wales should be notified . . . that no public post was to be held in Wales, except under very extraordinary circumstances, but by bilinguists' (I. Jones, 1908, p. 487).

The general thrust of the Welsh educational movement in the nineteenth century was not a movement from below, from the grassroots, but a process of building up, and consolidating, the position of a middle class. The people were called upon for support only when it was clear that the middle classes could not secure their goals unaided. The emphasis

placed on rewards to individual effort and achievement projected a vision of the social order in opposition to any collectivist conception. By stressing also that the thirst for
knowledge was a characteristically Welsh virtue which had its
tap-root in the communities of the Welsh countryside, the
dominant educational ideology directed attention away from
industrial Wales, and served to censure the collectivist traditions of labour as 'non-Welsh'.

CONCLUSION

We have been compelled to rely rather heavily on the pro-
grammatic statements of those who were actively involved in
the processes we have sought to analyse: our account is no
more than provisional, since many other constructions could
be, and were, placed upon Welshness during the period in
question, and much work remains to be done in rescuing
alternative traditions to those we have presented. It cannot be
too strongly stressed that the ideologies are deeply ingrained
within Welsh history writing itself. We have done no more
than tap the surface of the key issue, how the discourse of
nationalism was ordered.

Nationalism as a process of building up a system of shared
identifications involves two crucial elements: the formation of
social alliances and the articulation of either an alternative
hegemony or the maintenance of an existing hegemony. It is
important to emphasise that nationalism is not restricted to
subordinate groups. As an oppositional project nationalism
may be limited to the defensive control of existing institutions.
Nevertheless, the vision of an alternative society is usually
potentially present within the articulation of a 'national tradition' in which past, present and future states of society are
simultaneously imagined. The populist basis of nationalism
depends crucially on access to the means of communication.
Here intellectuals are vitally important both in having such
access and as 'remembrancers' who may build up alternative
selective traditions. It is particularly important to nationalist
strategy to control the means of cultural reproduction and
those institutions with the capacity for reproducing forms of

resistance. Lack of access to the normal channels of communication may lead to the proliferation of political symbolism and myth, a characteristic feature perhaps of all muted groups.

We have laid some stress on the flexibility of nationalist ideology, and the scope there is within it for some surprising changes of direction. It is unlikely that the 'raw materials' can be stretched indefinitely – the existing formation of nationalist beliefs and mythologies place limitations on subsequent developments and innovations: in Wales, nineteenth-century configurations continue to exercise a definite presence among contemporary nationalists. But within Wales, there is much to play for, since as one Welsh historian nicely puts it:

It has not been possible to promote what a French cynic declared to be the most important element in nationality, a general and unquestioning belief in false notions about the past history of a country (Rees, 1963, p. 16).

REFERENCES

Anon. 1849 *The Church in Wales. True Assertions and a serious warning* (London).

Boyce, D.G. (1982) 'Separatism and the Irish Nationalist Tradition', in C.H. Williams (ed.), pp. 75–104.

Brown, Terence (1981) *Ireland: A Social and Cultural History* (London: Fontana).

Cardiff Catalogue (1898) *Catalogue of Printed Literature in Welsh Department* (of Cardiff Free Libraries), ed. by John Ballinger and James Ifano Jones (Cardiff).

Conference (1870) *The Welsh Education Conference at Aberystwyth* (Oswestry).

Coupland, Sir R. (1954) *Welsh and Scottish Nationalism* (London: Collins).

Cymmrodorion (1887) *The Future Development of the Welsh Educational System. Proceedings of the Cymmrodorion Section of the National Eisteddfod of 1887* (London).

Davies, B.L. (1977) *Hugh Owen 1804–1881* (Cardiff: University of Wales Press).

Day, G. (1984) 'Development and National Consciousness: The Welsh Case', in H. Vermeulen and J. Boissevain (eds), *Ethnic Challenge: the Politics of Ethnicity in Europe* (Gottingen: Edition Herodot).

DWB (1959) *The Dictionary of Welsh Biography Down to 1940* (London: Honourable Society of Cymmrodorion).

Eley, Geoff. (1981) 'Nationalism and Social History', *Social History*, 6, pp. 83–107.

Ellis, E.L. (1972) *The University College of Wales, Aberystwyth 1872–1972* (Cardiff: University of Wales Press).

Emmett, Isabel (1982)' "Fe godwn ni eto": Stasis and Change in a Welsh Industrial Town' and 'Place, Community and Bilingualism in Blaenau Festiniog', in A.P. Cohen (ed.) *Belonging: Identity and Social Organisation in British Rural Cultures* (Manchester: Manchester University Press).

Evans, B.G. (ed.) (1885) *Prospectus of the Society for Utilising the Welsh Language* (Llangadock).

Gaventa, John (1980) *Power and Powerlessness* (Oxford: Clarendon Press).

Gray, R.Q. (1977) 'Bourgeois Hegemony in Victorian Britain', in J. Bloomfield (ed.) *Class, Hegemony and Party* (London: Lawrence & Wishart).

Howell, David (1978) *Land and People in Nineteenth Century Wales* (London: Routledge & Kegan Paul).

Hughes, T.J. ('Adfyfr') (1887a) *Landlordism in Wales* (Cardiff).

Hughes, T.J. ('Adfyfr') (1887b) *Neglected Wales* (London).

Jessop, Bob (1982) *The Capitalist State* (Oxford: Martin Robertson).

Jones, Bobi (1974) 'The Roots of Inferiority', *Planet*, 22, pp. 53–72.

Jones, E. Pan (n.d.) *Oes Gofion* (Bala).

Jones, Henry (1923) *Old Memories*, edited by Thomas Jones (London: Hodder & Stoughton).

Jones, Ifano (1908) 'Dan Isaac Davies and the Bilingual Movement', in J.V. Morgan (ed.), *Welsh Political and Educational Leaders in the Victorian Era* (London), pp. 432–93.

Jones, I.G. (1980) 'Language and Community in Nineteenth Century Wales', in D. Smith (ed.), pp. 47–71.

Jones, I.G. (1981) *Explorations and Explanations: Essays in the Social History of Victorian Wales* (Llandysul: Gwasg Gomer).

Jones, R.A. (1887) *The Land Question and a Land Bill* (Wrexham).

Jones, R. Merfyn (1981) *The North Wales Quarrymen 1874–1922*, (Cardiff: University of Wales Press).

Jones, R. Merfyn (1982) 'The State of the Nations', *Sociology of Wales*, V, pp. 14–20.

Jones, W.R. (1967) *Bilingualism in Welsh Education* (Cardiff: University of Wales Press).

Kiernan, V. (1976) 'Nationalist Movements and Social Classes', in A.D. Smith (ed.), pp. 110–133.

Lenin, V.I. (1967) 'Preliminary Draft Theses on the National and Colonial Questions' (1920), in *Selected Works*, vol. 3 (Moscow).

MacIver, D.N. (1982) 'The Paradox of Nationalism in Scotland', in C.H. Williams (ed.), pp. 105–144.

Morgan, K.O. (1981) *Rebirth of a Nation: Wales 1880–1980* (Oxford: Clarendon Press).

Morgan, Prys (1981) *The Eighteenth Century Renaissance* (Llandybie: Christopher Davies).

Morgan, R.H. (1888) *Disestablishment of the Church in Wales* (Wrexham).

Mouffe, C. (1979) *Gramsci and Marxist Theory* (London: Routledge & Kegan Paul).

National Eisteddfod (1866) *Programme*.

Orridge, A.W. (1982) '*Separatist and Autonomist Nationalisms*', in C.H. Williams (ed.), 43–74.

Parry, C. (1970) *The Radical Tradition in Welsh Politics – A Study of Liberal and Labour Politics in Gwynedd 1900–1920* (Hull: University of Hull Press).

Rees, J.F. (1963) *The Problem of Wales and Other Essays* (Cardiff: University of Wales Press).

Report (1871) *University College of Wales. Report and List of Subscribers* (London).

Salisbury, E.G. (1849) *Education for the Welsh* (privately circulated).

Sherrington, E. (1980) 'Welsh Nationalism, the French Revolution and the Influence of the French Right 1880–1930', in D. Smith (ed.), pp. 127–47.

Smith, A.D. (ed.) (1976) *Nationalist Movements* (London: Macmillan).

Smith, D. (ed.) (1980) *A People and a Proletariat: Essays in the History of Wales 1780–1980* (London: Pluto Press).

Vaughan, H.M. (1926) *The South Wales Squires* (London).

Vincent, J.E. (1896) *The Land Question in North Wales* (London).

Williams, C.H. (ed.) (1982) *National Separatism* (Cardiff: University of Wales Press).

Williams, G.A. (1980) *Madoc: The Making of a Myth* (London: Eyre Methuen).

Williams, G.A. (1982) *The Welsh in Their History* (London: Croom Helm).

Williams, Raymond (1977) *Marxism and Literature* (Oxford University Press).

Williams, Raymond (1981) 'For Britain, see Wales', *Times Higher Education Supplement*, 15 May.

Zubaida, S. (1977) 'Theories of Nationalism', in G. Littlejohn *et al.*, *Power and the State* (London: Croom Helm), pp. 52–71.

6 Spatial Policy as Territorial Politics: The Role of Spatial Coalitions in the Articulation of 'Spatial' Interests and in the Demand for Spatial Policy

C.G. PICKVANCE

This paper is intended as a contribution to two areas: state theory and the analysis of spatial policy. It is divided into three parts: first I outline the position taken here in relation to work in these two areas; then I introduce the concept of spatial coalition; finally I examine how it may be useful in understanding spatial policy.[1]

The term spatial policy is used here to mean policies which *explicitly* seek to give special treatment to activities occurring in delimited areas – which we shall call 'special treatment areas'. (Such treatment may consist of prohibitions or inducements.) In principle, spatial policy thus covers national parks and educational priority areas, but the focus here is mainly on regional policy and inner city policy under which incentives are given to firms in assisted regions or enterprise zones.

It is necessary to distinguish these policies from other state policies which have spatially differential effects, but where these are a by-product of a different goal, e.g. motorway building, aid to the steel industry, or national airports policy. (The spatial effects of these policies may be stressed more in federal political systems than in unitary systems.) Policies of this type are excluded here, for reasons which will be explained, but would be relevant if one were interested in the relation between the state and a particular region.

STATE THEORY AND SPATIAL POLICY

The position taken in this paper towards state theory is (a) that it should be capable of helping one understand particular types of policy and (b) that the analysis of state policy is valid as long as it embraces class relations and thus avoids functionalism.

The first point might seem self-evident but it is necessary to argue for it in opposition to the contrary view that theory can suggest in what circumstances state intervention will take place, but that nothing can be deduced from this about 'the form, extent and nature of state intervention in any one society' (Duncan, 1981, p. 235).

This is linked with the increasingly influential realist epistemology advocated by Keat and Urry (1975) and Bhaskar (1979). The positive aspect of this body of thought is its critique of the positivist search for laws at the level of empirical events. Instead, a level of real structures or mechanisms, whose causal powers exist by necessity, is proposed. In 'closed systems', that is, where no other structures interfere, there would be a direct relation between a structure and the level of empirical events. In 'open systems', however, that is, societies as they exist, a variety of structures or mechanisms co-exist and at the level of events their outcome is said to be 'contingent, and therefore only determinable through empirical research' (Sayer, 1981, p. 9). This view takes an extreme form in Massey's critique of industrial location model-building where Marxist theory is demoted to being 'a method and a framework of analysis' (1977, p. 32). It also undervalues the way theory guides empirical research and the potential of empirical material for theory-formation.

I would agree with the critique of positivism made by the

above writers but not with their claim that empirical out-comes in open systems are contingent and unpredictable. As Benton writes, within Bhaskar's own terms, 'what is to rule out the calculation of the resultant effects of the joint operation of a plurality of mechanisms?' (1981, p. 18). Carchedi (1983) is more critical of Bhaskar – for ignoring the interaction among several co-existent mechanisms – but like Benton argues that predictability of tendencies is possible. To illus-trate this, if we assume that the capitalist mode of production and the state are real structures,[2] and that a Marxian under-standing of their 'causal powers' is valid, then we can deduce that state interventions of certain sorts, for example system-atic nationalisation of all sectors of the economy, will not occur. The forces of capitalism may move in mysterious ways but they are not completely unpredictable. It is not being suggested that theory can tell us precisely what spatial policies will be adopted, when, and for which areas, but the claim that state theory should help one understand state policy is very different from Duncan's denial that any such deductions can be made, or the realists' blanket declaration of the contin-gency of empirical events.

The second position taken here towards state theory is that state policy is a valid object of analysis providing one takes class relations into account.

A general problem about studying state policy is that one risks being too much influenced by government labels. This applies particularly here, since our exclusion of policies that are not explicitly spatial means we are in fact defining our field of interest in terms of government labels: 'regional' policy, 'inner city' policy, etc. Topalov (1979) has eloquently argued that it is dangerous to take descriptions of state poli-cies as any guide to their content and that labels such as 'housing policy' or 'welfare policy' embody ready-made analy-ses which can be quite misleading. However, in the present case, hopefully, we will avoid this danger by using these policies as a starting point for an exploration of the interests involved.

But how much can one learn about the state from studying state policy? In other words, how do we answer Pendaries' question: 'can one reduce the analysis of the state to that of its policies?' (1979, p. 127). I would agree with Pendaries that an understanding of the class character of the state involves both the study of the effects[3] of state policy and of the class political relations underlying it. Failure to include the latter leads to a functionalist picture of the state in which its capacity to intervene effectively is unrestricted (see Pickvance, 1980; 1982). I shall argue that the class interests relating to spatial policy are to be sought at two levels: first, at the general level, where class relations will affect a government's predisposition to intervene in a given field at all, and secondly, within a specific region or city where class relations will affect the character of any intervention.

I now turn to the position taken in this paper in relation to the existing literature on spatial policy. Generally, this literature can be characterised by its 'top-down' perspective on spatial policy. In other words, spatial policy is referred back to changing government definitions of problems and priorities for their solution. In conventional writing these priorities are seen as autonomous products of government reflexion on the economic and political situation, whereas in Marxist writing they tend to be related to the 'needs of capital'. This top-down perspective is essential and I have no argument with it. However, it has led to a neglect of the 'bottom-up' pressures from 'cities', 'regions', etc. In this paper the top-down perspective is deliberately omitted and I shall focus exclusively on spatial policy as a response to a particular type of locally originating pressure.

This paper can therefore be seen as a sequel to a previous paper of mine (1981), which left a puzzle. In that paper I argued that despite the continuities in regional (and office) policy as judged by the legislation on which they are based, there had been major changes in the way they were operated, and that these changes could be seen as government responses to the crisis facing British capitalism. For example, in regional policy the original 'stick and carrot' notion by which restrictions were placed on factory location or expansions in the prosperous regions, and incentives were given to firms locating or expanding in the depressed regions, had largely disappeared by the 1970s. Incentives were now provided irrespective of the number of jobs created by the firms in question, and of whether they would have located in the depressed region in any case. I suggested that regional policy could best be seen as a large-scale subsidy to industrial capital.

However, this analysis left a puzzle: if the intention was to subsidise industrial capital, why was this not done exclusively through direct and explicit aid to industry? The scale of direct aid to private capital in all spheres is colossal: at £16000 million per year in grants, subsidies and tax reliefs, this sum exceeds government spending on the National Health Service or education. The question is why a relatively small sum, i.e., £500 million in 1982–3, should be provided under the name of regional policy.

I argued that the existence of a regional policy was not due to the alleged contradiction that 'the state must involve itself in the accumulation process but it must either mystify its policies by calling them something they are not, or it must try to conceal them' (O'Connor, 1973, p. 6). This suggestion is particularly inapplicable in a society where anti-capitalist feeling is weak and where aid to private capital is generally presented and accepted as in the general interest, i.e., to preserve jobs, to encourage 'wealth creation', etc. I still think this argument is quite correct. However, this ignored an alternative reason for support for industrial capital being provided under the regional label, namely that it is a response to 'bottom-up' pressures.[4] The argument of this paper will be that spatial policies should be seen as ways of providing state assistance to capital, not to conceal it from anti-capitalist sentiment, but in response to 'bottom-up' demands for intervention in spatial areas which are often made on a cross-class basis.

'BOTTOM-UP' PRESSURES: THE CONCEPT OF SPATIAL COALITION

In this section, I discuss a single element in the formation of spatial policy – 'bottom-up' pressures,[5] which I shall try and clarify by introducing the concept of spatial coalition. This term refers to an alliance which draws support from a variety of social classes and which seeks to promote what it defines as the interests of the area in question. The notion of coalition is the key one, since it suggests that the convergence of interests is not permanent. (The term 'local coalition' would be less clumsy but too restricted, since any area up to a region may be involved.) The precise demands which such coalitions make vary, but generally include the growth of the area. This appears synonymous with the welfare of all, and minimises attention to the divergent interests in the area. Characteristically, spatial coalitions press for the inclusion of the area within a special treatment area under a spatial policy.

This section is divided into five parts: (i) growth coalitions in urban politics; (ii) class and organisational levels of spatial coalitions; (iii) local class structure; (iv) the class basis of spatial coalitions; and (v) spatial coalitions as organisations.

Growth Coalitions in Urban Politics

The idea of 'spatial coalition' has a number of antecedents. The most obvious are in the field of urban politics, where various writers have studied coalitions around urban growth and redevelopment. Three writers will be considered here: Mollenkopf, Molotch and Saunders.[6]

Mollenkopf (1978) writes on post-war urban politics in the USA. He argues that from 1955 until the late 1960s, US cities were dominated by 'pro-growth coalitions' which pressed forward with urban renewal, roadbuilding and city centre redevelopment programmes. The main elements in these coalitions were urban renewal administrators, corporate executives (grouped into associations advocating urban redevelopment), growth-oriented mayors and, of more variable importance, city labour councils and construction trades councils, party organisations, real estate interests, etc. One of their main tasks was to obtain funds from state and federal government. The dominance of growth coalitions was only challenged in the late 1960s due to residents' protests against slum clearance, urban riots, middle-class opposition, and business and labour withdrawal in the face of politicisation. From our point of view, the important point is that in the 1955–65 period, an alliance could be formed around growth:

[A] growth platform could be touted as a panacoa. Since the negative consequences had not yet fully emerged, attention could be focussed on prospective rising tax bases, construction jobs and contracts, new housing, expanded central-city institutions. . . local business could see clearly the wide range of benefits which would accrue. Renewal, therefore, for a time commanded a working if not general consensus (Mollenkopf, 1978, pp. 136–7).

A second American writer is Molotch (1976) the title of whose article, 'The City as a Growth Machine' is self-explanatory. Molotch argues that 'a city, and more generally, any locality, is an areal expression of the interests of some land-based elite' (1976, p. 309) and it is in the interests of this elite to attract the maximum amount of growth to the city. His notion of 'interests' is somewhat vague, since it is used both broadly to refer to all who have interests in land (which would include all homeowners, i.e. the majority of the population) and narrowly to refer to those whose business is tied to growth, for example, developers, bankers, lawyers. He contrasts these 'parochial businessmen' with executives in externally controlled corporations who have 'no vested interest in the growth of the locality in question' (1976, p. 317). Molotch argues that growth is the key objective of local government, requiring it to exert pressure on higher levels of government to provide infrastructure to help it lure private firms. Molotch's argument is thus very closely related to that of Mollenkopf.

Finally, an example closer to home is Saunders's (1979) study of the commercial growth of Croydon. In effect, 'Croydon' exploited its location away from the centre of London but with good transport links to become a booming office and commercial centre. Saunders shows how this growth was sought in the name of free enterprise, civic pride and an expansion of the local property tax base. Who, after all, could be opposed to a package which promised increased commerce and prosperity with lower rates to boot? But what interests lay behind this action by 'Croydon'? The most subtle aspect of Saunders's analysis is his distinction between the manifest 'actor' (the council) and the broad basis of support from external interests on which it could rely.

Thus on the one hand,

the consistent support of town centre enterprises by the local authority (e.g. through its continuing support for further office development and its provision of productive infrastructure) has taken place *with little prompting from interests outside the town hall* (1979, p. 319, italics added).

Yet this action was only possible because of what Saunders describes as the 'political communion' between the local authority, middle-class interests and local business interests, (1979, p. 235), that is, a relation in which external interests do not need to exert pressure on the council, since there is a convergence of political values between them.[7] This reveals the importance of not treating the active agents of a spatial coalition as a measure of the extent of its support.

These three cases all describe spatial coalitions around urban growth. In all cases the council has a pre-eminent role and in the American cases business interests are very evident too.[8] The working class is only marginally involved in the American cases (through construction unions) and not at all in the British case. I would suggest that this configuration of support is because the prime goal of these coalitions was urban redevelopment rather than a growth in employment.

The spatial coalitions relevant to spatial policy have some similarities with these urban growth coalitions in that they are also concerned to exert pressure on higher levels of government to obtain funds to improve local facilities, and to attract private capital. The major difference is that their focal aim is growth in employment, and this I suggest accounts for their differing cross-class character.

Class and Organisational Levels of Spatial Coalitions

Having introduced the term 'spatial coalition' and illustrated some of its antecedents in urban politics, I will now try and outline what I see as its two main levels.

The term 'bottom-up pressures' implies some sort of homogeneous grass-roots political force. However, in reality such homogeneity does not exist since the political forces within any spatial unit are socially structured. It is useful to identify two levels of structuring: the class level and the organisational level. The former refers to local class structure, and the latter to organisational structures such as political parties, trade unions, local authorities, etc. It might seem logical to use spatial coalition to refer only to the organisations and class groupings *overtly* involved in promoting the 'interests of an area'. However, as our discussion of Saunders's study of Croydon showed, in situations of 'political communion', the overtly active social force (the council in his case) is only the tip of the iceberg of the effective coalition of interests.

To accommodate this point it would be best to distinguish between the manifest and latent levels of a spatial coalition, leaving the social forces involved at each level as an empirical variable. We shall adopt an inferior but more convenient solution by distinguishing between the class and organis- ational levels of a spatial coalition, that is, between the classes who support it whether or not this support is overt, and the organisational structures involved in it. We use the term level since on the whole class forces operate at the latent level, while manifestations of class forces (with the exception of voting patterns) take organisational forms and are hence part of the manifest level.

We will consider in turn: the locally existing pattern of class forces, the class basis of spatial coalitions, and the organis- ational level of spatial coalitions.

The Local Class Structure

The potential breadth of class support for a spatial coalition depends upon the local class structure. This can vary con- siderably according to the prevailing mode or modes of pro- duction in the broader society of which the spatial unit is part, and the spatial division of labour which allots particular economic activities to that spatial unit.

The relevance of the articulation of modes of production has been stressed by Lipietz (1977 and 1980) in his path-breaking work on the economic basis of regions. This work has been taken up by Dulong (1976; 1978) who sees changes in the combination of modes of production in a region as one basis for regionalist movements (see Kesselman, 1981). He makes this argument particularly with reference to the Breton regionalist movement which he attributes to the absorption of peasant farmers into the capitalist mode of production.

Apart from this case in which regionalism is seen as a phenomenon of the transition to capitalism, Dulong also refers to other cases where it is changes in the spatial division of labour *within* capitalism which are crucial to regionalism. The important work by Massey (1979), which acknowledges its debt to Lipietz (1977), is highly relevant here. The previous conventional wisdom stressed the dependence of the number of jobs and hence class composition of a spatial unit on the rise or fall of capitalist (and accompanying public sector) activity in the area. It was argued that capitalist restructuring was leading to the decline of old inner city areas as they lost out in the competition for new industry to sites on the periphery of existing cities, small towns and rural areas. Peripheral regions were seen as having an added attraction due to their higher levels of unemployment. The novelty of the Lipietz–Massey argument was to argue that focusing on the number of jobs was diverting attention from another aspect of restructuring. Namely, that the skill distribution of jobs was being altered by a new trend (observed by Massey in the electrical engineering industry) for firms to split up their activities between several sites in terms of the available labour supply: high-order managerial, executive and research activities would remain in a few major cities; tasks needing skilled manual labour would remain in the conurbations; and semi-skilled tasks (e.g. assembly work) would be located in peripheral regions. There is room for debate about these hypotheses – on the whole I suspect Massey underestimates the complexity of such spatial patterns – but it is this new dimension of spatial differentiation which is important.

This would lead to an understanding of class structure (i.e., fractions of capital, types of labour) in a given area in terms of two factors. First, the extent to which that area has a place in the developing mode of production, and what that place is (i.e., what type of jobs will be created there); and secondly, the historical precipitate of previous economic activities in the area. Thus, some areas will be attractive to multinational firms, while others will remain havens of small and medium capital.

Unfortunately, while studies of the spatial restructuring of capital have been relatively common – for example by Lovering (1978) and Cooke (1982) for Wales – its local-level implications for social and political structure have been less studied. Lovering uses the term 'headless capitalism' to depict the income and wealth distribution of Wales, which reveals a relative predominance of the working class. My interest would be in following out the implications of this for the local political order and the formation of spatial coalitions.

The Class Basis of Spatial Coalitions

We now turn to the question of the class basis of spatial coalitions. While local class structure sets a limit to this, it does not determine it. Two points are crucial here.

First, the class composition of the local area tells us little about the local social or political order. This depends on the shared traditions of militancy, moderation or deference. For example, the presence of multinational capital in an area may involve a variety of management styles (authoritarian, participatory, etc.) and this will affect employees' political attitudes. Dulong (1976) has used the term 'local society' to refer to this political dimension. In some cases – as in Brittany – he sees a long-standing type of 'local society' being eroded by the expansion of monopoly capital. (His perspective is to see regionalism as due to a crisis in the capacity of 'local society' to maintain political order in local areas on behalf of monopoly capital.) In others, monopoly capital enters some sort of alliance with pre-existing local élites. It may be that an understanding of local political orders will help explain why in some cases spatial coalitions emerge and in others they do not.[9]

Secondly, there is the question of regionalist consciousness – which overlaps with the question of ethnic and national identity (i.e., where a region is a nation but not a nation-state). Regionalism has a class dimension, in that it may be promoted by specific classes within the region, but its significance as a unifying force goes beyond this and it generally facilitates alliances between classes (Day and Suggett, 1983).

As a result of these two points, the involvement of different class interests in a spatial coalition is mediated. It cannot be derived from a purely economic analysis. However, it may be useful to indicate some strictly economic reasons for such involvement. In the case of urban growth coalitions, we saw that business interests were a consistent feature, unlike working-class interests, and suggested this was due to the distribution of economic benefits of urban redevelopment. In the case of spatial coalitions for employment growth, we suggest that while the working class forms a normal part of the class base, fractions of capital are a more variable element.[10]

The theoretical reason for this is that whereas the working class has an unequivocal interest in growth in employment,[11] this is only true for commercial capital among fractions of capital. Existing commercial capital will benefit from the higher turnover produced by higher employment – though eventually it could lead to new competitors – and can thus be expected to be active in spatial coalitions. (See Curtin and Varley's (1983) account of the attraction of industry to a town in the West of Ireland).

Existing industrial capital, however, may be economically opposed to the attraction of new firms, particularly if they compete for the same labour, and cases of industrial opposition to industrial development activity by councils in recent years illustrate this. Nevertheless, in some cases local industry has been organisationally involved in spatial coalitions. For example, Carney and Hudson (1978) provide a very interesting description of a spatial coalition in the North-East in the 1930s and early 1940s which had cross-class representation, and we discuss a similar Welsh case later on. Our argument would suggest that the only economic reason for industrial presence in spatial coalitions is a prudential one, i.e., to channel the coalition's demands so as not to threaten existing industry – as we shall suggest for the Welsh case. Industrial presence could also be symbolic, and detached from class support. There are solid political reasons, however, for an active industrial presence, for instance, the preservation of political stability (as possibly in the North-East case) and the strength of regionalist feeling. Clearly, the involvement of fractions of capital in the class base of spatial coalitions is best regarded as a problem requiring explanation.

Spatial Coalitions as Organisations

Finally, we turn to the organisational level of spatial co-alitions. The theoretical question here is what organisations are likely to act as part of a spatial coalition rather than make functional demands independent of spatial connotations. The first answer is: those organisations which have a spatial refer-ence. This covers a surprisingly wide range: (a) governmental institutions: devolved administrations (in the case of Wales and Scotland); metropolitan and shire county councils; and district councils; (b) Quangos: regional economic councils and planning boards; regional development bodies; new town development corporations; urban development corporations; and (c) others: MPs and local and regional groupings of MPs; area and regional levels of local authority associations (parti-san or otherwise); area and regional levels of trade unions and party organisation, etc.

The point about all these organisations is that they involve allegiance to a spatial area, and they can therefore be expected to be willing to enter spatial coalitions of appropriate scales. Indeed, those among them with the largest vested interests (such as the governmental institutions) are likely to be a consistent element in spatial coalitions compared say to trade union regional bodies whose involvement may be more related to economic conditions. Hence, what appear to be 'bottom-up' demands by spatial coalitions may be shaped by governmental pressures, and are an aspect of central – local government relations.

Finally, the role of spatial coalitions depends on national traditions of territorial politics and ultimately on patterns of state formation. Different countries vary in the extent to which the spatial allocation of resources is determined by bargaining between national and sub-national units of government. In federal political systems, and particularly those where the units constitute nations, this bargaining is most explicit, and territorial politics is a way of life. In Britain, however, the high degree of central control over local government policy and finance would suggest that the scope for territorial politics was limited. (This is not entirely due to its having a unitary system since, as Ashford (1982) documents, France, another unitary state, has a far more strongly developed system of local – central bargaining than Britain.)

In fact, it would be wrong to conclude that territorial politics is ruled out in Britain by centralisaton. First, the degree of centralisation allows considerable discretion by councils since most central government grant is not tied to specific purposes (transport and police funds are the exception); most central policy advice is not mandatory; and councils can levy rates at levels they set themselves, even though they may be penalised in some cases: considerable political bargaining is therefore possible about the distribution of spending within this framework. Secondly, although the distribution of central government funds to local councils is based on an 'objective' formula, it is well known that this formula is itself the product of bargaining between central and local government. (This led to the shift of funding to the metropolitan areas under Labour and a reverse shift back to the shire counties under the present Conservative government). Finally, and most important for us, is that central government itself administers a set of policies which is precisely a method of distributing resources via territorial politics and provides a further reason for the formation of spatial coalitions. This is, of course, spatial policy. I would thus agree with Tarrow that centralisation of control over policy and finance has not destroyed territorial politics and may even, as he suggests, 'lead citizens at the periphery to turn more and more to the local, regional, and primordial identities around them' (1978, p. 22).

In this section we hope to have explained what is meant by spatial coalition, and the need to distinguish between the class structure of the area in question, the classes which support the spatial coalition, and the organisations which take visible roles in it.

SPATIAL COALITIONS AND SPATIAL POLICY

We now discuss the significance of spatial coalitions in relation to spatial policy. The section is divided into three parts:

(i) the reciprocal influence between spatial coalitions and spatial policy; (ii) the scale of spatial coalitions and special treatment areas; and (iii) a Welsh example.

The Reciprocal Influence Between Spatial Coalitions and Spatial Policy

The two directions of influence here will be considered in turn. On the one hand, I would argue that spatial policy has a major influence on the articulation of 'spatial' interests because of its agenda-setting or demand-channelling function. In other words, the fact that spatial policies allocate special treatment on an areal basis is an incentive to spatial coalition formation and territorial politics since it invites excluded areas to present cases for their inclusion, e.g., as Development Areas, Inner City Partnership Areas, or Enterprise Zones. At the same time, the existence of spatial policies discourages the formulation of demands of other, perhaps more radical kinds – though not their total abandonment.

The demand-channelling function means that any spatial coalition which is uncertain about how to formulate its demands will tend to opt for a request for inclusion in a special treatment area, as will those spatial coalitions which are committed to making such demands perhaps because they were formerly included in a special treatment area. Thus in 1981 Manchester City Council responded to the forthcoming removal of Intermediate Area status from most of Lancashire – which would also bring about the loss to it of EEC assisted area funds – by demanding the redesignation of the City with this status. (It also asked for the recalculation of the formula for fixing 'block grant'.)

From the government's point of view spatial policies provide a standard and accepted response to any spatial coalition which has not learnt the 'rules of the game': namely, it is invited to make a case for its inclusion in one area-based scheme or another.

On the other hand, I would suggest that the existence of spatial policy is a factor in the creation and persistence of spatial coalitions, since the legitimacy of a demand will depend on the breadth of support it has. In this way, state policy may encourage the creation of cross-class coalitions and discourage single-class based demands.

The Scale of Spatial Coalitions and Special Treatment Areas

It follows from the idea of a reciprocal relation between spatial coalitions and spatial policy that the spatial scales of each may be related too, and that spatial policy may influence and pose problems for the scale of spatial coalitions. (The reverse relation, i.e., the idea that the scale of spatial coalitions influences the scale of special treatment areas, seems unlikely.) This is because the scales of the special treatment areas under spatial policy act as an 'opportunity structure' which influences the formation of spatial coalitions. I shall mainly be concerned here with the correspondence between such areas and the scales of local government units as one prominent element in spatial coalitions.

Many spatial scales already have coalition elements representing them, for example, district councils and county councils. But others, such as regions, may have fewer or they may consist of Quangos rather than government bodies. In such cases, new coalitions may emerge in response to a new scale of special treatment area in which inclusion is being sought. Thus, whereas existing government units may be prominent in demands for enterprise zone status, a demand to be included as an assisted area may require the formation of a new coalition. The ease with which coalitions can join together (or split) to alter their spatial scale to make spatial policy demands is thus an important variable. Where changes are difficult, the incentive will be to press for policies corresponding to the existing spatial scale of the coalition. This is clearly related to the geographical structure of class relations as manifested in organisations, and to sentiments of local identity, which may discourage co-operation and spatial expansion of a coalition.

The possible effects of the opportunity structure embodied in existing inner city and regional policy for coalition formation can be seen by asking whether current governmental units correspond to the scale of the special treatment areas.

Inner city partnership areas are mostly specific to a single local authority and coalitions based at this level are obviously appropriate. On the other hand, while some enterprise zones are limited in the same way, others cross district council boundaries, for instance, Newcastle/Gateshead, Salford/ Trafford, the Medway Towns. This suggests that there is a real problem for spatial coalitions seeking enterprise zone status.[12] They can choose (a) to go it alone with perhaps smaller chances of success but in the hope that no other enterprise zone will be set up nearby, or (b) join up with neighbouring councils with perhaps a greater chance of success, but in the knowledge that the benefit will be diffused due to the large area designated as an enterprise zone. The choices open are partly constrained by the 1980 Finance Act which sets as a condition that enterprise zones should show immediate results without surrounding towns being affected – the exact reverse of a growth pole! – but this leaves a lot of scope for argument.

Finally, the case of regional policy poses a similar problem, since the areas designated for special treatment are also mixed in scale at the present time. Compared with inner city policy the scales are all larger, and single local authorities are not the only units in question. As far as I know this is not an aspect of regional policy that has been much commented upon.

If for simplicity we consider only the post-1966 period, a number of trends can be identified. There has been a multiplication of types of special treatment area with the addition of Special Development Areas (SDAs) in 1967 to the Development Areas (DAs) of 1966, and the introduction of Intermediate Areas (IAs) in 1970. At that point Development Areas were mostly large, covering several counties if not whole regions, while SDAs were smaller than counties in size; IAs were intermediate in size. After 1972, IAs became larger. But since 1977, following the inner city debate which drew attention to intra-regional differences, both DAs and IAs have been eaten away at, a process which was dramatically continued in 1979 with the halving of the special treatment areas (Keeble, 1976; McCallum, 1979; Townsend, 1980).

The year 1977 thus marks a break in the opportunity structure between the 1966–77 period when most areas were large – the exception being SDAs – and the 1977–83 period when the typical scale has been reduced. This shift is mainly due to the new and more differentiated conception of the spatial problem introduced as the inner city 'problem' emerged. I would argue that it changed the task of spatial coalitions. No longer were coalitions required over large spatial scales. The name of the regional policy game changed from regional scale special treatment areas to county and sub-county levels. (This has implications for the *raison d'être* of regional level bodies.)

So far we have assumed that the designation of special treatment areas was a matter for territorial politics, i.e., for negotiation between spatial coalitions and government. I consider this is a realistic assumption. However, if areas were designated on the basis of an objective criterion it could be argued that territorial politics was irrelevant – though it could equally be argued that such a criterion was a way for govern-ment to cope with a multiplicity of spatial coalitions. The major example of this in regional policy is the 1960–66 period when Development Districts (DDs) replaced the old large Development Areas dating from 1945 and the small 1958 DATAC areas. These DDs were many in number and small in size and it was generally believed that designation was based on the local unemployment rate exceeding 4½ per cent. However, with this exception, for the whole of the period since the declaration of the first Special Areas in 1934, there has been considerable flexibility in regional policy areas, and hence scope for the action of spatial coalitions.

In this context it is worth mentioning the detailed analysis of post-1979 regional policy areas by Townsend (1980). He argues that each type of special treatment area tends to coincide with a broad band of unemployment level: IAs with the 6.6–7.1 per cent band, DAs with the 7.2–9.5 per cent band, and SDAs with the over 10 per cent category. This suggestion is borne out best among the SDAs (79 per cent of which lie in the 'right' band), less well by DAs (64 per cent), and poorly for the IAs (24 per cent). Interestingly, Town-send acknowledges the role of pressures from the Scottish and Welsh Secretaries for exceptional treatment for 'their' areas. Thus the role of objective criteria – and by implication the possibly lesser role for spatial coalitions – is far from clear cut in this case.

A Welsh Example

So far the argument of this section has been somewhat hypothetical. We conclude, therefore, by referring briefly to the closest approximation to what we have in mind: an account of local mobilisation in response to, and in demand of, spatial policy.

This occurs in the important article on Wales by Rees and Lambert (1981).[13] The authors use the term 'regionalist consensus' to refer to an agreed view of South Wales's economic problems and their solutions, a view shared by 'organized labour and capital and the major political parties'. Significantly, they add that the 'role of the state in moulding and sustaining this "regionalist consensus" has been crucial' (1981, p. 125). I would see this consensus as the collective view of a (regional) coalition in which government units were important.

Rees and Lambert show how at the political level this view met with considerable government support: a whole series of Welsh economic planning and development institutions was set up from 1968 onwards – a trend which reflected the demand for devolution. At the economic level, however, they note that the state either supported or did not intervene in a series of industrial location decisions, which favoured already developed areas in Wales rather than those defined by the 'regionalist consensus' as most in need of jobs. Rees and Lambert argue that Welsh nationalism was thus used by the state to legitimise the divisive effects of the economic processes it fostered.

Rees and Lambert do not provide all the evidence relevant to an analysis of regional-level interest articulation, but it seems that the coalition which presented the 'regionalist' consensus view was making demands on a number of fronts: creation of regional institutions, use of nationalised industry policy, as well as spatial (regional) policy. This suggests that pressures for institution creation (reflecting Welsh nationalism and possibly local government interests here) may relegate spatial policy to a secondary role. (Though in this case it was inapt to meet the demand for jobs to be provided in the valleys rather than for the coastal area, since the same industrial incentives would apply in both cases.)

One might try to relate Rees and Lambert's analysis to capital restructuring. Without following all of Dulong's analysis with its state monopoly capitalism framework, one might ask what class interests underlay the 'regionalist consensus' and in particular what fractions of capital were involved. If it was not led by large capital, which as we suggested earlier was unlikely, then could the paticipation of small and medium capital(?) be an attempt to preserve their own economic position by diverting new growth to areas which were marginal to them. As Lebas hypothesises, the arrival of large-scale industrial capital in an area may cause a 'crisis [for] the local commercial and industrial bourgeoisie' (1978, p. 257). In this case, *their* involvement (if more than symbolic) in the regional coalition may have been not so much to attract growth (the aim of the councils and trade unions) but to ensure that if it came, it would not challenge their interests. This can only be speculation but it is suggestive of the questions raised by the role of spatial coalitions.

In this section, we hope to have indicated the way in which spatial policy has a demand-channelling function by providing an incentive for the articulation of 'spatial' interests into spatial coalitions demanding special treatment area status. In particular, we showed how the range of spatial policy scales could be seen as an opportunity structure encouraging coalition formation at the corresponding scale or causing problems for existing spatial coalitions.

The major conclusion I wish to draw from this is that the channelling of demands into territorial politics is a major reason for the continuity and increased diversity of spatial policy in Britain.

CONCLUSION

Finally, let us return to the starting point of this paper and consider its contribution to the literatures on state theory and spatial policy.

This paper only partly exploits the lessons of spatial policy for *state theory*, since we have deliberately ignored the economic and some of the political effects of such policy. However, our focus on spatial coalitions draws attention to two points relevant to state theory. First, that the effects of spatial policy cannot be reduced to the economic since the management of demands from such coalitions is a political effect. And secondly, that spatial coalitions are one type of class relation affecting state intervention, and one which cannot be reduced to a single class. In particular, one might argue that the need for spatial policy obstructs the state from a pure function of aiding private capital irrespective of its spatial location. Finally, the paper as a whole can be seen as an essay in middle-range theory since it does not simply set out conditions in which some state intervention takes place, and treat its character as contingent, but brings some of the forces shaping its character into the analysis.

In relation to *spatial policy* this paper represents a departure from previous work which has analysed spatial policy in terms of economic forces, government conceptions of the spatial problem, and party politics. Only the latter reveals an exception to the 'top down' perspective.[14] What this work fails to do, in my view, is to provide an adequate explanation of why spatial policies exist. In terms of scale of economic aid to private capital, spatial policies are insignificant – totalling some £500 million per year for regional policy, and perhaps £50 million for inner city policy, compared with total aid to private capital of £16 000 million. Indeed, strictly economic considerations might suggest the abolition of spatial policy on the grounds that the sheer scale of economic devastation was now so widespread that a spatially concentrated approach was inappropriate. In addition, the multiplication of types of special treatment area could be seen as counterproductive since their effect on economic activity is likely to be on its spatial distribution and not on its total amount. (The latest addition to the gamut of types of area, the freeport, announced as this paper was being written is a more explicit attempt to add to the total level of activity).

And while the evolution of spatial policy clearly reflects changing conceptions of the spatial problem – e.g., in the post-1977 recognition of the inner city and of intra-regional differences – such changes in ideology are best seen as responses to economic and political situations, rather than as autonomous developments.

Thus one is driven back to the political sphere in order to explain the persistence of spatial policy. The main argument of this paper is that national party politics and the attempt to prevent the emergence of nationalist parties are not a sufficient explanation and that territorial politics plays a key role. In other words, it is because demands are articulated through *spatial* coalitions, and because spatial policy provides a well-adapted means of meeting these demands that spatial policy persists. Although I have suggested that the precise scale of spatial coalitions responds to spatial policy, the demand for spatial policy is permanent. It is in order to meet *these* demands and not to conceal the 'accumulation' function of the state that spatial policy persists.

In conclusion, the aim of this paper has not been to put forward a substitute for existing approaches to spatial policy. The role of broad economic forces, changing ideologies of the spatial problem, and party politics, which have been neglected here, are all undoubtedly important. Rather, it has been to draw attention to an equally important but neglected dimension, that of territorial politics, and hopefully thereby to widen the research agenda in the area of spatial policy.

NOTES

1. I would like to thank Phil Amis, Nick Buck, Peter Fitzpatrick, Ian Gordon, Tim Harrington and Kevin Lavery at the University of Kent, for their helpful comments on the first draft of this paper, and Doug Ashford, Pierre Filion and conference participants for their responses to the circulated version.
2. The key problem for realism is how real structures and their causal powers are identified. The scarcity of discussion of this problem suggests that some sort of privileged access 'behind the scenes' obviates the need to *debate* the possible real structures and their powers.
3. However, we should not expect the 'character' of the state revealed by studying the effects of state policy to be simple or uniform, but contradictory. All policies will represent class compromises of some sort but will more closely reflect the interests of fractions of capital, while others will tend to reflect 'working-class' interests as advocated by labour and party organisation. (This phrasing conceals a fundamental ambiguity which is never resolved in Marxian accounts. Policies may reflect the interests of capital because capital is 'strong' – which I would suggest to be true for banking and oil capital in Britain – or because it is 'weak'

– which I would argue in the case of non-oil industrial capital in Britain. The former case implies an instrumental view of the state; in the latter case capital's interests are promoted by the state because it lacks the dynamism to promote them itself, and because their pursuit is seen as being in the national interest.) The class compromise will reflect the past and present state of class relations. Thus the growth of state intervention in Britain has not been a mechanistic response to the changing 'needs of capital' but reflects the impulsion of labour organisations too, and is always subject to counter-offensives by employer organisations, as at present. It follows that I reject the argument that all policies can be expected to reveal an interest of some fraction of capital to the same extent, if probed deeply enough. The study of state policy effects should reveal their differential character which reflects the different class compromises in each case.

4. It follows that the statement in my earlier paper that 'the "regional" element of the policy is completely subsidiary, and is an example of the way that thinking in terms of spatial units can conceal the real social processes involved' (1981, p. 241) is inaccurate. The regional element diverts attention from the 'aid to private capital' function of regional policy, but I will argue that it is a response to 'bottom-up' pressures for spatial policy which are very real social processes. My attention was drawn to the importance of these pressures by Kevin Morgan commenting on the earlier paper. (See Morgan, (1980, fn. 51). Morgan's discussion of pressures for regional policy in Wales refers to the demand for devolved institutions, the success of Plaid Cymru, and Labour's concern for the security of the seats of its Welsh MPs.)

5. In so doing, I am not denying the importance of national-level class relations, or processes of problem definition and policy formation within central government and political parties.

6. Also relevant is Strauss's seminal study of urban imagery and in particular his discussion of the role of professional boosters and local Chambers of Commerce in the competition between towns for economic growth. (1961, pp. 200–6) See also Logan (1978).

7. In fact, there is some ambiguity about which business interests formed part of this 'political communion' since Saunders later describes small local business interests as having been 'left out in the cold during the redevelopment years' (1979, p. 323) which suggests they were outside the political communion. The 'local business' interests which were inside it may resemble Molotch's 'growth-related professionals'.

8. The difference between this and the British case where external interests are not manifest is probably best seen as due to a difference of political ideology rather than of effective patterns of power. In other words, openness to business influence is seen as a virtue in American urban politics, whereas in Britain it is seen as an intrusion to be kept out of sight: it is quite possible that effective business power is similar in extent in both cases (Dunleavy, 1980, pp. 150–6).

9. This relates to the more general issue of why it is that certain areas make no demands for spatial policy or are slow in making them (e.g.,

the belated case made by Yorkshire and the North-West for Intermediate Area status in regional policy.) Is it purely for economically rational reasons – i.e., interests in the area feel their economic case is poor – or could it be that in some areas there are political problems in mounting spatial coalitions?

10. Cf. Urry's concept of 'local social movement' which 'embraces a variety of classes although much of the initial strength will probably be generated by the labour movement' (1981, p. 469). Apart from this Urry's concept refers to a very different reality: (a) for him such movements seek to protect the locality *against capital and the state*, whereas for me spatial coalitions often work through state agencies and favour capital; (b) he defines the locality as the 'local labour market' i.e., only one of the areas to which spatial coalition refers; and (c) he writes of a 'local homogenization of class interests as in the case of Castells's urban social movements' whereas I see spatial coalitions as alliances among classes which do not involve such a convergence of interests. Cf. Harvey's term 'territorially based alliance' (1982, p. 420) and Hadjimichalis's (1983) term 'regional social movement'.

11. The main exception to this is in commuter suburbs and villages and retirement areas where protection of the environment is more important than job provision.

12. The emphasis of this paper is on upward demands. The fact that in certain cases the location of enterprise zones has been against local wishes indicates that central priorities play a role too. These are part of a tradition of by-passing local government, i.g., via housing associations, Urban Development Corporations, etc.

13. O'Dowd's (1983) interesting analysis of the regionalist consensus in Northern Ireland has similarities with the Welsh case, but he places greater emphasis on the role of government in it, and its effects in diverting attention from the political situation.

14. Labour enthusiasm for spatial policy is usually related to its desire to reward its inner city and regional political support. Conservative continuities with Labour policy may be seen as an attempt to woo Labour voters. But in both cases the desire to deter support for Welsh and Scottish nationalist parties cannot be overestimated.

REFERENCES

Ashford, D. E. (1982) *British Dogmatism and French Pragmatism* (London: George Allen Unwin).

Benton, T. (1981) 'Some comments on Roy Bhaskar's "The Possibility of Naturalism" ', *Radical Philosophy*, 27, pp. 13–21.

Bhaskar, R. (1979) *The Possibility of Naturalism* (Brighton: Harvester).

Carchedi, G. (1983) 'A Critical Note on Bhaskar and Systems Theory', *Radical Philosophy*, 33, pp. 27–30.

Carney, J. and Hudson, R. (1978) 'Capital, Politics and Ideology: The North East of England 1870–1946', *Antipode*, 10, 2, pp. 64–78.

Cooke, P. (1982) 'Dependency, Supply Factors and Uneven Development in Wales and Other Problem Regions', *Regional Studies*, 16, pp. 211–27.

Curtin, C. and Varley, A. (1983) 'Bringing Industry to the Periphery: A West of Ireland Case Study'. Paper to BSA Annual Conference, Cardiff.

Day, G. and Suggett, R. (1983) Conceptions of Wales and Welshness: Aspects of Nationalism in Nineteenth-Century Wales'. Paper to BSA Annual Conference, Cardiff. (Chapter 5 in this book.)

Dulong, R. (1976) 'La crise du rapport Etat/Société locale vue au travers de la politique régionale', in N. Poulantzas (ed.), *La crise de l'état* (Paris: PUF).

Dulong, R. (1978) *Les régions, l'état et la société locale* (Paris: PUF).

Duncan, S.S. (1981) 'Housing Policy, the Methodology of Levels, and Urban Research: The Case of Castells, *International Journal of Urban and Regional Research*, 5, pp. 231–54.

Dunleavy, P. (1980) *Urban Political Analysis* (London: Macmillan).

Hadjimichalis, C. (1983) 'Regional Crisis: The State and Regional Social Movements in Southern Europe', in D. Seers and K. Ostrom (ed) *The Crisis of the European Regions* (London: Macmillan).

Harvey, D. (1982) *The Limits to Capital* (Oxford: Basil Blackwell).

Keat, R. and Urry, J. (1975) *Social Theory as Science* (London: Routledge & Kegan Paul).

Keeble, D. (1976) *Industrial Location and Planning in the UK* (London: Methuen).

Kesselman, M. (1981) 'Regionalism and Monopoly Capital – A New Approach to the Study of Local Power', *International Journal of Urban and Regional Research*, 5, pp. 107–17.

Lebas, E. (1978) 'Movement of Capital and Locality: Issues Raised by the Study of Local Power Structures', in M. Harloe (ed.), *Conference on Urban Change and Conflict 1977* (London: Centre for Environmental Studies).

Lipietz, A. (1977) *Le capital et son espace* (Paris: Maspero).

Lipietz, A. (1980) 'The Structuration of Space, the Problem of Land and Spatial Policy', in J. Carney *et al.*, *Regions in Crisis* (London: Croom Helm).

Logan, J. R. (1978) 'Growth, Politics and the Stratification of Places', *American Journal of Sociology*, 84, pp. 404–16.

Lovering, J. (1978) 'The Theory of the "Internal Colony" and the Political Economy of Wales', *Review of Radical Political Economics*, 10, 3, pp. 55–67.

McCallum, J. D. (1979) 'The Development of British Regional Policy', in D. Maclennan and J. B. Parr (eds) *Regional Policy* (London: Martin Robertson).

Massey, D. (1977) *Industrial Location Theory Reconsidered.* (Unit 25 in Course D204.) (Milton Keynes: Open University Press).

Massey, D. (1979) 'In What Sense a Regional Problem?' *Regional Studies*, 13, pp. 233–43.

Mollenkopf, J. H. (1978) 'The Postwar Politics of Urban Development', in W.K. Tabb and L. Sawers (eds) *Marxism and the Metropolis* (New York: Oxford University Press).

Molotch, H. (1976) 'The City as a Growth Machine: Toward a Political Economy of Place', *American Journal of Sociology*, 82, pp. 309–32.

Morgan, K. (1980) 'The Reformulation of the Regional Question, Regional Policy and the British state', *University of Sussex Urban and Regional Studies Working Paper No. 18.*

O'Connor, J. (1973) *The Fiscal Crisis of the State* (New York: St Martins Press).

O'Dowd, L. (1983) 'The Crisis of Regional Strategy: Ideology and the State in Northern Ireland'. Paper to BSA Annual Conference. (Chapter 7 in this book.)

Pendaries, J-R. (1979) 'Etat, économie et politique chez Jean Lojkine', *International Journal of Urban and Regional Research*, 3, pp. 125–32.

Pickvance, C. G. (1980) 'Theories of the State and Theories of Urban Crisis', *Current Perspectives in Social Theory*, 1, pp. 31–54.

Pickvance, C. G. (1981) 'Policies as Chameleons: An Interpretation of Regional Policy and Office Policy in Britain', in M. Dear and A. J. Scott (eds) *Urbanisation and Urban Planning in Capitalist Society* (London and New York: Methuen).

Pickvance, C. G. (1982) *The State and Collective Consumption* (Unit 24 in Course D202.) (Milton Keynes: Open University Press).

Rees, G. and Lambert, J. (1981) 'Nationalism as Legitimation? Notes Towards a Political Economy of Regional Development in South Wales', in M. Harloe (ed) *New Perspectives in Urban Change and Conflict* (London: Heinemann).

Saunders, P. (1979) *Urban Politics: a sociological interpretation* (London: Hutchinson).

Sayer, A. (1981) 'Abstraction: A Realist Interpretation', *Radical Philosophy*, 28, pp. 6–15.

Strauss, A. L. (1961) *Images of the American City* (New York: Free Press).

Tarrow, S. (1978) 'Introduction', in Tarrow, S., Katzenstein, P. and Graziano, L. (eds) *Territorial Politics in Industrial Nations* (New York: Praeger).

Topalov, C. (1979) 'Can Housing Policy Be an object of Research?' *International Journal of Urban and Regional Research*, 3, pp. 445–51.

Townsend, A. R. (1980) 'Unemployment Geography and the New Government's "regional" aid', *Area*, 12, pp. 9–18.

Urry, J. (1981) 'Localities, Regions and Social Class', *International Journal of Urban and Regional Research*, 5, pp. 455–74.

7 The Crisis of Regional Strategy: Ideology and the State in Northern Ireland

LIAM O'DOWD

Most Western European states are committed to regional policies with two manifest and interrelated aims: (i) the alleviation of spatial concentrations of unemployment and (ii) the 'modernisation' of local industrial production. The high ideological profile of these policies would appear to be disproportionate to the actual commitment of state resources to regional strategies so designated. They have been less than successful, to say the least, in removing spatial disparities and, indeed, the rest of the state's economic policy may have more profound spatial effects.

Why then do regional strategies[1] exist and why do they provoke so much analysis and debate? The political economy of space and state theory provide one set of answers. These approaches stress the determining effect of changing patterns of accumulation on international, national and regional space (see, for example, Carney *et al.*, 1980; Dunford *et al.*, 1981; Massey and Meegan, 1982; Urry, 1981). Capitalist accumulation is seen as dynamic, contradictory, and necessarily uneven in spatial terms, a product of class struggle and the reproduction of class relations. Furthermore, they have sought to specify the state's role, including regional strategy, in managing the transition from one regime of accumulation to another, that is, in facilitating a contradictory process, of which the state is itself a part product, and which it does not ultimately control (for an overview see Lebas, 1982, especially, pp.43–65; 100–107). Mainstream social science, on the other hand, is more likely to accept the state's definition of the regional question, in its own terms. It does share with the more critical approaches, however, a mass of data on industrial location and shifting patterns of (un)employment. Similarly, it attributes a key role to manufacturing industry in shaping space (e.g., Dunford, 1977; Fothergill and Gudgin, 1982).

Both sets of perspectives implicitly recognise the ideological force of regional strategy. To put it crudely, political economy seeks to challenge it by asking alternative questions. Mainstream social science, on the other hand, broadly accepts the official problematic while monitoring its operation. Yet, this means that the ideology of regional strategy is seldom studied explicitly in its own right.

This chapter suggests that the ideology of regional strategy has a dual dimension. On the one hand, it can obscure the contradictions of economic strategy by conflating the interests of capital and labour at regional level. On the other hand, it has a signposting effect. It reveals the importance of spatial politics and the nature of the forces which shape space, be they classes, ethnic movements or political organisations. Above all, regional strategy points to the often underestimated significance of 'territorial strategy' for the legitimacy of the state itself, a legitimacy which is often threatened by the problems of managing socio-economic transition.

I have chosen to examine regional ideology via a case study of Northern Ireland, where spatial divisions are particularly problematical and spatial politics especially intense. Yet, here, as elsewhere, the (British) state has had to respond to the changing international division of labour. Since 1945 this has meant managing the transition from an economy built around nineteenth-century competitive capitalism to one shaped by contemporary monopoly capital. As elsewhere, regional strategy is part of an official state ideology which seeks to compartmentalise 'pure economics' or 'market forces' from politics. The state attempts to mobilise support or consensus behind a strategy presented as a technical adaptation to changing economic conditions. In the process, the state is

presented as neutral arbiter encouraging industrial modernisation to offset the decline in employment brought about by
the decline of traditional firms.

Northern Ireland would appear to be a potentially informa-
tive case study in that the regional strategy applied has been
that of the UK as a whole, with some modifications to allow
for higher industrial incentives and different administrative
arrangements. It has long been designated as a 'peripheral'
area, with a 'regional problem' which ranks highest on most
conventional indices of disadvantage within the UK. It combines three common attributes of a 'region': administrative
unity; a structural concentration of declining industries; and a
measure of political – ethnic distinctiveness. In particular, it
has proved to be a hostile arena for the technocratic ideology
of state management and for projections of the state as a
'neutral arbiter'.

Government reports and statements provide the thread
linking the various parts of the following discussion. They
have set the parameters for much of the analysis and political
debate on regional development and are the most accessible
expressions of official ideology. The discussion is organised
around three themes: (i) the role of the Stormont administration in applying British regional strategy prior to 1970–2;
(ii) the attempts of the Direct Rule administration to
strengthen the faltering ideology of regional development, via
the formation of a 'regionalist consensus', and the restructuring of the local state apparatus; and (iii) the increasingly
apparent limitations of regional strategy in the light of mass
closures of multinational enterprises, deepening political
polarisation, and the Conservatives' new economic policy
after 1979.

REGIONAL STRATEGY UNDER STORMONT

As in Britain (see Dunford *et al.*, 1981, p. 397; Pickvance,
1981), early regional strategy was seen as a means of alleviat-
ing unemployment. Initial post-war measures were piecemeal
and restricted, despite the exceptionally high unemployment
rates in Northern Ireland. (Several useful general accounts
are available, e.g., Wiener, 1980; Parson, 1980; Harvey and

Rea, 1982, pp. 74–91.) Just as the earlier more comprehensive planning proposals were abandoned in Britain, so also the 1944 *Report on the Location of Industry in Northern Ireland* was shelved and was not to be resurrected in any form until the promulgation of the Matthew–Wilson plans in the 1960s. The first significant legislation on regional policy was the *Industrial Development Act (NI), 1945*, which was modelled on the *Great Britain Distribution of Industry Act, 1945*. This was the first act to make state assistance to industry in Northern Ireland conditional on job creation. It provided for interest relief grants, rates exemptions, provision of sites and premises, compulsory acquisition of land or premises, and financial assistance to improve basic services. Subsequent acts in the early 1950s implemented re-equipment and modernisation grants not tied to employment creation.

The Unionist party's enthusiasm for an active and co-ordinated regional strategy was limited to say the least; a viewpoint shared by its key supporters in local industry and commerce. Local capital made little use of the existing incentives, and the low-wage linen complex, in particular, strongly resented state help to incoming industry which was increasing competition for local labour (O'Dowd, 1980, pp. 36–7). The internal Unionist debate over regional strategy was illustrated by the publication of what is still the most comprehensive work on the local economy (Isles and Cuthbert, 1957). Commissioned by the Stormont government in 1948, completed in 1955, and published reluctantly two years later, it was quite critical of the inactivity of government and local entrepreneurs. It highlighted the degree to which the Northern Ireland economy was integrated into the UK as a whole and sought to undermine the economic case of those Unionists who were toying with 'Dominion status' as a buffer against creeping socialism in Britain (Isles and Cuthbert, 1957, pp. 402–29). The authors suggested a more active regional strategy and the encouraging of emigration to Britain when other methods failed. The Hall Report (1962), maintaining the careful technocratic tone of the earlier report, reiterated its argument that the 'regional problem' was mainly due to the 'natural disadvantages of remoteness, size and lack of local raw materials and energy sources'. Despite favouring 'increased competitiveness' and the continued attraction of external investment, it made few new proposals.

The eventual and reluctant decision to initiate the more far-reaching strategies of the 1960s was due to a number of pressures. First, mass redundancies among skilled Protestant shipbuilding and engineering workers in the early 1960s. For a brief period, there were signs of electoral defections to the Northern Ireland Labour Party, which was drawing some cross-sectarian support in Belfast (Bew *et al.*, 1979, chapter 5). Secondly, the period 1959–62 marked a transition to a more active regional policy in Britain (Pickvance, 1981, pp. 238–9). Finally, a small group of civil servants, in close touch with British developments, were pressing for administrative reform and a more rational physical planning strategy. In this, they got some support from the new leaders of the Unionist party, O'Neill, Faulkner and Craig (see Faulkner, 1978; Oliver, 1978, pp. 80–91).

The Matthew Report (1963) on the Belfast Region and Wilson's (1965) economic development plan were a major boost to those wishing to mobilise support behind 'regional improvement' and 'modernisation'. They were predicated on accelerating the attraction of increasingly mobile international investment to Northern Ireland. Furthermore, they projected a technocratic rhetoric of planning and efficiency, under the aegis of Unionism, which seemed to make the sectarian language of local politics redundant.

In some respects, the new planning departures can be seen as an attempt to impose a spatial order on a process underway since the late 1940s. A number of multinationals had already located in the environs of Belfast, partially compensating for the contraction of employment in agriculture, engineering and linen. Yet, aggregate unemployment at no time approached the 'full employment' figures in the rest of the UK. The 1960s seemed to mark a watershed, however. Although the local economy continued to lose jobs faster than any other UK region, the planners could claim credit for a higher rate of new employment creation than anywhere else (Moore *et al.*, 1978; Simpson, 1983). The Wilson (1965) Plan had set a target for the 'creation' of 30 000 new jobs between 1964 and 1969. In the event, the Northern Ireland Development Programme

(1970, p. 71) was able to claim nearly 29 000. These employment figures were a poor and profoundly misleading indication of the total impact of the new regional strategy. A
regional strategy appealing to common interests and objectives had no pervasive local nationalism to draw on to divert
attention from new forms of uneven development and associated administrative reform. The contrast here with the Welsh
experience, as described by Rees and Lambert (1981, p. 136),
is illuminating. In Wales, the same broad regional strategy
was able to appeal to nationalism to mobilise consensus
behind a restructuring of space and the local state apparatus.
To understand the different trajectory of regional ideology in
Northern Ireland, it is necessary to look briefly at the nature
of the Unionist state.

Northern Ireland was established in 1920, not as the culmi-
nation of a movement to initiate economic and political
change, but as an attempt to defend and preserve a social
formation based on the uneven spatial development of
nineteenth-century competitive capitalism, British imperialism, and Protestant dominance. Despite the declining global
role of British imperialism, the other two elements remained
remarkably intact until the early 1960s, despite many vicissi-
tudes. The key to this stability lay in the class and political
relations between overwhelmingly Protestant industrial capital and skilled workers, the Orange Order and the Unionist
state institutions. The general aim of defending the Union was
in the interests of nearly all sections of capital. Individual
capitalists were heavily represented in all Unionist cabinets
and even in the 1960s had frequent and easy access to Unionist ministers (Greenberg, 1980). The other elements of the
Unionist class alliance were firmly, if sometimes uneasily,
integrated via paternalism and Orange clientelism in the
workplace and state patronage and employment practices (see
Buckland, 1979; Farrell, 1980).

The initial acquiescence, and subsequent more positive
support, of the British government for this unique form of
devolution was also central to its impressive stability. The
legal and administrative terms of devolution served to minimise the political articulation of class conflict within Unionism. Revenue raising, a potential area of conflict, was largely a

matter for Westminster. The local administration was largely responsible for expenditure, within broad guidelines laid down by the central state and this helped to lubricate the mechanisms of political patronage.

One factor, however, appeared at once to threaten political stability while helping to maintain the political integration of Unionism. The 'democratic' viability of the state meant ensuring the permanent minority status of Catholic Nationalists, on whom the Partition settlement had been imposed in conditions of civil war between 1920 and 1922. Nevertheless, as Greenberg (1980, p. 248) rightly observes, neither the Unionist state nor any major sector of (Protestant) manufacturing depended crucially on the 'manipulation and control of Catholic labour mobility or suppression of Catholic political and trade union organisation'. Catholic labour, especially males, were poorly represented in manufacturing industry, and over-represented in construction, agriculture and services in semi-skilled and unskilled occupations. They were also heavily over-represented among the unemployed and among emigrants (O'Dowd, 1980; Hepburn, 1983; Simpson, 1983). The Catholic middle class was mainly composed of farmers, teachers, clergy and small businessmen, largely servicing their own 'community'. Under these conditions, the maintenance of Unionist economic dominance could be left to the operation of 'market forces'. Yet, Catholics remained, numerically at least (33 per cent), a substantial disaffected minority, with consistently higher birthrates. They continued to oppose the legitimacy of Partition by constitutional, and occasionally by violent means. They even had numerical majorities in many areas west of the Bann. Thus the detailed *political* control of the Catholic population, outside the workplace, seemed to be of paramount importance to the survival and stability of Northern Ireland. Herein lay the final and crucial specificity of devolved government, that is, its responsibility for security via the courts, police and paramilitary B-Specials, all of which were closely identified with the Unionist Party.[2] The technocratic or social democratic compartmentalisation of 'economics', 'politics' and legal coercion had little purchase in Northern Ireland.

The strategy of political control was, in crucial respects, a territorial strategy. Colonisation and successive waves of capital accumulation had laid down a complex and interlocking network of Protestant and Catholic areas. The Border maximised the area under Unionist control. It seemed to ensure a permanent Protestant majority while freezing and institutionalising the internal divisions. After 1920, the whole thrust of local administration was to defend this arrangement via Special Powers legislation, B-Specials, housing allocation policy, franchise manipulation and discriminatory employment practices. The resultant stability meant the *outcome* conformed to the interests of traditional and incoming capital. They were not necessarily as wedded to the precise means of control as were grass-roots supporters of the status quo, who wished to preserve their distinct advantages in employment and their more marginal advantages in areas such as housing.

It is against this background, therefore, that the impact of the new regional strategy must be judged. First, it appeared to move the Unionist state away from a defensive to an initiating role and left it with a tricky ideological task of reconciling continuing Unionist hegemony with major structural change. Secondly, the Matthew Plan was the first to involve *both* spatial manipulation and industrial inducement to further capital accumulation (Parson, 1980, p. 80). At first, 'objective' planning requirements seemed to coincide with the political interests of Unionism. Matthew applied the conventional planning wisdom of the time, albeit with weak technocratic justification (Gillespie, 1977; Bew *et al.*, 1979, p. 160). Stormont quickly implemented many of his proposals, notably the stop-line for Belfast, the designation of growth centres at Craigavon and Antrim/Ballymena and of other secondary centres in the environs of Belfast. Wilson's extension of the growth centre concept to six secondary or 'key' centres west of the Bann was also accepted. The two major growth centres were designated as 'New Towns' in 1965 and, in response to pressure, Derry was also so designated in 1968. Meanwhile, Belfast Corporation appointed traffic consultants and physical planners to restructure Belfast in line with the overall regional strategy.

The destabilising ramifications of the new strategy soon became clear. First, it focused rising Catholic dissent on Stormont, now apparently bent on modernising exclusion and discrimination. The emphasis on developing east of the Bann, where 75 per cent of all Protestants and less than 50 per cent of all Catholics lived, was seen as a 'new plantation of Ulster'. This impression was confirmed by the location of the New University in Coleraine, rather than in Derry; the isolation of Omagh and Newry through railway rationalisation; the designation of Protestant centres as 'New Towns'; and above all, by the siting of incoming industry in Protestant areas. Whatever the neutral language and technocratic criteria of the planners, locational decisions were immediately translated into the sectarian rhetoric of local politics (see Hoare, 1981). Even where Catholics seemed to be located favourably, as in West Belfast, they signally failed to benefit in terms of manufacturing jobs. At the zenith of regional strategy in Northern Ireland in 1971, Catholics were still over twice as likely to be unemployed as Protestants (Fair Employment Agency, 1978) and over twice as likely to emigrate (Simpson, 1983, p. 102). Whatever the merits of the 'conspiracy to discriminate' theory, there is no evidence that the Unionist state saw the amelioration of Catholic structural disadvantage as a major object of regional strategy. Instead, Unionist politicians reaffirmed publicly the irrelevance of Protestant–Catholic comparisons to a programme of adapting Northern Ireland as a whole to the changing world economy. There were good reasons why they took this stance, as the Unionist political alliance was beginning to show ominous signs of internal dissension.

Not the least of these signs was the thrust of regional strategy to rationalise the highly decentralised system of territorial control at local government level. Matthew (1963, pp. 15, 46) questioned the planning expertise of local councils, and civil servants and modernising politicians sought to concentrate planning powers at regional level, while reducing the number of authorities (Tomlinson, 1980). As early as 1965, some planning powers had been bureaucratised with the setting up of the New Town Commissions. There was by now, however, a growing revolt against localised Unionist control from an entirely different source – the Civil Rights Movement, which began to attack the various manifestations of discrimination. This movement became the first largely Catholic movement in nearly fifty years to enlist the support of a British

(Labour) government by demanding 'democratic' reforms: 'One Man, One Vote'; fairer housing allocation; and reform of the local security apparatus. The Unionist state now appeared to be threatened on many fronts – from the Civil Rights Movement, the British government, and from the 'modernisers' within its own ranks. Among the latter were the Northern Ireland Chamber of Commerce and Industry and other elements of the Protestant middle class who supported the limited O'Neill reforms in the hope of preventing further political instability. But already popular Protestant reaction was beginning to set in and the Unionist party began to fragment.

The 1960s regional strategy had largely solved the problem of Protestant unemployment in the Belfast Region. The Civil Rights Movement, while opposed by working-class Protestants as a threat to the state, served to highlight the class priorities which were built into the regional strategy. The latter seemed to place a higher priority on motorway development than housing renewal in Belfast, and the cheap high-rise housing provided under the Belfast plan for Protestants was seen to be no better than its Catholic counterpart (Wiener, 1980). Protestants in the west of the Province had benefited little from incoming capital and were now to have their local powers reduced to appease the 'enemies of the state'. Class and sectarian pressures were leading to the disintegration of 'public order' and local political control, forcing the British state to reassert its own responsibility for Northern Ireland.

DIRECT RULE AND 'REGIONALIST CONSENSUS'

Direct Rule from Westminster did seem to mark a radical break with the past, at least in terms of the formal politics and official ideology of the state. In retrospect, however, it is the continuities with the Stormont period which are most striking. In particular, the Northern Ireland Office (NIO) sought to consolidate and extend the regional strategy pursued by Stormont, while attempting to mobilise a broader, 'regionalist consensus' behind it. In many respects, this policy took a similar form to the tried and trusted methods which had been frequently used to combat regional dissent, and incipient separatism, within Great Britain itself.

This policy proceeded on a number of fronts. First, the centralising and bureaucratising thrust of the 1960s regional strategy, which the Unionist party had failed to bring to fruition, was now realised. Here, the existence of the Northern Ireland civil service was important. Its leading figures had long been the most consistent advocates of rationalising local administration along British lines (Oliver, 1978; Green, 1979). In practice, this policy went somewhat further than similar developments in Britain in response to the threat posed by mass working-class unrest, particularly in Belfast and Derry. The fact that much of the conflict was intra-working class did little to minimise the threat to political stability at this point. The plans made to reform local government (Northern Ireland Government, 1970) were now implemented in a somewhat altered form. A succession of bodies were added to the recently established Northern Ireland Housing Executive, including Health and Social Services Boards, Education and Library Boards and a Ministry of Development (later the Department of the Environment). These assumed most of the powers previously held by the local authorities. The latter were reduced from seventy to twenty-six and left with residual powers of street cleaning and managing cemeteries and recreational centres. The new state agencies were staffed by civil servants and ministerial appointees with minority representation from elected representatives. With the removal of policing powers from Stormont, the local parliament was prorogued and economic, political and policing powers centralised under a British Secretary of State at the NIO.

In 1973, there was a short-lived attempt link a reconstructed local parliament to the overall regional strategy. Significantly, the 'Powersharing Executive' was to collapse as a result of failure to mobilise working-class support. It failed to undermine support for the IRA in Catholic areas and was eventually brought down by a general strike, led by key Protestant workers, and supported by the middle, petit bourgeois, tier of the old Unionist alliance. While this indicated the class basis of the new 'improved' regional strategy, it also demonstrated that, at best, working-class action had only a limited veto effect. The institutional basis of the regional strategy remained intact. Local politicians were reduced to sending delegations to the NIO and to advising the administration in state agencies, local councils and such bodies such as the Northern Ireland Convention (1974) or the current Assembly.

Although, at the time, British response to the Northern Ireland crisis seemed *ad hoc* and reluctant, even to those operating policy, it nevertheless took a recognisable and consistent form. In structure, it differed little from the regional development strategies, pursued in Britain, France or Federal Germany, of creating regional institutions insulated from disturbing and destabilising local influences (see e.g., Dulong, 1978). Elected bodies in Northern Ireland assumed the role of what Hirsch (1981, p. 604) has termed 'symbolic conflict processing mechanisms'. Yet, clearly, the immediate impetus for restructuring the local state did not come solely from perceptions of the requirements of monopoly capital, although it was linked in a complex manner to the state's *formulation* of what these requirements were.

When Labour came to power in 1974, its Northern Ireland ministers recognised the limitations which local working-class opposition had placed on regional strategy. They sought to broaden the basis of a 'regionalist consensus' which would incorporate significant elements of the working class behind the aims of economic development and reducing regional social inequalities. This appeared to have some potential as a means of marginalising the 'intractable' politics of sectarianism and the 'national question'. Paradoxically, although economic, political and military/security powers were now more centralised and co-ordinated than ever before, the thrust of Labourist ideology was to split the 'Northern Ireland Problem' technocratically into its discrete, constituent parts – economic, political and military. For Secretaries of State Rees and Mason this meant engaging local politicians in desultory and inconclusive discussions on 'political initiatives' while concentrating on the 'twin enemies of unemployment and terrorism'. The Northern Ireland Information Service began to issue daily press releases, often reproduced verbatim in the local press, on the activities of ministers in 'selling Northern Ireland' to potential foreign investors, bringing local social services in line with the rest of the UK, and in counteracting the IRA. At times, these bulletins read like league tables of monies spent, jobs 'created' or 'saved', people arrested and quantities of arms discovered (see O'Dowd *et al.*, 1982).

Particular attention was devoted to developing a local corporate consensus on the economy. Ministers encouraged frequent consultation among local trade union leaders, the local branch of the CBI, and the NIO. The Northern Ireland Economic Council (NIEC) was reorganised as a consultative forum to incorporate these interests. The major economic report of the period (Quigley, 1976) reflected the trend of government thinking, even if many of its recommendations were ignored. Based on a fuller analysis of regional statistics than previous reports, it advanced a more differentiated view of regional strategy as incorporating 'labour market strategy' as well as 'industrial promotion' and its associated spatial strategy. Quigley (1976, p. 69) acknowledged that the regional effects of national policy may be more important than the deliberately conceived instruments of regional policy. This was an implicit recognition that the most substantial basis for Labour's regional policy was increased public expenditure, especially on social services, to ensure parity with the rest of the UK. This was particularly important as external investment had almost dried up, and unemployment was mounting, with redundancies and closures among existing state-assisted plants.

Under Labour, public expenditure became ever more crucial to the management of the local economy. One of the results was a massive increase in service employment, especially in the public sector which by 1983 accounted for 45 per cent of total employment, compared to 35 per cent in 1974 (Fothergill and Gudgin, 1982, p. 38; O'Dowd, 1982, p. 102). Public sector expansion was mainly in female part-time employment in the education and health services (Rowthorn, 1981, p. 13). Budget priorities shifted in favour of social security payments and law and order and away from earlier spending on capital projects (Harvey and Rea, 1982).

One result was the emergence of spatial politics in a new

form. At the height of the civil unrest in the early 1970s, a vast number of localised community groups, tenants associations and defence committees had developed, especially in Belfast, in the context of intimidation, population movements and 'no-go areas'. These were typically urban, working-class, and divided sharply on sectarian grounds. Sometimes actually encouraged by the local administration as a means of managing the conflict in the early 1970s (Rolston, 1980), they now began to exert pressure on the new state agencies over specific issues such as housing, urban renewal, motorway construction and welfare rights. While this was the 'politics of bread and butter issues', implicit in Labour's regional consensus, it scarcely undermined the territorial politics of sectarian division.[3] As Labour, under Mason, began to develop ever tougher 'security policies' through 'criminalisation of terrorism' by abolishing political status in the prisons, through saturation of Catholic areas by greatly expanded[4] and almost totally Protestant security forces, the limits of 'regionalist consensus' became abundantly clear.

THE CRISIS OF REGIONAL STRATEGY

The core elements of post-War regional strategy in Northern Ireland had come to show signs of disintegration from the early 1970s. Manufacturing employment had declined only slightly between 1959 and 1974. In the next five years, it declined by 3.3 per cent per annum, a rate which rose to 9.2 per cent between 1979 and 1982 (NIEC, 1983, p. 15). Over 70 000 manufacturing jobs disappeared between 1971 and 1983 (a decline of 40 per cent). In the three years to 1982 over 100 manufacturing plants closed with a loss of 28 000 jobs – 20 per cent of the 1979 total (see House of Commons Industry and Trade Committee Evidence, 1982). Unemployment doubled to 63 000 between 1970 and 1979 and doubled again by 1982 to stand currently at over 20 per cent (see Department of Economic Development Statistics). Redundancies far outstripped new job promotions, despite massive subsidisation of existing and new firms such as the shipyards (NIEC, 1983, pp. 42–3), Courtaulds and De Lorean. The last two were spectacular and costly failures and reflected the increasing desperation of the promotional agencies in the 1970s (see House of Commons Report from the Committee of Public Accounts, 21.5.80). The key multinational firms, around which the 1960s growth centres were constructed, began to close, one by one: Courtaulds in Carrickfergus and Derry; ICI in Carrickfergus; Enkalon in Antrim; Goodyear in Craigavon; Standard Telephone and Cables in Larne and Enniskillen; and Michelin in Newtownabbey. Unemployment, already high in peripheral and largely Catholic areas west of the Bann, now got substantially higher, reaching well over 30 per cent in many areas and affecting previously low unemployment areas in the Protestant environs of Belfast. The 1981 Census indicates dramatic disparities in the spatial distribution of unemployment, on both a class and sectarian basis. This suggests that a regional strategy stressing common interests and objectives is unlikely to receive popular acquiescence, much less active support.

Unlike the period prior to 1970, the official discussion of regional strategy now registers, however obliquely, the material basis of sectarian division. Quigley (1976) thus can advance a 'dual economy thesis' referring to the growing disparity between the (largely Catholic) area west of the Bann and the (heavily Protestant) area to the east. Specific locational decisions, such as the siting of De Lorean and the Enterprise Zones, have been aimed ostentatiously at bridging Catholic and Protestant space, while delivering little in terms of new employment. Fair Employment Agency reports have demonstrated the continued exclusion of Catholics from manufacturing (especially in engineering) and their continued absence from the decision-making levels of the Civil Service (despite signs of increased recruitment at lower levels).[5] The activities of the Agency have provoked sustained pressure from all levels of Unionist politics for its abolition, and indifference from Catholic politicians on account of its ineffectiveness.

The official language of regional strategy obscures the material basis of sectarian division, in part because regional development has been portrayed as an alternative way forward. To take it into account explicitly would be to run the risk of 'contaminating' economic strategy with local politics. Yet the 'collapse' of regional strategy itself must be explained.

This is accomplished, in part, by translating local political conflict into a rather undifferentiated variable called the 'security situation' or 'political instability'. This variable is then assessed not so much in terms of its economic causes, as in terms of effects. Above all, 'political instability' is seen as a deterrent to overseas investment (see e.g., Quigley, 1976, pp. 15, 66; Ulster College Group, 1982, p. 24). The independent effect of this 'factor' is often highlighted by the much better record of the Irish Republic in attracting multinational investment under identical international economic conditions. Hence, the NIEC (1983, p. 54) estimate that job promotions in the Republic were five times the Northern total, although their survival rate is similar. Also, frequent estimations are made of job losses specifically traceable to the Troubles, most of which approximate Rowthorn's (1981) estimate of 24 000.

Increasingly, the 'political instability' or the 'Troubles' have been portrayed as a problem of perception and business confidence that can, in fact, be combatted. The NIEC (1980, p. 27), in particular, attacks the distorted media image of the province – 'the quite unnecessary preoccupation with the security situation'. Polls commissioned by economic agencies support the 'bad image' hypothesis and the NIEC lobbies the BBC on the subject, claiming in one report that 'our economy would be much stronger if, for example, television coverage of industry portrayed the true situation'. The Northern Ireland Chamber of Commerce have undertaken their own campaign to demonstrate the 'normality' of life in the province. All this may be read as part of the consistent attempt to compartmentalise 'economics' and 'politics'. Comparisons with the Republic, and proposals for more co-operation and trade (noticeably absent from regional strategy until recently) are encouraged, provided it has 'nothing to do with politics' (see, e.g., Northern Ireland Chamber of Commerce evidence to the House of Commons Industry and Trade Committee, 1982).

Yet, at times, the official ideology of regional development demonstrated considerable ambiguity on the precise nature of the relationship between economic strategy and local politics. The Development Programme produced in 1970 shows evidence of a typical vacillation on this point. In one paragraph

the authors confess to a feeling of irrelevance when considering growth centres and stop-lines as Belfast was erupting. Yet,
in the very next paragraph they reinterpret the 'Troubles' in
terms of a demand for houses and jobs, demands to which the
development strategy was highly relevant (1970, pp. 8–9; 26).

There are, however, increasingly apparent reasons why
local political demands cannot be reinterpreted as demands
for 'jobs and houses'. The thrust of Conservative policy since
1979 has been that state regional strategy cannot, and should
not, deliver jobs on any large scale. Official ideology now
stresses the virtues of self-reliance, competitiveness and the
'spirit of enterprise'. Although 'regional policy' expenditures
were not reduced in line with Conservative practice in Britain
(Pickvance, 1981), the ideology of regional development has
been modified. As Conservative strategy is geared to accom-
modating the UK *as a whole* to the changing international
division of labour, one line of argument is that 'getting the
national economy right' will have trickle down effects for
regions like Northern Ireland. The other emphasis is the stress
on local enterprise and indigenous small business. The
Northern Ireland Government (1981) statement of aims
clearly reflected altered priorities by placing the 'establishment of small businesses' on top of the list, followed by
'making existing businesses competitive' and, finally, attracting overseas investment. The Industrial Development Board
(IDB), the new streamlined promotional agency set up to
promote jobs on commercial lines, has conceded that it is
shifting the emphasis to helping 'indigenous industry', while
admitting that this will make little impression on unemployment (*Irish Times*, 5.10.82: interview with Saxon Tate).

In Northern Ireland, at least, the significant reduction of
mass unemployment is no longer the major explicit rationale
of regional strategy. Loosening the 'constraints on capital' and
on the 'indigenous spirit of enterprise' via Enterprise Zones,
local enterprise agencies and small business programmes
produces few jobs, if much diverting ideological debate. In
appealing to the revival of local capital, the government is
relying on a sector which has accounted for only 20 per cent of
job years in 'state assisted industry' since 1945 (NIEC, 1983,
p. 27). Yet, the policy of attracting external (monopoly)

capital is also seen to have failed and Westminster MPs are increasingly scrutinising the cost effectiveness of the small number of jobs promoted (House of Commons Report of the Committee on Public Accounts, 21.5.80). Tighter controls on public expenditure remove the option of expanding public sector employment which fell for the first time in at least fifteen years in 1981 (Nothern Ireland Abstract of Statistics). Employment in Northern Ireland manufacturing industry is now less than 20 per cent of total employment, less than half public sector service employment. Despite continuing 'intensive aid' for remaining manufacturing industry, the state is finding it increasingly difficult to manage the accelerated restructuring of capital.[6]

The onus for reproducing capitalist social relations has fallen increasingly on the state. This, in effect, means a manifestly political strategy. Accordingly, Conservative Direct Rule has put a new emphasis on elected politicians and on breaking the 'political deadlock' as a means of 'sustained improvement in the economy and in security' (Prior, 5.4.82 – Northern Ireland Information Services (NIIS)) The Secretary of State has even suggested that the new Northern Ireland Assembly might be a 'political enterprise zone' for Northern Ireland (Prior, 10.11.82 – NIIS). This emphasis on 'local politics' seems to reverse a long-term marginalisation of 'politics' in the ideology of regional strategy. That it is scarcely a politics of consensus is immediately apparent from the rise of Sinn Fein and the alienation of the Social Democratic and Labour Party (SDLP) from local political institutions.

SUMMARY AND CONCLUSIONS

There has been a marked, if contradictory, progression in regional strategy in Northern Ireland which official ideology at once registers and obscures. The core of this strategy has been the *state's formulation* of the requirements of monopoly capital in the specific conditions of the province. In the 1950s and the 1960s, it was, in the first instance, a response to the failure of local capital to maintain employment levels. Secondly, it was a response to popular, and often territorially based, class and sectarian pressures. It sought to meet these pressures within the constraints set by the class and sectarian nature of the Stormont statelet itself. Success was limited and ambiguous. A relatively large number of jobs were 'created' by incoming investment, but Stormont failed to manage the associated political transition because of its own in-built constraints. Direct Rule sought to relax these constraints from a 'neutral arbiter' position by completing the restructuring of the local state apparatus and expanding state regulation of the economy and public sector employment.

The full contradictions of regional strategy under Stormont, and under Direct Rule until 1979, have only become apparent in its redefinition by the Conservative government in the past four years. Combatting mass unemployment has been dropped as the primary and manifest aim of regional policy in favour of encouraging small indigenous capital. There is now a reduced emphasis on bureaucratic and technocratic ideology. Local elected representatives are being encouraged again as part of the new official ideology of regional self-reliance. Political instability is being emphasised as a major obstacle to some future, and rather hazily defined, economic revival. Yet, this instability is often defined merely in terms of the 'bad image' of Northern Ireland which can only be fully overcome by agreement among the local 'constitutional' parties.

The reorientation of official ideology fits uneasily with a situation in which the state has ever growing responsibility for reproducing capitalist social relations. This is pursued within state employment, in expanded youth training schemes and, in more coercive form, in the policing of working-class estates. Sectarian relations are being reproduced simultaneously, through security policies at one end of the spectrum and the selective employment of Catholics in the public sector at the other.[7] The struggle between the IRA and the security forces has sharpened the long established topography of sectarian division, especially west of the Bann and in urban working-class areas. While the British government have not conceded Unionist demands to build a 'Berlin wall' on the Border, it has inceasingly asserted the territorial legitimacy of the state and the nature of the Border as a 'UK land frontier'. This offsets, partially at least, the delegitimising effects of a failed regional strategy among Protestants.

The more general implications of the Northern Ireland experience are perhaps twofold: (i) it illustrates the destabilising effects of state-subsidised monopoly capital and the political problems of managing its early withdrawal in the wake of global restructuring; (ii) the specificity of the province in the UK context may lie in its potential as an experimental laboratory for dealing with territorially focused expressions of class, national and racial unrest elsewhere. In this respect, there are signs that earlier practices of applying 'mainland' strategies of management to Northern Ireland, are now being reversed.

On a more general theoretical level, this case study seems to question the utility of deriving state policy from the 'objective requirements' of capital abstractly stated. In any specific area, these 'requirements' are only partially clear, and are often contradictory and politically destabilising. In any case, they change with each phase in the restructuring of the spatial basis of global capital accumulation. The specificity of the state resides, however, in the way it attempts *to formulate* what these 'requirements' are, in response to specific historical conditions.

NOTES

1. Regional strategy is defined here as the battery of measures and institutions used to promote industrial development through loans, grants and subsidies to individual firms to locate, expand or remain in an area. It also includes state provision of physical infrastructure in the form of industrial estates, advance factories, roads, port facilities, growth centres and 'new towns' as well as selective controls on investment in more prosperous regions.

2. It was Westminster's removal of local security powers which precipitated the fall of the Stormont parliament when the Unionist party resigned en bloc in protest.

3. This point is reinforced by the successful mobilisation (and by Paisley's Democratic Unionist Party, to a lesser extent) around the spatial politics of social provision.

4. Between 1974 and 1979, 56 per cent of the total expansion in male public sector employment was due to the increase in police and prison service employment. This was a direct result of Labour's policy of 'Ulsterisation' and 'criminalising terrorism'. As these services employ very few Catholics, they involve an important economic subsidy to one

side of the sectarian divide, whatever their other political and ideological implications.

5. A cross-section of Fair Employment Agency research is reported in Cormack and Osborne (1983). See also the recently published study of 23 000 civil servants (Fair Employment Agency, 1983).

6. Some idea of the dynamics of capitalist enterprise and the role of state intervention can be gauged from the NIEC (1983, pp. 16–21) which shows that 137 000 jobs were 'created' in 'state-assisted' enterprise between 1945 and 1982. Only 45 000 of these jobs survive. The average duration of employment in projects opened prior to 1965 was nine years and this fell sharply for projects opened after 1970. These figures understate the state underpinning of capital in Northern Ireland as the definition of 'state assistance' excludes 'standard capital grants' which are not subject to the creation of employment.

7. The Fair Employment Agency (1983) reports a very uneven distribution of Catholics in the Northern Ireland Civil Service ranging from highs of 40 per cent and 33 per cent in Health and Social Services and Manpower, respectively, to lows of 10 per cent and 19 per cent in the Police Authority and Education, respectively. Of 133 posts, at Assistant Secretary level or higher, only 11 were occupied by Catholics (1983, p. 14). In the 1970s, Catholics were recruited in greater numbers than before but these appointments have been disproportionately female and lower grade jobs. Even here, the importance of sectarian territory is emphasised as there are very few Catholics in the single establishment departments in Protestant East Belfast and North Down (1983, p. 64).

REFERENCES

Bew, P., Gibbon, P., and Patterson, H. (1979) *The State in Northern Ireland* (Manchester: Manchester University Press).

Buckland, P. (1979) *The Factory of Grievances: Devolved Government in Northern Ireland* (Dublin: Gill and Macmillan).

Carney, J., Hudson, R., and Lewis, J. (eds) (1980) *Regions in Crisis* (London: Croom Helm).

Cormack, R. J. and Osborne, R. D. (eds) (1983) *Religion, Education and Employment: Aspects of Equal Opportunity in Northern Ireland* (Belfast: Appletree Press).

Dulong, R. (1978) *Les Régions, l'État et la Société Locale* (Paris: Presses Universitaires de France).

Dunford, M. (1977) 'The Restructuring of Industrial Space', *International Journal of Urban and Regional Research*, 1, (3), pp. 510–20.

Dunford, M., Geddes, M. and Perrons, D. (1981) 'Regional Policy and the Crisis in the UK: A Long-Run Perspective', *International Journal of Urban and Regional Research*, 5, (3), pp. 377–410.

Fair Employment Agency (FEA) (1978) *An Industrial and Occupational Profile of the Two Sections of the Population in Northern Ireland* (Belfast: FEA).

Fair Employment-Agency (1983) *Report of an Investigation by the FEA for Northern Ireland into the Non-Industrial Northern Ireland Civil Service* (Belfast: FEA).

Farrell, M. (1980) *Northern Ireland: The Orange State* (London: Pluto Press).

Faulkner, B. (1978) *Memoirs of a Statesman* (London: Weidenfeld and Nicolson).

Fothergill, S. and Gudgin, G. (1982) *Unequal Growth* (London: Heinemann).

Gillespie, A. (1977) *Growth Centres and Regional Development in Northern Ireland* (University of Cambridge, unpublished Ph. D).

Green, A. J. (1979) *Devolution and Public Finance: Stormont from 1921 to 1972*, University of Strathclyde, Studies in Public Policy, 48.

Greenberg, S. B. (1980) *Race and State in Capitalist Development* (New Haven: Yale University Press).

Hall Report (1962) *Report of the Joint Working Party on the Economy of Northern Ireland*, Cmnd. 446, Belfast: HMSO.

Harvey, S. and Rea, D. (1982) *The Northern Ireland Economy*, (Belfast: Ulster College).

Hepburn, A. C. (1983) 'Employment and Religion in Belfast, 1901–1951', in R. J. Cormack and R. D. Osborne (eds) *Religion, Education and Employment* (Belfast: Appletree Press).

Hirsch, J. (1981) 'The Apparatus of the State, the Reproduction of Capital and Urban Conflicts', in M. Dear and A. J. Scott (eds) *Urbanisation and Urban Planning in Capitalist Society* (London: Methuen).

Hoare, A. G. (1981) 'Why They Go Where They Go: The Political Imagery of Industrial Location', *Transactions of the British Institute of Geographers*, 6, pp. 152–175.

Isles, K. S. and Cuthbert, N. (1957) *An Economic Survey of Northern Ireland* (Belfast: HMSO).

Lebas, E., (1982) 'Urban and Regional Sociology in Advanced Industrial Societies', *Current Sociology* 30, (1), pp. 1–271.

Massey, D. and Meegan, R. (1982) *The Anatomy of Job Loss* (London: Methuen).

Matthew, R. (1963) *Belfast Regional Survey and Plan*, Cmnd. 451, (Matthew Report) (Belfast: HMSO).

Moore, B., Rhodes, J. and Tarling, R. (1978) 'Industrial Policy and Economic Development: The Experience of Northern Ireland and the Republic of Ireland', *Cambridge Journal of Economics*, 2, pp. 99–114.

Northern Ireland Development Programme, (1970) (Belfast: HMSO).

Northern Ireland Government. (1970) *Report of the Review Body on Local Government in Northern Ireland*, Cmnd. 546 (Macrory Report) (Belfast: HMSO).

Northern Ireland Government (1981) *Industrial Development in Northern Ireland: A Framework for Action* (Belfast: HMSO).

Northern Ireland Information Services (NIIS). Press Releases.

NIEC (Northern Ireland Economic Council), (1980) *Annual Report* (Belfast: NIEC).

NIEC (1983) *The Duration of Industrial Development Assisted Employment*, 40 (Belfast: NIEC).

O'Dowd, L. (1980) 'Regional Policy', in L. O'Dowd, B. Rolston and M. Tomlinson, *Northern Ireland: Between Civil Rights and Civil War* (London: Zed Press).

O'Dowd, L. (1982) 'Regionalism and Social Change in Northern Ireland', in M. Kelly, L. O'Dowd and J. Wickham (eds) *Power, Conflict and Inequality* (Dublin: Turoe Press).

O'Dowd, L., Rolston, B. and Tomlinson, M. (1982) 'From Labour to the Tories: The Ideology of Containment in Northern Ireland', *Capital and Class*, 18, pp. 72–90.

Oliver, J. (1978) *Working at Stormont* (Dublin: Institute of Public Administration).

Parson, D. (1980) 'Spatial Underdevelopment: The Strategy of Accumulation in Northern Ireland', *Antipode*, 12, (1).

Pickvance, C.G. (1981) 'Policies as Chameleons: An Interpretation of Regional Policy and Office Policy in Britain', in M. Dear and A.J. Scott (eds) *Urbanisation and Urban Planning in Capitalist Society* (London: Methuen).

Quigley, W. G. (1976) *Economic and Industrial Strategy for Northern Ireland*, Report by Review Team (Quigley Report) (Belfast: HMSO).

Rees, G. and Lambert, J. (1981) 'Nationalism as Legitimation? Notes Towards a Political Economy of Regional Development in South Wales', in M. Harloe (ed.) *New Perspectives in Urban Change and Conflict* (London: Heinemann).

Rolston, B. (1980) 'Community Politics', in L. O'Dowd *et al.*, *Northern Ireland: Between Civil Rights and Civil War*. (London: Zed Press).

Rowthorn, B. (1981) 'Northern Ireland: An Economy in Crisis', *Cambridge Journal of Economics*, 5, (1), pp. 1–31.

Simpson, J. (1983) 'Economic Development: Cause or Effect in the Northern Ireland Conflict', in J. Darby (ed.) *Northern Ireland: The Background to the Conflict* (Belfast: Appletree Press).

Tomlinson, M. (1980) 'The Relegation of Local Government', in L. O'Dowd *et al.*, *Northern Ireland: Between Civil Rights and Civil War* (London: Zed Press).

Ulster College Group (1982) *Unemployment* (Belfast: Ulster College).

Urry, J. (1981) 'Localities, Regions and Social Class', *International Journal of Urban and Regional Research*, 5, (4), pp. 455–74.

Wiener, R. (1980) *The Rape and Plunder of the Shankill* (Belfast: Farset Press).

Wilson, T. (1965) *Economic Development in Northern Ireland*, Cmnd 479, (Wilson Report) (Belfast: HMSO).

8 Small Enterprises, the Recession and the 'Disappearing Working Class'

CHRIS GERRY

There would seem to be every reason to make an explicit link between the national-level impact of the recession on both the numerical size of the employed population and on the size and composition of the small business sector. However, it may at first seem curious to connect so explicitly the respective fates of the world economy, the small business sector and the working class in this short and, admittedly, speculative essay.

Nevertheless, the connection can and should be made. The main aim of this essay is twofold. One objective which, despite its *secondary* importance, should nevertheless be dealt with first, is that of showing how a careful analysis of the recession's impact on small businesses in general and, in particular, specific types of small enterprise (to be identified below) will help in the assessment of the full effect which worldwide capitalist crisis has had on levels of employment and its sectoral distribution. Secondly, and more importantly, this essay seeks to indicate (on a more qualitative, but nonetheless crucial level of analysis) the effect that the recession and associated government policies may have had on the level of consciousness of the working class, and how a number of writers 'on the Left' have interpreted this impact.

The reason why this essay has been deliberately designated as 'speculative' is that it proposes an *inversion* of the form in which the problematic of 'alternative forms of production', the rise of the 'black economy' and similar phenomena associated with the current recession and 'de-industrialisation' has so far generally been posed. Rather than seeing the emergence of new lifestyles, new forms of organisation of production and consumption, and new vehicles for political expression as deliberate strategies on the part of potential victims of the recession, this essay will provide a number of indications which could lead us to draw the conclusion that, *to some extent*, such endeavours can be located within the overall strategy of the ruling class (i.e., those *managing* the recession in the expectation of renewed capitalist accumulation in the future). The current situation facing various types of 'traditional' and 'emergent' small enterprises is used as a specific example from which such a conclusion might be drawn. Consequently, the essay provides much more in the way of proposals for future analysis than the results of research already completed.

A concrete example will adequately set the scene for the comments which follow. If one were to calculate the level of real-wage reductions necessary to re-establish the international competitiveness of some of the major Western economies (and recent austerity measures and other policies in Poland, Romania and other CMEA economies indicate that the same applies to Eastern Europe), it is likely that, under the present conditions of international recession, the figure for the UK economy would be somewhere between 15 and 20 per cent. It is difficult to believe that such a reduction could be achieved quickly enough through a single measure, and the political consequences of a rapid offensive on real and even money wages could be extremely threatening for the ruling class. Thus it is rather appealing to examine the different measures which could be successfully combined in order to push the real incomes of the majority of the working population down to an internationally competitive level. This essay concentrates on one such measure, the stimulation of small enterprises as a pole of attraction to both the unemployed and the ostensibly up-and-coming generation of new capitalists.

RECESSION AND THE SMALL ENTERPRISE SECTOR

The gloomy predictions of those who see the current form of technological advance as the enemy of workers, rather than their saviour, may only be half right but, nevertheless, the future of many of the unemployed in the Western capitalist economies (and those still to enter the labour market for the first time) remains bleak indeed. Will they become permanent welfare recipients? Or will they be involved in some sort of rather marginal 'self-employment'?

If, in this context, the traditional forms of small enterprise are allowed or even encouraged to flourish, and 'new' forms emerge or are promoted, then wage-employment of some sort would tend to proliferate in the small business sector, rather than in the traditional, large-scale industrial enterprises. Were a more thriving small enterprise sector to be supplemented by an increase in 'new' forms of self- and collective-employment (e.g., in co-operatives, community enterprises, etc.), a substantial quantitative and qualitative transformation of the sectoral distribution and importance of both self-employment and wage-employment could be foreseen. The sphere of 'self-employment' as conventionally understood (Scott, 1979) has already become a significant arena of struggle between those who have been displaced from their traditional and relatively stable modes of income generation (on the one hand) and the state (on the other hand).

The current world recession has seen a substantial acceleration in the internationalisation of capital and the relocation of capitalist production, due to the fact that profitability has been severely squeezed. This process is part and parcel of the heightened competition made necessary by the continued search for profit under conditions of declining world demand (Glyn and Harrison, 1980, pp. 5–33). In this context, new types of small enterprises have proliferated within 'national' economies, at the same time as large national and transnational companies have initiated their own responses to the crisis. These responses have characteristically included the 'externalisation' of a significant part of the labour and labour-associated costs previously borne by large companies, either by making workers redundant (with or without the introduction of technological innovation) and/or by 'farming out' work previously undertaken within the large company to smaller pre-existing or even specially created enterprises.

Additionally, other small enterprises (more commonly associated with what has been termed the 'black economy') have appeared, as sections of the unemployed (unable to maintain subcontractual links with their former employers, and unable to find alternative wage employment) have established for themselves less 'formal' modes of income generation, not necessarily in conformity with current health and safety, registration, fiscal or other regulations and requirements imposed by the state. Aside from these two types of small enterprises (former employees becoming dependent subcontractors, and 'black' occupations which infringe social security, fiscal and other norms), another form of small enterprise has emerged, or flourished, as a result of the recent boom in microcomputers, biotechnology, etc., and the service activities associated with them. Finally, there are the already established or newly initiated enterprises of a more 'traditional' character (in retail distribution, transport, construction, personal services, etc.) which have managed to survive the intensification of competition associated with the deepening crisis.

It should be emphasised at the outset, however, that this preliminary classification ignores the very substantial 'rump' of small enterprises spread across virtually all branches and sectors of manufacturing and services, which has continued to play a very significant role in the provision of commodities for the domestic market and for export. More importantly, these conventionally defined small enterprises continue to employ a very substantial proportion of wage- and salary-earners; estimates vary (according to the definitions and techniques used) from 2.5 to 5 million employees in the UK. These relatively small companies have also been seriously affected by the recession and have experienced bankruptcy, severe reductions in the demand for their products, and may even have attempted some of the labour-related, technological or other forms of restructuring more normally associated with large industrial concerns.

The comments which follow refer in particular to the types

of newly emerging or reconstituted small enterprises (legitimate and 'black') mentioned above, rather than to the 'rump'
of relatively 'classical' small-scale enterprises. Nevertheless, to
the extent that policies favouring *or* discriminating against
small enterprises (of whatever variety) will be forthcoming as
part of state-promoted restructuring, some of the trends indicated below may well have significance for that 'rump' in the
longer term. This emergence and/or reconstitution of particular types of small enterprises raise at least two important
questions.

First, to the extent that the 'black economy' constitutes (or
will constitute) a significant component of the small business
sector (broadly defined in terms of both numbers employed
and value added), the state will wish to ensure that any initial
fiscal losses it may incur due to non-registration, fraud, etc.,
can be progressively reduced to manageable proportions.
Paradoxically, this may mean that increased personnel would
have to be deployed inside the Civil Service, so as to improve
the 'policing' of the 'new self-employed', at a time when public
sector employment in general is subject to substantial financial and manpower cuts.

Secondly, to the extent that small businesses, whether they
are created on an inadvertent or a voluntary basis under
conditions of economic recession, may increasingly adopt
'unconventional' organisational and institutional forms (e.g.,
workers' co-operatives, autonomous producers, voluntary associations for the provision of basic wage-goods such as housing, etc.), it will be in the state's interests to ensure that the
institutional, legal and 'policing' provisions which govern the
role, status and scope of such new forms are constantly
monitored, improved and updated in order to guarantee that
those involved continue to respond to the state's fiscal, economic and ideological initiatives, in a direction consistent with
the interests of the ruling class.

André Gorz (1982) concludes that there will indeed be a
struggle for the political 'space' which such new organisational forms will create. This essay attempts, among other
things, to argue that the struggle between these new (and
not-so-new) forms and the state will also be over the distribution of the economic surplus produced by such enterprises.

The struggle is not primarily over whether or not to promote smaller 'national' firms (and if so, to what extent); it is fundamentally concerned with providing the surest foundation for the renewed growth of capital, whatever form of restructuring this may require. A 'dependent renaissance' of the smaller-scale enterprise sector is, under current conditions, absolutely vital to any strategy of rapidly accelerating accumulation. While the post-War boom years saw a trend towards a relative dissolution of the smaller enterprise in many sectors, the deepening crisis of the mid-seventies onwards has seen their flourishing in a number of quite different branches of economic activity, ranging from the 'high tech' micro-electronics sector to the 'alternative' (co-operative, individual/artisanal) organisations found in some of the declining traditional branches of production.

It is therefore to be expected that the struggle for the largest share of the surplus generated by such new 'smaller' enterprises will take on different forms, and will be characterised by different tactics on both sides (i.e. state *and* small enterprises), according to the type of enterprise in question (i.e., legitimate/traditional, legitimate/technological, legitimate/'alternative', or 'black') and upon the specific economic and political circumstances of the moment. For example, while 'high tech' micro-enterprises linked to the consumer-, immediate-goods or machinery/robotics markets will probably play a very important role in supporting (both with inputs and in terms of risks and costs) any industrial growth and restructuring in the UK, and therefore will need to be both controlled *and* encouraged, the promotion offered to co-operatives, management-buy-out and other 'rescue operations' in the more traditional and declining sectors may be more apparent than real, more cosmetic (in terms of catering to regional, unemployed and other lobbies) than concrete. Thus, the debate over the current status and future role of small enterprises is an important one, with considerable implications for both class analysis and class politics.

In the run-up to the 1979 UK general election, small business and its promotion became one of the more prominent topics of debate, discussion and party manifestoes. All the major political parties vied with each other for the votes of both the 'traditional' small entrepreneur (shopkeepers, tradesmen, small specialist manufacturers, transport operators, builders, etc.) and the small, but growing, caucus of 'hi-tech' would-be entrepreneurs. *The Guardian* newspaper had already established its weekly Small Business Page with the appealing acorn logo (a reference to the adage that 'from acorns do great oaks grow') and, since then, many more of the 'quality newspapers' have followed suit.

As the recession intensified, the bourgeois press gave emphasis to articles and editorials dealing with 'the shape of post-industrial society' and 'life without work', as well as the new opportunities which were becoming available for the establishment of 'a firm of one's own' in the era of new technology. The press attributed great dynamism to what was, after all, a minute portion of the small business community. As the apparent bottom of the recession was reached, without any strong evidence of a future upturn manifesting itself, more references were made to the sponsored efforts and/or self-activity of those who had been made redundant (Local Enterprise Schemes, Business Start-Up Programmes, etc.) as well as those who had unsuccessfully attempted to enter the wage-labour market for the first time ('teenage' entrepreneurs, self-help alternatives to Youth Opportunity and Training Schemes).

It would be naïve and simplistic to suggest that all the major political parties (and the classes, and more-or-less-distinct combinations of capitals on whose behalf such political formations speak) had to a greater or lesser extent come to the same conclusion: namely, that greater priority and support should be accorded those enterprises which not only offer the best opportunities for profit-making or foreign-exchange earning under the current conditions, but also those which may be able to generate some degree of 'national' economic and employment growth, thereby mitigating some of the worst 'national' impact of the recession. Rather, the depth and character of the crisis has made it necessary for the ruling class to make provision for the burden of 'economic recovery' to be borne to an unprecedented extent, not merely by the working class (in the form of unemployment and reduced real incomes), but also sections of that amorphous 'middle class', in the form of opportunities to establish or consolidate enterprises intimately connected with the hoped-for upturn in economic activity; opportunities which will almost certainly involve a substantial transfer of risks and costs from the largest national and multinational companies to the above-mentioned firms. Regardless of the ideological 'trimmings', the objective is the same across the board, with differences of emphasis regarding the precise degree to which different classes and class-fractions will benefit from or bear the cost of the process of capitalist restructuring.

In the currently hostile and depressed international economic climate, it has so far been the larger enterprises with a capacity for the international mobilisation and transfer of assets and resources which have set the tone for the overall process of restructuring and relocating production. Consequently, it is to be expected that such a process of restructuring (involving, e.g., support for fractions of international capital whose presence in the UK is to be encouraged or consolidated via the provision of both cheapened labour-power and a private support network of small enterprises able to service cheaply technologically advanced national privatised branches of industry, as well as selected branches of multinational or 'foreign' capitalist production) would be capable of creating new niches for small enterprises, just as many of the more traditional niches had been narrowed in previous periods of boom and capital concentration.

The response of transnational capitalist enterprises to the economic recession has been to pursue some or all of the following policies (with varying degrees of success):

(1) The national rationalisation and international relocation of production (Massey and Meegan, 1982).
(2) The restriction and/or shifting of major product lines.
(3) The introduction of new technology (without or alongside productivity deals and job-losses) facilitated by the downturn in labour militancy.
(4) The conversion of substantial blocs of industrial capital into finance capital (particularly during the period of internationally extremely high interest rates).
(5) The re-appropriation of productive capacity which had

previously been relinquished in favour of 'national' capital in the now heavily indebted 'newly industrialised countries' (Mexico, for example).

As part of its strategy to lift both 'national' and internationalised branches of capitalist production out of their protracted recession, the ruling classes of the advanced countries must make improvements to the levels of nationally generated and retained surplus; however, the effect should not be mistaken for the cause. Whatever new 'national' growth takes place will be the by-product of the major strategy, i.e., that of bringing large, internationalised capital out of its crisis. Modifications in the priority accorded the relatively small 'national' or even 'alternative' enterprise (e.g., co-operatives) will constitute neither the dominant trend nor the principal objective of the strategy. Nevertheless, the weight to be attached to 'national growth policies' will vary according to the degree of cohesion between, on the one hand, small capitalists' economic interests and, on the other hand, either the political vehicle they adopt for the furtherance of their cause, or the political grouping which adopts small businessmen as a part of its political constituency. Given the fragmented and heterogeneous nature of the economic branches in which small firms are concentrated, and the propensity of small entrepreneurs to adopt equivocal and vacillating political stances (across a broad spectrum of petit bourgeois and bourgeois parties) great cohesion is unlikely. The more nationally focused efforts of the ruling class will nevertheless tend to emphasise several quite distinct sectors of the national economy (in which the smaller enterprise is well represented) for quite different reasons:

(1) The sector of relatively 'backward' and weakened enterprises (both privately and 'publicly' owned), which is principally but not exclusively oriented towards the domestic market.
(2) Financial, advisory and technical service enterprises, principally but not exclusively oriented towards the demands of large transnational companies active in the country in question and/or oriented towards the export

market (i.e., 'invisibles', technological advice, and related services); these enterprises may not be 'small' in terms of capital or labour employed.

(3) Other components of the small business sector believed to have the potential for rapidly generating a relatively high rate of accumulation and/or relatively substantial employment growth, regardless of their branch of production.

It may be in this (relatively medium-term) sense that governments have come to recognise that smaller capitalist enterprises have a 'positive' role to play in the preservation of some sort of 'national' accumulation process. After all, despite the fact that the nation state (whether developed capitalist, 'Third World' or, to a lesser extent, 'centrally planned') has become increasingly impotent relative to the progressively more internationalised world economic system, individual governments nevertheless must both materially and ideologically attempt to mould and/or respond to the political and social processes taking place within their own national boundaries. No national government can afford to ignore completely the interests which are bound up in the 'national' economy, no matter how involved in or dependent on the internationalised economy the class fractions it represents may be. It is precisely in this context – the contradiction between increasing involvement in the international economy and political dependence upon a nationally–territorially defined social and political structure – that the debate on small scale enterprises has to be seen.

Many of the surviving 'national' branches of production in the UK (including nationalised industries) have been disproportionately weakened by shrinking domestic and overseas demand for their products, heightened competition and, to some extent, by government policy itself. A higher profile given to the promotion of smaller enterprises, co-operatives, etc., is likely to intensify further competition in the home market between 'nationally oriented enterprises' themselves and between the latter and transnationals seeking to penetrate further that national market. This does not augur well for the type of results often naïvely predicted by those who foresee a new hey-day for the smaller enterprise and the boot-strap capitalist. Doubtless, there will be redoubled demands for protectionist domestic trade policies from some quarters, combined with appeals for more government help in penetrating overseas (and particularly Third World) markets: hence the recent appearance of policies in the UK and Western Europe which appear to be simultaneously 'open' for certain branches of production and 'protectionist' for others.

FAREWELL TO THE WORKING CLASS, WELCOME SMALL ENTREPRENEUR?

What has been the response of 'the Left' to the debate on 'the future of work' in general, and the resurgence of a wide range of legitimate, 'alternative' and 'black' small-scale activities? Two recently published contributions are worthy of mention, not because they address themselves specifically to this question, but because they demand of socialists a fundamental rethink in both theoretical and practical political terms. The reassessment for which Bahro (1982) and Gorz (1982) ask focuses upon the capacity of the contemporary working class to act as the major agency of current political struggle, future social transformation and the eventual construction of a socialist society.

In recent articles, Eric Hobsbawm (1982; 1983) has echoed the controversy raised by Gorz and Bahro, with particular reference to the British situation. In their separate ways, each of three above-mentioned authors poses crucial questions relating to some or all of the following issues: 'national' economic decline; increasing unemployment in the advanced capitalist countries; the likely impact of the 'new' technology (microchips, 'robotics', etc.) on future patterns of employment; the current and much-debated decline in the consciousness and militancy of the working class; the decline of the traditional 'labour' and left social-democratic parties; and the corresponding rise of the 'new parties of the recession', such as the Greens in West Germany and Britain's Social Democrat Party (SDP).

Nevertheless, the *relations* between these processes associated with the recession are not given sufficient emphasis by Gorz, Bahro and Hobsbawm; nor have these authors suggested any concrete proposals and/or solutions, except for rather vague discussions of possible political realignments, embracing traditional sections of the labour movement along with myriad other 'interest' groups. Thus, certain strategies are proposed, but these are, in themselves, extremely problematical. The common thread of the three contributions is the thesis that the working class as such (i.e., as conventionally defined, in particular, by Marxists) has been, or is being, superseded as the agency for any future socialist transformation of society. Conspicuous by its absence in these contributions has been any real sense of the *connections* between the growth of 'new technology'; savage reductions in employment; the growth of legitimate small enterprises as well as that of the 'black economy'; the proliferation of 'moonlighting' and 'hobbling' among the unemployed; the Conservative government's privatisation strategy; the cuts in public expenditure; and the restructuring of what is still euphemistically called 'British' capital, within and outside UK national boundaries.

For Gorz, this 'supersession' can be explained by the particular form, scale and pervasiveness of the contemporary capitalist labour process, which renders workers' traditional forms of struggle and organisation (as well as their level of consciousness) inappropriate to the tasks of transforming society; in particular, due to the effects of 'de-skilling', the anti-revolutionary attitudes of most skilled workers, the reformism of modern trade unions, and the massive scale and internationalised nature of capitalist production units.

For Bahro, the supersession of the working class as a revolutionary agency of change is explained in terms of the eclipsing of 'internal' (i.e. class) contradictions by 'external' ones: namely, between 'East' and 'West' over nuclear arms; and between 'North' and 'South' over the global distribution of wealth which is produced and reproduced by the contemporary, capitalist international division of labour. As a consequence, Bahro sees the struggle of mankind for survival itself as the pre-eminent concern, rather than any specific struggle of the working class for political and economic supremacy. The political implications of this thesis are that movements which are based narrowly upon the working class and (or?) its representatives are doomed to failure: broader movements based upon all those who feel threatened by nuclear attack and/or man-made ecological disasters, it is argued, are the only ones with any real hope of success.

For Hobsbawm, the decline in the political and revolutionary role likely to be played by the working class in the transformation of society has been the result of two interconnected factors: the substantial increases in its material standard of living during the post-World War Two long boom; and the qualitative impact on consciousness originating in the ostensible quantitative contraction of the class, as industrial employment has tended to give way (in the West) to a more pervasive white-collar, service-oriented type of employment.

A large number of criticisms can be levelled at this view of the 'shrinking working class', only a few of which can be dealt with here. Briefly, however, the following points should be stressed:

(1) So-called 'national' working classes may be shrinking numerically, due to the currently high levels of unemployment, and the impact (albeit slower than predicted) of new technology; but this ignores the fact that even during the current world crisis, the size of the 'world' working class, corresponding to the highly internationalised world economic system, is undoubtedly continuing to grow.

(2) The purely numerical strength of the working class is a highly inaccurate measure of its political strength and level of consciousness. UK manufacturing employment now constitutes less than half of the total wage-labour force but, as long as one is operating outside the conceptual framework of bourgeois democracy (in which so-called political power is normatively correlated with numerical strength, as expressed in voting patterns), it is entirely legitimate to cite such cases as the Russian Revolution, in which a working class both absolutely and relatively smaller than that currently found in the UK (approximately 3 million) was instrumental in the Bolshevik seizure of power. Thus, the high (though relatively diminished) membership of the UK working class still constitutes a potential political force of considerable, indeed potentially determining, significance.

(3) The assumption that white-collar or 'service-sector' work-
     ers are in some way *less* working class, or have fundamen-
     tally different or lower levels of political consciousness
     cannot be made without reference to some empirical
     evidence; aside from the fact that an historically chang-
     ing, rather than a static ahistorical, social category is
     under scrutiny here, the most cursory glance at recent
     acts of industrial militancy in the white-collar and service
     sector is sufficient to invalidate this assumption. Ex-
     amples of white-collar militancy in the era of the so-called
     'decline of the working class' abound: in the late 1960s,
     following dockers' and dustmen's strike actions, there
     were the first teachers' strikes; in the early 1970s, civil
     servants and local government officers took industrial
     action and a major civil servants' dispute took place in
     1982.

Clearly, an evaluation of the 'shrinking working class thesis'
is absolutely central to the theme under discussion here: do we
say 'farewell to the working class' as such and, thereafter,
embark upon a search for some other donkey on which to pin
the 'revolutionary' tail? Perhaps it would be more constructive
to ask whether, both now and in the past, our confidence in
being able to specify correctly the location and boundaries of
the working class has been misplaced?

The restoration of socialists' confidence in being able to
identify, politically adapt to and – most important of all –
influence the changing material and ideological contours of
the working class, of course involves a move away from
restrictively mechanical and dogmatic formulae for 'class
membership'; but it does not necessarily mean throwing the
working-class 'baby' out with the stagnant analytical 'bath
water'. We need to question just how sensitive to changes in
capitalism itself have been our previous class analyses.
Having made that reassessment, the historical trends in the
boundaries of the working class *of* itself can be dialectically
related to changes in the class *for* itself, i.e., its willingness and
capacity to enter into struggle with the ruling class.

None of this added sensitivity to changing material and
ideological circumstances need prejudice the rigour which

should characterise any analysis of political and socio-economic change. Gorz, Bahro and Hobsbawm appear to be saying that a new route to socialism is required, and that a prerequisite of this redirection is the discovery of a new 'vehicle'. Despite the 'new' route, vehicle and 'guides', the 'old' map (of class contours, boundaries and potentialities) continues to be used with (misplaced) confidence. If the working class is shrinking, are we then to talk with equal confidence (and not for the first time) of a 'new' capitalism? How easily this terminology elides with that of those who purvey the concept of the 'post-industrial society'. The crucial point is that Marxist analysis and the socialist transformation, which it seeks both to inform and bring about, requires a continuous process of analytical map-correction which results from concrete experience and cannot be reduced to a simple process of abstract theorising.

Gorz, Bahro and Hobsbawm, in their various ways, challenge the relevance of the working class to contemporary political struggles and, in the final analysis, its role in the overthrow of capitalism and the construction of socialism. And yet, there are only very vague references to the likely identity and characteristics of those who would assume (or share) the burden of responsibility for this historical transformation. Gorz speaks continuously of 'the movement'; Bahro of the Greens and even the 'Multicoloureds'; while Hobsbawm is content to refer to the 'broad unity' which will be required between all progressive groups (among which he includes the majority of reformists). At best, they suggest that the working class alone cannot fulfil the role of the revolutionary agency of social transformation. At worst, the working class disappears into the background of such a project, and is supplanted by, rather than supplemented by, various other social groups (with allegedly 'cross-class' characteristics), such as the peace movement, environmentalists and, indeed, all those who adhere in principle to social democratic ideas. It is perhaps Gorz who comes closest to identifying those whom he believes will play the role of agents of 'revolutionary change' when he refers to a new 'non-class of non-proletarians', though further than this he appears unwilling to move.

Clearly, not all of those who have either been forced out of wage employment or who have voluntarily switched from the positions classically occupied by workers in the capitalist labour process, have subsequently found it possible to transform themselves into small- or medium-sized entrepreneurs in the private sector. It may have been the aspiration of some, but it turned out to be the reality for relatively few. Schoolleavers, for example, have often found themselves working for small (and some not-so-small) capitalists, as a new type of contract labour inspired by the Youth Opportunities Scheme (YOP) and its variants. Equally, not all of those badly affected by the recession have been wage employees: many small businesses (and a not inconsiderable number of major companies) have disappeared. The birth and death rates of small enterprises appear to have more or less matched one another in recent years, indicating a process of proliferation through high turnover, rather than through numerical expansion of small businesses. Seen from a longer historical perspective, the number of 'small companies' (employing less than 100 workers) has declined from around 300 000 in the 1930s to around 70 000 in 1973.

Does this mean that ex-entrepreneurs have been proletarianised by the recession, or have they merely been made redundant? If they have moved into wage-employment, have they retained strong ideological residues of their previous 'autonomous' status, despite the fact that they are now selling their labour power to capital? Does this also mean that many ex-employees, having been made redundant, have moved into the lowest echelons of self-employment, trading their previously proletarian status for a 'middle class' one? The lack of information, analysis and, above all, clarity in many of the studies of small businesses makes the investigation of such questions extremely difficult – hence the crucial importance of analysing this sector, not merely as an academic exercise but, more importantly, as a means of evaluating some of the predictions and policies derived from the thesis of 'the disappearing working class'.

Such an analysis of the small business sector would help to clarify many of the processes and interconnections mentioned (but posed in fragmented form) by Gorz, Bahro and

Hobsbawm. In this way, a more accurate assessment could be made of the strengths and weaknesses of the working class, the 'labour movement' and its representatives. Only after such an assessment will it be possible to make judgements concerning the ostensible decline of the working class and its politics. Perhaps the conclusion will be drawn that it is the politics of some of the self-styled spokespersons of that movement that has become marginal to the realities of the contemporary working class; it cannot have gone unnoticed that the title of Gorz's book 'Farewell to the Working Class' is ambiguous, in as much as it can be interpreted either as an elegy to a spent political force, or as a proclamation of a personal class trajectory.

A serious answer to the questions posed by Gorz, Bahro and Hobsbawm would require that the different layers, strata and segments of contemporary society (heterogeneous as they undoubtedly are in class terms) be analysed 'in action' and 'in formation'. In other words, both these groups and the working class itself need to be assessed in the very process of responding politically, organisationally and economically to the current crisis, taking both offensive and defensive initiatives in order to adapt to and challenge the conditions and processes which have been produced by the state's 'management' of the recession in favour of the restructuring (rather than the supersession) of capitalism.

One of the implications of seeing these various social layers 'in formation' or 'in motion' would be that an analysis would be required of the emergence and activities of what might be called the 'new parties of the recession', such as the Greens in West Germany and, in a very different way, the SDP in Britain. These new political groupings are themselves engaged in struggle: the policies which they currently espouse may have some impact in the near future, not only to the extent that some of these parties may be able to exert some influence on (or in) government, but also in as much as they hope, through such policy-proposals and objectives, to draw voters and members away from the traditional bourgeois, petit bourgeois and reformist 'labour' parties (and, incidentally, away from any revolutionary party explicitly espousing the overthrow of capitalism).

For Hobsbawm, for example, any rebuilding of confidence and combativity on the Left in the current circumstances would require a substantial redefinition of what constitutes 'the Left', enabling larger components of traditional and 'new' social democracy to be both ideologically and materially incorporated. Such a formula is currently rejected by Bahro on the grounds that West German social democracy is already in terminal decline and has nevertheless maintained an overt hostility to Green theory, practice and policies. For him, it is the extra-parliamentary movements and the 'unorthodox' political parties which constitute the potential political breeding ground of the Greens; incorporating these groups under the Green umbrella could allow considerable influence to be exerted by the Green Party inside the Bundestag, perhaps becoming an effective and autonomous opposition pressing for radical change. Only Gorz, however, emphasises the fact that this will inevitably involve a struggle, though he fails to raise seriously the question of political power in his discussion.

> The State can only cease to be an apparatus of dominion over society and become an instrument enabling society to exercise power over itself with a view to its own restructuring, if society is already permeated by social struggles that open up areas of autonomy, keeping both the dominant class and the power of the State apparatus in check. The establishment of new types of social relations, new ways of producing, associating, working and consuming is the fundamental precondition of any political transformation. The dynamic of social struggles is the lever by which society can act upon itself and establish a new range of freedoms, a new state and a new system of law (1982, p. 116).

Yet Gorz remains vague about the form these 'new ways' of producing and organising will take, how they will be created and co-ordinated, and by whom. Though he identifies political power (albeit implicitly) as the main objective of 'social struggles', he does not shed much light on the process by which this power will be either ceded (by the bourgeoisie) or seized (by his 'non-class of non-proletarians', one assumes).

Gorz also remains equivocal concerning the way in which these initiatives will manage to keep state power in check, which is partly due to the fact that he underestimates the extent to which any of the 'alternatives', 'initiatives' and other options currently on offer have been formulated by institutions of the very state he seeks to capture, precisely in order to prevent the emergence of any *real* autonomy being expressed by the mass of the population.

The debate over the so-called 'disappearing working class' and its alleged supersession as an agency of social transformation has a serious deficiency: its lack of a rigorous and comprehensive analysis of the small enterprise sphere, its forms of persistence/adaption and its scope for accumulation. In order to provide such an analysis in the terms outlined above, it is important that the small business sector (and, though not identical, Gorz's own 'sphere of autonomy') be seen as a current and future battleground (in material and ideological terms) between classes. Such an approach would demand an examination of the strengths and weaknesses, strategy and tactics of groups which sought to carve out their own autonomy (whether in a 'new' form, or an old one). A *more important focus of attention, however, should be the strategems and weaponry deployed by the ruling class* to ensure that this sphere of autonomy neither suffocates for lack of accumulation opportunities (because this would place an insurmountable burden on larger capitalist enterprises to accumulate at rates which they are currently unable to attain and in markets which they cannot readily expand) nor develops a level of real (rather than merely formal) autonomy which might prejudice the benefits which the ruling class gains from its economic and juridical relations with small units of production.

RECESSION, RESTRUCTURING AND THE 'DISGUISED PROLETARIAT'

If massive unemployment can be seen, then, as part of the same process of capitalist restructuring on a world scale, of which recent technological initiatives also form an important part, then the depressing predictions concerning the future of the currently unemployed, those yet to attempt to find wage employment and, indeed, those still with wage-work, should be viewed in a somewhat different light from the semi-obscurity which much of the recent literature has cast on this subject.

This sphere of both 'new' self-employment and wage-work has already become a significant area of struggle between those displaced from their traditional and, in the past, relatively stable modes of income generation, on the one hand, and the state, on the other. For example, Rank Xerox announced plans in 1983 to make many of its middle managers partially autonomous, by helping them to set up consultancy firms which would provide services to companies (including Rank Xerox) outside the two or three days for which the managers were to remain contractually tied to the company. Thus, additional services (over and above the absolute minimum) are provided at individually competitive consultancy rates, without the 'inconvenience' of the social and other costs (e.g., perquisites) normally associated with management and other employment.

The 'sphere of autonomy' generated by capitalist crisis (to some extent state-managed as part of the capitalist restructuring which is vital to the system's recovery) will be extremely heterogeneous, especially in terms of the degree of 'autonomy' characterising its constituent enterprises and activities. Small enterprises established by the former employees of major firms and continuing in the same sub-branch of activity, may be 'fully autonomous' only on the surface. Their new-found freedom would amount to little more than being an extension of the factory for which they previously worked (though now bearing many more of the direct and indirect costs and risks) and, though formally self-employed, the majority of such small businessmen would be almost as integrated into their former company's activities as they were as salaried staff. But they would now, in all likelihood, be employers themselves, and therefore able to pass on the cost burdens which they had recently begun to shoulder. And who, ultimately, would experience the lack of autonomy implicit in lower real wages, weakened or non-existent bargaining power, and the ideological backward step of working under more

'personalised' relations of production, but the relative minority of redundant workers who are fortunate to find wage-
work in this new and booming sector?

Though it is still too early to estimate the real material
impact of the recession and the plethora of make-work,
reduce-the-unemployment-statistics, provide-cheap-labour
and promote-new-business schemes (such as YOPs, Enterprise Zones, science parks, small business promotion, etc.)
there is little doubt that, even were no real quantitative
success to be achieved in the creation of a small business
sector able (if not always willing) to absorb many of the
labour and labour-associated costs of the larger capitalist
companies, it might nevertheless have an appreciable ideological impact. Were such a strategy to be relatively successful
in providing cost-reductions and cost-transfers, it would have
simultaneously achieved two objectives. First, the strategy
would have resuscitated and revitalised a number of mechanisms of exploitation (chain subcontracting, outworking,
monopsonistic subcontracting between many micro-
enterprises and one large buyer of semi-finished goods, etc.)
which previously were somewhat residual in the majority of
branches of industry. Secondly, the strategy would have encouraged the emergence of a 'new' work-ethic, namely that of
self-employment (despite its often low degree of autonomy) as
a form of income generation increasingly more typical than
wage-employment.

Such a scenario has obvious dangers for large sections of the
currently employed, the unemployed, and those yet to try
their 'luck' in the labour market; it also threatens those who
have actively criticised and struggled against the policies and
strategies which have accompanied the current economic
recession. The danger here is that 'the Left' will be easily
satisfied with a purely intellectual search for its 'lost' working
class, and will continue to search long after the above-
mentioned tendencies have become concrete.

Those analysing the impact of the recession from a Left
perspective should resist the temptation to say 'farewell to the
working class', and should seriously reconsider their statements concerning the immanent disappearance of that class as
an economic and political force with which to contend. They

should perhaps consider the possibility that a phenomenon which has accompanied the current recession and high levels of unemployment is the emergence of a 'disguised proletariat' (Gerry, 1980; Gerry and Birkbeck, 1981) outside the major factories and offices, ignored by and ignoring the Trade Union movement, whose objective conditions are highly similar to those we associate with classical capitalist exploitation, yet whose ideological position is increasingly individualist and petit bourgeois, rather than collectivist and proletarian.

The analysis of this 'disguised proletariat' has its roots firmly in classical Marxist propositions concerning the industrial reserve army, rather than in the political alliances between bishops and bricklayers proposed by Left reformists and Eurocommunists. This same analysis has also been enriched by recent debates concerning classes in contemporary capitalist society (see e.g., Wright, 1976). From this perspective, it appears that, rather than confronting a working class whose physical presence and/or influence is shrinking to the point of disappearance, the working class is merely becoming 'less visible' to those whose reformism has been left standing by the speed and depth of the recent capitalist crisis and subsequent downturn in political militancy and struggle.

A large proportion of those in 'disguised wage employment', working *with* but not (in any contractual or juridical sense) *for* capital, will appear to occupy the ground which is commonly (but incorrectly) identified with the legitimate small enterprise sector and/or the less-legitimate so-called 'black economy'. Here we come full circle: back to the need to analyse the current role, position and dynamic of the small enterprise sector in the context of profound economic recession and capitalist restructuring, remembering that the focus of analysis will be units of production in which the relations between micro-entrepreneurs and their workers will be central, and in which the relations established between such enterprises and the *rest* of capitalist production and exchange will be vital to our understanding.

If the traditional parties and/or the 'new parties of the recession' are eager to capture these social layers as a political constituency, then the existing and up-and-coming generation of micro-entrepreneurs have to be offered at least some minimal material incentives within an acceptable, attractive and relevant ideological framework, in order that such support is forthcoming. This will be rather difficult to achieve in the current context of capitalist restructuring, but it is a nettle which must be grasped if the battle for the 'hearts and minds' of new micro-entrepreneurs *and* their workers is to be won by a political coalition *different* from that which today dominates the state, and offering a different social distribution of the new, higher level of accumulation.

Socialists must not only be aware of the likely implications of a ruling-class victory in this process of capitalist restructuring and the ideological inroads made into the working class it implies; they must also be aware of the implications of a social democratic or 'alternative' victory and its limitations. By initiating the investigation of an important strand in the bourgeoisie's current strategy, we should hope for and work towards not merely new theoretical conclusions, but also a real political response to the threat. The quality and direction of such a political response will depend crucially on what sort of analytical approach is adopted, however. If political action is rooted in the notion of a 'disappearing working class', its parameters will be quite different from political action rooted in an approach which takes account of the shifts in workers' (and others') consciousness resulting from the recession and of the corresponding ruling-class strategy, but which does not accord *subjective* aspects of consciousness supremacy over the *objective* factors which condition that consciousness. In other words, we must understand the nature of the current crisis and recession; understand how the small business sector fits into it (from the structural and the strategic viewpoints); and be aware of the dangers of confusing a concrete strategy for restructuring capitalism with some sort of renaissance of the small, self-employed 'master' and the corresponding 'withering away' of the working class.

REFERENCES

Bahro, Rudolf (1982) *Socialism and Survival: Articles, Essays & Talks, 1979–1982* (London: Heretic Books).

Gerry, Chris (1980) 'Petite Production Marchande ou Salariat Déguisé? Quelques Réflexions' *Revue Tiers Monde*, vol. XXI, No. 82.

Gerry, Chris and Birkbeck, Chris (1981) 'The Petty Producer in Third World Cities: Petit Bourgeois or 'Disguised Proletarian'? in Frank Bechhofer and Brian Elliott (eds) *The Petite Bourgeoisie: Comparative Studies of the Uneasy Stratum* (London: Macmillan).

Glyn, Andrew and Harrison, John (1980) *The British Economic Disaster* (London: Pluto).

Gorz, André (1982) *Farewell to the Working Class: An Essay in Post-industrial Socialism*, (London: Pluto).

Hobsbawm, Eric (1982) 'The State of the Left in Western Europe' in *Marxism Today*, October, pp. 8–15 (also in *The Guardian*, 27 September, in condensed form).

Hobsbawm, Eric (1983) 'Falklands Fallout', in *Marxism Today*, January, pp. 13–19 (also in *The Guardian*, 20 December, in condensed form).

Massey, Doreen and Meegan, Richard (1982) *The Anatomy of Job Loss: The How, Why and Where of Employment Decline* (London: Methuen).

Scott, Alison MacEwan (1979) 'Who are the Self-Employed', in Ray Bromley and Chris Gerry (eds) *Casual Work & Poverty in Third World Cities* (Chichester: John Wiley).

Wright, Eric Ohlin (1976) 'Class Boundaries in Advanced Capitalist Societies', in *New Left Review*, 98, July–August, pp. 3–41.

9 Marxism and the Environment: A View From the Periphery

M.R. REDCLIFT

The emergence of the Green Movement in Europe has focused attention on the environment as the most neglected aspect of Marxist theory. The Greens' message is important for a number of reasons. First, they represent a new constellation of forces on the Left. Unlike the peace movement of the 1960s, the anti-nuclear movement in Europe today, by incorporating radical ecology and the feminist critique of patriarchy, seeks to problematise industrial society itself. Secondly, at another, deeper level the Green Movement is both a product *of* Marxism and a challenge *to* Marxism. The new ecological politics is a logical, if unexpected, outcome of Marxism's attachment to the institutional forms and processes of monopoly capitalism. From a Green perspective the 'growth model' which lies at the heart of industrial capitalism is shared by Left and Right. The issues of alienation from work and the socially engineered dependence on the consumption of unnecessary goods are seldom raised by the orthodox Left, but they are central planks in the Green alternative (Bahro 1982a, 1982b; Gorz, 1982).

This paper examines the roots of this reorientation on the European Left, within the context of alternative development models. The environmentalist case, particularly that of the radical Greens, rests on a distinctive understanding of the role the South's resources play in sustaining the industrial model,

and the complicity of working-class organisations in its legitimation. The neglect of environmental and resource issues in
Marxist thought helps to explain the force which radical
environmentalism has brought to its current critique of underdevelopment. Just as the Brandt Committee has sought an
accommodation between North and South, around a programme designed to extend the life of the international economic order, the radical Greens seek a more credible model
than that of orthodox Marxist political economy. Beginning
with an examination of the way in which Marxist theory has
treated the environment, the paper moves on to examine the
neglect of the environment in the sociology of development.
The relationship between Marxism and the environment should
not be confined to developed countries, but should also embrace
underdeveloped countries where, until recently, the 'environment' was treated as if it was of no consequence to the
development process. The argument put forward is that the
analysis of underdevelopment needs to come to grips with
environmental issues, before the contribution of the periphery
to the central industrialised countries can be properly appreci-
ated. Although the periphery does not have a voice at the
centre of the environmental debate, the efforts of the Green
Movement in Europe represent an attempt to bring about a
dialogue between North and South about the wider implications of development for both. The writing of the radical
Greens is thus important for two reasons. First, it forms part
of the current critique of developed capitalism in a period of
economic recession. Secondly, it seeks to widen the discussion
of underdevelopment, by including in the discourse aspects of
that process which have been ignored by all but a handful of
social scientists working in the Marxian tradition.

THE ENVIRONMENT IN MARXIST THOUGHT

An awareness that activists on the Left in Western Europe
have sought to incorporate a concern with the environment in
their political agenda, has led Soviet apologists to argue that
Marx, Lenin and Engels were the intellectual precursors of
today's Greens:

Little wonder that many scientists are turning again and again to Marxist – Leninist theory, and finding in it specific propositions applicable to the relationship between society and nature (Khozin, 1979, p. 31).

The truth is less obvious and more interesting. Late nineteenth-century social theorists were better read in the natural sciences than most of their successors today. Marx was familiar with soil science and plant biology, and made use of his studies in writing about population and ground rent. Nevertheless, like most of his contemporaries, Marx was writing at a time when biologically related social theories were prominent. The search for ways of disposing of these theories led the 'founding fathers' of sociology in several directions, as Buttel has observed (1983, p. 11). It led Marx into a confrontation with Malthusian notions of scarcity. It led Durkheim into a critique of Herbert Spencer's positivism. Weber, for his part, proposed a synchronic view of human civilisation in place of an evolutionary perspective. Marx was not exceptional in attaching more importance to Man's ability to transcend Nature than to the need for conformity with natural laws.

There is more substance in the claim that Engels sought to re-examine Man's responsibilities to nature. Engels, alone among Marxist writers, recognised the dangers which might be posed by Man's demands on the physical environment. This emerges clearly from the two essays, written in 1875 and 1876, entitled 'Introduction to the Dialectics of Nature' and 'The Part Played by Labour in the Transition from Ape to Man'. In the second of these essays Engels writes:

Let us not, however, flatter ourselves over much on account of our human victories over nature. For each such victory nature takes its revenge on us . . . we are reminded that we by no means rule over nature, like someone standing outside nature, but that we belong to nature and exist in its midst, and that all over mastery of it consists in the fact that we have the advantage over all other creatures of being able to learn its laws and apply them correctly (Engels 1970, p. 362).

Lenin elaborated on this view in his work, *Materialism and Empirio-Criticism*, seeking to draw from it evidence that historical materialism was uniquely compatible with natural science (Lenin, 1952, p. 69). He noted that Engels had constantly referred to the 'laws of nature', without considering it necessary to explain the generally known propositions of materialism (Lenin, 1952, p. 156). There are also fragments in *Capital*, where Marx expresses a preference for what we would call 'sustainable development', but they scarcely constitute evidence that this was a central concern of his (Marx, 1971, p. 820). We cannot but conclude that Marx and Engels were creatures of their age, and although a nascent environmentalism was developing in North America at the time (Dasmann, 1975, p. 3), the late nineteenth-century preoccupation was primarily with the origins of economic growth and the mechanisms needed to sustain it.

This emphasis in early political economy on the liberating aspects of economic growth, made a separation between development theory (in both its Neoclassical and Marxist versions) and environmentalism inevitable. Early Marxism shared a fascination with capitalism's success at achieving economic growth. The analysis of economic crises under capitalism did not provoke doubts about the value of growth, although capitalist society's ability to ensure the necessary conditions for growth was increasingly questioned. Since capitalist economies had been most dynamic under high growth conditions, the 'problem' could not include growth itself. Marx's borrowing from the classical political economists, notably Ricardo, included an explicit attachment to economic growth as a means of realising human potential. It is sometimes forgotten that the early political economists wrote within a broadly humanistic tradition, and their interest in trade and manufacturing was partly motivated by the philosophical search for ways of maximising human happiness (de Silva, 1982). Physical resource use was inevitably linked to the primary search for human improvement. The exhaustion of natural resources the loss of ecological balance and with it, the species, the implications of technological reductionism, were all concerns which lay in the future.

ENVIRONMENTALISM IN SEARCH
OF SOCIAL THEORY

The historical roots of environmentalism in North America and Europe need not detain us here (O'Riordan, 1976; Lowe and Warboys, 1980, Dasmann, 1975). The developing science of ecology had been married, not always willingly, to a long-standing concern with the conservation of landscape and the production of amenity values. For some, like Frank Fraser Darling in his 1969 Reith Lectures, the starting point was the effect of development upon nature and the need to preserve 'wilderness' (Fraser Darling, 1970). For others in the Anglo-Saxon world, 'environmentalism' expressed the need 'to restore to nature the wealth that we borrow from it' (Commoner, 1972, p. 299). As civilisation had become oppressed by growth it had lost its restorative equilibrium with nature (Meadows, 1974). The pressure of population on biological systems, their 'carrying capacity', could no longer be 'accommodated' in traditional ways (Brown, 1978). Only through global solutions to global problems could mankind arrest the process described so eloquently by Simmons as the 'political thraldom' of the rich northern consumers over the poor southern producers (Simmons, 1974).

There are a number of core ideas in contemporary environmentalism which merit discussion. First, the conviction that the 'carrying capacity' of the earth's resources is reduced by the 'ultimate limits' of these resources (Dasmann, 1975, p. 36). Secondly, there is the 'biological magnification' argument, that food chains magnify toxic substances imperilling the survival of other species (Bull, 1982; Van den Bosch 1980). Thirdly, it is the view of many observers that economic development, pursued for its own sake, has distributive consequences far removed from industrial society (Ward, 1979; Eckholm, 1976 and 1982). Fourthly, as expressed by Norman Myers in his seminal book *The Sinking Ark*, there is the conviction that our own survival depends, critically, on the disappearance of other natural species (Myers, 1979). At a fundamental level, the environmentalist perspective also poses questions about the use to which science is put, substituting 'better science' for 'more science' in the canons of contemporary policy (Lowe and Warboys, 1980). The range of environmental concern does not stop at such normative pronouncements. The view that is taken of Nature encompasses every aspect of human history since the Middle Ages (Thomas, 1983).

Just as remarkable as the range of environmental concern, and the urgency with which it is expounded, is the search for a social theory which is both consistent with ecological principles and which could provide human agents with a way of averting ecocatastrophe. Most environmentalist writing places emphasis on the need for political decisions in laying the basis for sustainable development. However, there is considerable confusion over the likelihood, and efficacy, of better environmental policy. Unable to avoid the temptation to build 'the social factor' into their environmental advocacy, most authors nevertheless fail to identify both the *agency*, without which nothing can be achieved, and the *mechanism* through which environmentalist policies will be implemented.

The conviction that Man is capable of reversing environmental depredation rests on assumptions about political will for which there is little evidence. Commoner (1972), for example, cites the ability to *adapt to* technology as evidence of a much more questionable ability to *control* it. Similarly, Riddell (1981) argues that a better allocative system, based on environmental resources, is the only solution to Man's self-destruction. However, the resource-conscious pantheism that he espouses as 'ecodevelopment' is rooted in personal convictions rather than historical analysis. Before achieving the 'realistic alternative goals' available to society, we must be clear about what they are and united in pursuing them (Meadows, 1974). Unfortunately, despite the need for concerted action, human societies seldom restrict freedom for environmental motives. There are few imperatives to social action in the working of the biosphere, even if we ignore the warnings that exist (Eckholm, 1982, p. 209). Most social organisation is geared to improving access to goods and services, or ensuring that their 'collective consumption' enables society to produce, socially and reproductively (Castells, 1977). Except for short-term private gain, people show a marked reluctance to organise politically for environmental ends. Stretton's (1976) axiom, that 'people cannot change the way they use resources without changing their relations with each other', contains a basic truth which is nonetheless elusive.

The search for a social theory which would turn analysis into praxis eludes most writers. It has been suggested that better conservation might begin by penalising the groups that do the polluting (Fraser Darling, 1970, p. 29). However, most legislative controls on pollution are more modest, and depend upon the consent of the guilty party (Sandbach, 1980). More fundamentally, an awareness of environmental dangers also implies a willingness to forfeit real advances in income for rather less tangible environmental benefits. It is not difficult to see which of these 'will be the less unacceptable' (O'Riordan, 1976, p. 309). The domain assumptions of environmentalism may be acceptable to much of the population of industrial societies, as Cotgrove argues (1982). However, two questions remain unanswered: how *strongly* do people agree with environmental objectives, and what do these objectives require them to *do?*

THE RECONSTRUCTION OF DEVELOPMENT PARADIGMS

Earlier in this paper it was suggested that there was an affinity between Marxist and Classical political economy in their emphasis on economic growth. The availability of natural resources was clearly a prerequisite for economic development, but the implications for the natural environment of resource scarcity and advanced technology have received attention only in recent times. It is remarkable that environmentalist thinking has had little influence upon the development paradigms, whose common origins we found in nineteenth-century political economy.

The recent discussion of development has taken issue with the view that it is a linear process, originating in the centre but eventually manifested in the periphery. Neo-Marxist writing, in particular, sought to demonstrate that peripheral areas were once central to capitalist accumulation (Frank, 1967; 1969). In the view of the 'world-system theorists' the development of capitalism itself needed to be set in this context. The crisis of capitalism arose from a contradiction between the continued production of surplus in the periphery, and the requirement that this surplus be consumed, if necessary through redistributive policies (Wallerstein, 1980). Another school, represented by writers such as Amin and Emmanuel, identified the process of underdevelopment with the terms of exchange between centre and periphery, rather than the evolution of the global system (Amin, 1974; Emmanuel, 1973). Their work sought to clarify the nature of capitalist accumulation in the periphery by seeking to explain the mechanism through which value was transferred to the centre. At the same time French Marxist anthropologists like Godelier (1977) and Rey (1973) became interested in non-capitalist production relations under capitalist world conditions, and the articulation of modes of production to which this gave rise. Much of the current writing in the sociology of development seeks to elaborate on different elements in these perspectives, analysing the specific historical circumstances in which underdevelopment occurs (Kitching, 1980; Leys, 1977; Long and Roberts, 1979; Lopes, 1978) or seeking to explain the continued importance of petty commodity production in peripheral societies (Banaji, 1977; Bernstein, 1977; Goodman and Redclift, 1981).

Considering the breadth and depth of much Marxist writing on development, it is all the more remarkable that changes in the natural environment have received such scant attention. The international dimension of the environment/ resource crisis has been particularly badly served. Most social scientists working within a political economy framework have confined their attention to trade relations, investment policies and the transfer of industrial technology. The conversion of vegetable into animal protein for consumption in the North, and the energy conversion factor in petroleum-dependent food production, are among a number of processes with considerable distributional importance that have been largely neglected by the Marxist tradition. The concentration on production relations has led social scientists to neglect the patterns of consumption, and exchange, to which these give rise. Few writers in the sociology of development have interpreted underdevelopment as an effect, not only of capital's rapaciousness but also of our consumption habits and the technologies used to feed these habits.

One of the few who has taken the environment seriously is Foster-Carter. Over a decade ago, in a far-sighted essay, he drew attention to the neglect of the environment in Marxist writing on development (Foster- Carter, 1974). He suggested, echoing Malcolm Caldwell's path-breaking studies, that the way natural resources are being depleted in the drive to industrialise casts doubts on the sustainability of development in both rich and poor countries (Foster-Carter, 1974, p. 93; Caldwell, 1971). Caldwell, working within a Marxist frame-work, had argued that transcending both underdevelopment *and* overdevelopment required a better appreciation of 'the objective natural limits in our manipulation of our environment' (Caldwell, 1977, p. 9). The Green Movement in Europe, as we shall see, represents an attempt to cast the argument about development and underdevelopment in these terms.

Neoclassical development theory has also experienced dif-ficulties in rising to the environmentalist challenge. A para-digm shift has not taken place, but 'mature' Neoclassical theory has been broadened under the influence of economists interested in challenging the conventional wisdoms of much development theory, often by utilising 'sociological' categories (Sen, 1981; Bauer, 1981). The major contribution to the development debate has come from the Brandt Committee's report, which makes a number of illuminating references to the part the destruction of the natural environment plays in the creation of rural poverty (Brandt, 1980, pp. 47, 73). Interestingly, the major report from the international agencies concerned specifically with the environment, the World Con-servation Strategy, seems to have been written in total ignor-ance of Brandt's findings (World Conservation Strategy, 1980). In view of this fact, it is worth reflecting briefly on the nature of the environmental crisis in the South, and its implications for the way in which 'centre' and 'periphery' are perceived.

The empirical problems afflicting the South's environment and resources have been documented in a series of publi-cations (Eckholm, 1982; Global 2000, 1982; UNEP, 1981;

Myers, 1979). Two kinds of problem area can be identified, corresponding to different levels of technology and demographic structure. The first are areas which are marginal to commercial agricultural development, where peasant producers and pastoralists are forced back on increasingly fragile ecosystems. The results of intensive production in resource-poor regions include eroded soils and depleted forest cover, as land is taken into production which cannot support the population. Desertification and deforestation are both serious problems not only for much of Africa, but for other regions of the world such as the Andes and Himalayan foothills. In tropical areas the loss of forests is especially grave, since most of the nutrients are present in the biomass rather than the soils beneath.

The environmental crisis is not confined to marginal areas and the tropical forests, however. Most regions in which commercial agriculture is practised experience other, equally important threats to ecosystem stability. The heavy dependence on chemically-based fertilisers and insecticides has depleted many irrigated rice-producing zones of their fish, traditionally an important source of protein to rice farmers. Similarly, the maintenance of irrigation systems has proved particularly costly with increased salinisation, in the face of pressing alternative demands for water use. Insect and plant life have suffered as a result of crop-spraying, and the human toll from diseases associated with chemical inputs is also significant (Bull, 1982.)

It is also important to emphasise the effects of changes in land-use, corresponding to shifts in income distribution, on the environment. Croplands that could have been devoted to crops for direct human consumption have been transferred to forage crops, such as soya and sorghum. The beneficiaries of new crop production technologies are those in the South with high enough incomes to afford meat in their diet, and those in the North who eat animal products from the South. In addition, large tracts of land under natural forest, or peasant production, have either been exploited by lumber companies or they have been utilised by cattle ranchers, with accompanying problems for the local agricultural population and the urban masses deprived of cheap food. The development of the land frontier usually means a replication of the structures of inequality found in the more populated zones, compounded by geographical access and practical violence.

RUDOLPH BAHRO AND THE GREEN MOVEMENT

A concern with sustainable development is a comparatively recent phenomenon, and one that has rarely been shown by Marxist theorists. The Green Movement stems from different antecedents in the radical tradition. This section discusses some of the problems that lie in the path of radical environmentalism, focusing on the work of Rudolph Bahro. Can the perspective of the Greens be married with the Marxist tradition in political economy? To what extent does Bahro successfully incorporate the periphery in his account of the crisis confronting the industrialised countries?

Among the issues raised by Bahro, the following deserve particular attention. First, he questions the relationship between personal lifestyles and political practice in the developed countries. Secondly, he argues that the ecological crisis dictates new political priorities for the Left. Thirdly, and most provocatively, he outlines some revisions in Marxist thinking which the current crises in North and South make necessary. *Socialism and Survival* is a curious book, engaging the reader by the passion and conviction of its advocacy, while disappointing those who look to the Radical Greens for a thoroughly worked-out body of theory. As E.P. Thompson writes in the Preface, Bahro's vision 'does not refute the utopian mode'. If there were echoes of William Morris in Bahro's previous book, *The Alternative in Eastern Europe* (1978), there is more than a hint of Proudhon, Thoreau and the European anarchist tradition in the pages of *Socialism and Survival*.

Bahro's 'personal politics' is personal in the sense that the individual's behaviour is expected to be compatible with their wider ideological stance. Bahro seeks consistency between political positions and personal behaviour, including radically altered patterns of personal consumption and the commitment to feminist ideals. It is also 'personal' in a different sense, since altered consciousness is seen to rest on 'conversion' (his word) to a more ecological politics. As we shall see, this view departs radically from most Marxist thinking which views objective class interests as primary in determining the outcome of structural change (Bottomore, 1982).

The renunciation of the production–consumption ethos of advanced capitalism is a prerequisite for personal fulfilment in these societies. What is required is not 'emancipation in economics [but] emancipation *from* economics' (1982a, p. 33). The psychological underpinnings of capitalism have enabled the leisure-time which technology affords us to be converted into yet another opportunity for the consumption of unnecessary goods. In as much as capitalism has 'freed' the worker from the worst excesses of the labour process, it has sought to occupy his free time with 'compensatory needs', that bring neither happiness nor personal fulfilment. The contrived demand for ever more consumer goods pushes back the day when socialism can be 'afforded', and, by depleting the resources of poor people in the South, creates a more onerous and threatening form of exploitation than that which existed under nineteenth-century factory conditions in Europe. Alienated labour and 'the loss of emotional connection' between individuals in the North is mirrored in the South by increasing economic dependency and the loss of control over nature.

Another set of issues with which Bahro is concerned are the priorities on the European Left. In his view mankind's survival is under threat both from nuclear annihilation and the environmental crisis in the South. This dictates a new system of priorities, since socialism can never be achieved until the threat of nuclear war and ecocatastrophe have been averted. The immediate injustices of advanced capitalism are thus afforded a lower priority than the wider injustices implicit in the East–West, North–South conflicts:

> We can no longer behave as if the fate of us all depended on the outcome of domestic class struggles over wage levels, or on what party is dominant in the state. The tremendous contradiction on the North–South and East–West axes, which are inseparably bound together, overspill this context (1982a, p. 20).

In Bahro's view our survival depends upon our ability to put existing development processes into reverse. In the North, society needs to be effectively *de*-industrialised, rather than *re*-industrialised, if only because the false competition between industrial nations provokes environmental depredation in the South. The first move should be nuclear disarmament, ending the artificial stimulus that the armanents industry produces, in both Western capitalist, and Eastern bloc, economies. Disarmament and a new world economic order are essential first steps towards resolving the ecological crisis.

Support for the present world economic order implies a deception aimed at both ourselves and people in the South. We are deceived into believing that the commodity world that we find around is a *necessary* condition of human existence (p. 27). Its defence lies in the constantly increasing nuclear arsenal at our goverment's command. But even more objectionable is the deception we are practising on the South. Through complicity with capitalist industrial society we are following a model of development which the South cannot emulate. The expanded reproduction of capital requires the South's resources for *our* development; it has not the capacity to 'develop' the South in its own interest.

The third, and perhaps most provocative, element in Bahro's writing is his critique of contemporary Marxist thinking and practice. In this critique he pulls together several strands in contemporary thought which, although at odds with the dominant ideology of capitalist society, are still insufficiently reflected in Marxism. To some extent they suggest, and Bahro supports this view explicitly, that Marxism's historical legacy has reduced its current efficacy (p. 49).

Bahro's critique of contemporary Marxism is more thorough going than he seems to realise. Few important ideas escape his attention. The belief in the revolutionary potential of the proletariat is one example. Bahro feels this concept represents a considerable 'theoretical obstacle' to clear thinking, since the proletariat 'is not functioning in the way we were led to expect' (p. 63). In his view the principal contradictions of capitalism are not observed in 'the institutionalised class struggle' within the developed countries, but in nuclear re-armament and the ecological crisis. The centre of gravity has shifted, as it were, from the workplace to the world stage.

The proletariat's role is more problematical than any of the classical Marxists suggested. As Bahro writes:

The idea of the world-historic mission of the working class assumes that its class interests are directly identical not only with those of its nation as a whole, but also with those of all humanity (Bahro, 1982a, p. 64).

He feels that the evidence for this proposition is limited. On the one hand, it is not clear that, historically, any single, subordinated class 'has by itself anticipated the impending new order' (p. 65). Should we make an exception for the proletariat? On the other hand, the orthodox Marxist conception of 'worker' is reductionist, denying a wider human status which, given the worker's reluctance to act like a revolutionary, many Marxists actually begrudge him (p. 67). It is liberating the individual that provides the springboard to human liberation. The 'idea that it is enough to refer to the "class standpoint" in order to attain the level of a movement for general emancipation, no longer applies' (p. 112).

The other essential stand in this re-evaluation of class is Bahro's insistence that 'the alienated structure of people's needs' is inseparably linked to economic exploitation. Thus, 'it is only because capitalism exists . . . that the working people in the rich countries still have a relative need for rising incomes' (p. 26). Although expressed as a solecism – if capitalism did *not* exist neither would the working class – Bahro is giving expression to a deep-seated dissatisfaction with industrial capitalism. How much of labour under capitalism is socially useful? How can socialism replace expropriation with social appropriation, freeing the individual from the double-bind imposed by authoritarian structures and the creation of surplus value?

Reading Bahro, one is struck by the fact that much contemporary sociology fails to make the necessary links between what is happening to northern industrial society and development in the South. One wonders, specifically, whether the increased sophistication with which we handle the different dimensions of the international economy has not induced a blindness to shifting values and class aspirations in our own societies. Within the very broad brush-strokes of Bahro's writing can be discerned a new perspective, if not a new paradigm. Put simply, this is that the environmentalist consciousness developing in Europe, shorn of the parochialism evident in the American and British literatures, offers a radically different critique of underdevelopment.

From what has been written it is also clear that Bahro and the Greens hold a view of the 'mutual interest' between North and South that is radically different from that of much recent development theory, as expressed in reports like that of the Brandt Commission. The difference between these approaches can be expressed in diagrammatic form. Both positions draw attention to the impending crisis in the world economic system, but the analysis which each provides of this crisis, and the prescriptions offered, are so divergent that the Greens' analysis could be said to invert that of the Brandt Commission.

The 'North-South dialogue': two definitions.
of mutual interest

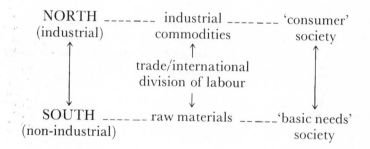

NORTH _____ industrial _____ 'consumer'
(industrial)   commodities   society

                    trade/international
                    division of labour

SOUTH _____ raw materials _____'basic needs'
(non-industrial)   society

(1) *Brandt* (1980; 1981)

    A. The North is facing a crisis of under-production/ consumption. This is the basis of the industrial recession. In both North and South there is a failure of demand, but for *different goods* (consumer society versus basic needs society).

    B. The solution for the North is to make the South richer through increased trade, bringing increased demand for industrial goods.

C. Improved economic growth in the South, stimulated by trade, will help reduce poverty there, and improve provision of basic needs in the South.

(2) *Radical Environmentalism* (Bahro, 1982a)

A. The North is over-producing and over-consuming the *wrong* goods, particularly armaments. This is the basis of the ecological crisis.

B. The solution for the North is to de-industrialise, reducing competition within the North to produce unnecessary consumer goods. This will also reduce inequality in the North.

C. Reducing growth in the North would reduce demand for raw materials in the South, and help resource conservation there.

D. The ecological crisis is a product of industrial growth in the North. Only ecological action, towards alternative social provision can meet basic needs in the South (urban squatting, appropriate technology, preventive medicine).

CLOSING THE CIRCLE: THE PROBLEM OF HUMAN AGENCY

The perspective of the radical Greens departs from both orthodox Marxism and more politically conservative environmentalism. They start with the premise that unless the environmental crisis is averted, no other important social goals will be achieved. What prevents necessary measures being taken to avert the crisis is not so much a lack of earnestness on the part of development agencies as conservative environmentalists suggest. Rather, it is in the interest of the industrial countries to maintain a North – South relationship, in which the progressive destruction of the environment is an inevitable consequence.

A decade ago, the response of the Left to the environmentalists' position was weak partly because it was universalistic. The destruction of the environment in the South was not total or irredeemable. Capitalism proceeded by uneven and combined development, depleting some resource systems more than others, and leaving in its wake important distributive consequences. *Some* people's resource base was destroyed to the benefit of others. The environmentalists, by refusing to characterise the process as capitalist, could offer no clues to the way it worked.

This accusation cannot be levelled at the radical Greens, such as Bahro. They argue that it is capitalist industrialisation that poses the threat to peace and development. They also recognise that the costs of environmental destruction will not be equally borne. However, they see in capitalism no inbuilt capacity to resolve its own contradictions. Nor do they place their faith in the enlightenment of international development agencies, or interested individuals in the North, to ensure human survival.

Bahro suggests that several processes provide grounds for optimism. First, the South's attempts to resist exploitation by making common commodity agreements, modelled on OPEC. Secondly, the pressure being mounted by trade unions in the North for a reduction in the working week and a better working environment. Thirdly, the 'alternative' lifestyles based on co-operative arrangements for production and living, which have blossomed in the developed countries since the 1960s.

Taken together these points are little more than straws in the wind. Common commodity agreements have often come unstuck partly because some countries benefit more from the curtailment of production in *other* countries than they would from a voluntary agreement to produce less. Evidence of pressure for a reduction in the working week by some sections of labour is more than compensated for by those who continue to work overtime in an effort to maximise household income. Indeed, the industrial recession has meant that household heads in employment in the United Kingdom are *more* likely to include other income earners than formerly (*Social Trends*, 1983). The 'alternative' lifestyles that have blossomed since

the 1960s have not taken the political initiative from conservative forces in the developed countries of Western Europe and
North America. In place of greater personal freedom, it could
be objected, these societies have nurtured the New Right. The
central dilemma of Bahro's thought, like that of other re-
visionist voices on the Left, is that most people are not
prepared to be led to the new Jerusalem.

The perspective outlined by Bahro is likely to remain
utopian until such time as a better accommodation is found
between the stirrings of radical environmentalism and the
organised ranks of labour and the unemployed. If we move,
with Bahro, from 'class interests to life interests' we need to
win the support of those whose lives are currently at issue.
Since class assumes so little importance in Bahro's writing,
the burden for social and economic change falls, inexorably,
on the individual. The individual is unlikely to make a declaration of faith in the Green position until the Greens have
outlined detailed proposals for bringing work to the North
without pushing the South into greater economic dependency.
If, as the Greens suggest, the advantages for both in considering their common interests are conditional upon changes in
northern economies, what do these changes mean for the
individuals in the North who will be converted to radical
environmentalism by economic necessity rather than an act of
faith?

The strengths of the Green's position are also its weaknesses. Their argument rests on personal convictions about
survival that not everybody shares, and the *urgency* of which
can be challenged. In addition, it is unclear how consciousness of the need to resolve the ecological crisis, will lead to
action to solve it. By exorcising determinism so completely
from their Marxism, Bahro and the Greens can be charged
with depriving their arguments of historical conviction.

At the same time, the radical Greens do present a challenge
to both Marxist and environmentalist orthodoxies. In seeking
to revert our attention to basic needs, rather than contrived
consumption; in seeking to revise domestic priorities in the
light of the global resource crisis, the radical Greens invoke
the development experience of the South. It is in this sense
that Bahro and the radical Greens provide a challenge to

those of us who, having declared an interest in the environment, fail to see it adequately reflected in Marxism. The challenge is nothing less than the replacement of both over-development and underdevelopment. The radical Greens are surely right to insist that the periphery finds a voice in the future of industrial society.

REFERENCES

Amin, S. (1974) *Accumulation on a World Scale* (New York: Monthly Review Press).

Bahro, R. (1978) *The Alternative in Eastern Europe* (London: New Left Books).

Bahro, R. (1982a) *Socialism and Survival* (London: Heretic Books).

Bahro, R. (1982b) 'Capitalism's Global Crises', *New Statesman*, 17–24 December.

Banaji, J. (1977) 'Modes of Production in a Materialist Conception of History', *Capital and Class*, vol. 3, pp. 1–44.

Bauer, P.T. (1981) *Equality, the Third World and Economic Delusion* (London: Methuen).

Bernstein, H. (1977) 'Notes on Capital and Peasantry', *Review of African Economy*, no. 10, pp. 60–73.

Bottomore, T. (1982) 'Degrees of Determination', *Times Literary Supplement*, 12 March.

Brandt Commission (1980) *North-South: A Programme for Survival* (London: Pan Books).

Brandt Commission (1981) *Towards One World? International Responses to the Brandt Report* (London: Temple Smith).

Brown, Lester R. (1978) *The Twenty-Ninth Day* (New York: Norton).

Bull, David (1982) *A Growing Problem: Pesticides and the Third World Poor* (Oxford: OXFAM).

Buttel, F., (1983) 'Sociology and the Environment: The Winding Road Toward Human Ecology' (Cornell University, unpublished ms.).

Caldwell, M. (1971) 'Oil Imperialism in South-East Asia', *Journal of Contemporary Asia*, 1 3.

Caldwell, M. (1977) *The Wealth of Some Nations* (London: Zed Press).

Castells, M. (1977) *The Urban Question* (London: Edward Arnold).

Commoner, B. (1972) *The Closing Circle* (London: Jonathan Cape).

Cotgrove, S. (1982) *Catastrophe or Cornucopia* (Chichester: Wiley).

Dasmann, R.F. (1975) *The Conservation Alternative* (Chichester: Wiley).

de Silva, S.B.D. (1982) *The Political Economy of Underdevelopment* (London: Routledge and Kegan Paul).

Eckholm, E.P. (1976) *Losing Ground* (Oxford: Pergamon).

Eckholm, E.P. (1982) *Down to Earth* (London: Pluto Press).

Emmanuel, A. (1973) *Unequal Exchange* (Paris: Maspero).

Engels, F. (1970), in Marx, K. and Engels, F. *Selected Works* (one volume) (Moscow).

Foster-Carter, A. (1974) 'Neo-Marxist Approaches to Development and Underdevelopment', in E. de Kadt & G. Williams (eds) *Sociology and Development* (London: Tavistock).

Frank, A.G. (1967) *Capitalism and Underdevelopment in Latin America* (New York: Monthly Review Press).

Frank, A.G. (1969) *Latin America: Underdevelopment or Revolution* (New York: Monthly Review Press).

Fraser Darling, F. (1970) *Wilderness and Plenty* (1969 Reith Lectures) (London: BBC Publications).

Global 2000 (1982) *Report to the President* (Harmondsworth: Penguin Books).

Godelier, M. (1977) *Perspectives in Marxist Anthropology* (Cambridge University Press).

Goodman, D. and Redclift, M. (1981) *From Peasant to Proletarian: Capitalist Development and Agrarian Transitions,* (Oxford: Basil Blackwell).

Gorz, A (1982) *Farewell to the Working Class* (London: Pluto Press).

Khozin, G. (1979) *The Biosphere and Politics* (Moscow: Progress Publishers).

Kitching, G. (1980) *Class and Economic Change in Kenya: The Making of an African Petite-Bourgeoisie 1905-1970* (New Haven, Conn: Yale University Press).

Lenin, V.I. (1952) *Materialism and Empirio-Criticism* (Moscow).

Leys, Colin (1977) *Underdevelopment in Kenya: The Political Economy of Neo-Colonialism 1964-1971* (London: Heinemann).

Long, N. and Roberts, B. (1979) (eds) *Peasant Cooperation and Capitalist Farming in Central Peru* (Austin: University of Texas Press).

Lopes, B.J.R. (1978) 'Capitalist Development and Agrarian Structure in Brazil', *International Journal of Urban and Regional Research,* 2, 1, pp. 1-11.

Lowe, P. and Warboys, M. (1980) 'Ecology and Ideology', in F. H. Buttel and H. Newby (eds) *The Rural Sociology of the Advanced Societies* (London: Croom Helm).

Marx, K. (1971) *Capital,* vol. III (Moscow).

Meadows, D. *et al.* (1974) *The Limits to Growth* (London: Pan Books).

Myers, Norman, (1979) *The Sinking Ark* (Oxford: Pergamon).

O'Riordan, T. (1976) *Environmentalism* (London: Pion).

Rey, P. P. (1973) *Les Alliances de Classes* (Paris: Maspero).

Riddell, R. (1981) *Ecodevelopment* (Farnborough: Gower).

Sandbach, F. (1980) *Environment, Ideology and Policy* (Oxford: Basil Blackwell).

Sen, A. (1981) *Poverty and Famines: An Essay on Entitlement and Deprivation* (London: Oxford University Press).

Simmons, I. (1974) *The Ecology of Natural Resources* (London: Edward Arnold).

Social Trends, (1983) (London: HMSO).

Stretton, H. (1976) *Capitalism, Socialism and the Environment* (Cambridge University Press).

Thomas, Keith (1983) *Man and the Natural World* (London: Allen Lane).

UNEP (United Nations Environment Programme) (1981) *Environment and Development in Africa* (Oxford: Pergamon).

Van den Bosch, R. (1980) *The Pesticide Conspiracy* (Chalmington, Dorset: Prism Press).

Wallerstein, I. (1980) *The Modern World System* vol. II (New York: Academic Press).

Ward, B. (1979) *Progress for a Small Planet* (Harmondsworth: Penguin Books).

World Conservation Strategy, (1980) IUCN, UNEP, and WWF.